Enforced Disappearances in
International Human Rights

Enforced Disappearances in International Human Rights

María Fernanda Pérez Solla

Foreword by Manfred Nowak

McFarland & Company, Inc., Publishers

Jefferson, North Carolina, and London

LIBRARY OF CONGRESS CATALOGUING-IN-PUBLICATION DATA

Pérez Solla, María Fernanda, 1973–
     Enforced disappearances in international human rights / María
Fernanda Pérez Solla ; foreword by Manfred Nowak.
          p.   cm.
     Includes bibliographical references and index.

     ISBN-13: 978-0-7864-2325-5
     (softcover : 50# alkaline paper) ∞

     1. Disappeared persons.   2. Disappeared persons —
Legal status, laws, etc.   3. Human rights.   I. Title.
HV6322.P47   2006
362.87 — dc22   2006000863

British Library cataloguing data are available

Cover image ©2006 Photodisc

Manufactured in the United States of America

*McFarland & Company, Inc., Publishers
     Box 611, Jefferson, North Carolina 28640
     www.mcfarlandpub.com*

Contents

Foreword

by Manfred Nowak

In the middle of the night, a group of heavily armed men break into your house, force your husband or son out of his bed, push him into an army jeep without number plates and drive him to an unknown destination. The next morning you inquire with the local police, the closest military office, the mayor of your town or even with the minister of interior, but you always receive the same answer: All authorities deny that your husband or son has been detained by public officials, and they pretend to have no idea whatsoever about the fate or whereabouts of your loved one. But in reality, your husband or son has been kidnapped by state security forces or paramilitary groups closely associated with them, and is being detained incommunicado for a prolonged period of time in a secret destination and interrogation center, subjected to the most cruel practices of torture. He may be clandestinely killed.

This is a typical scenario of an enforced or involuntary disappearance as it emerged in Latin America during the military dictatorships of the late 1960s and 1970s and later spread to other regions of the world, notably Asia. For the authorities, the practice of enforced disappearances serves the purpose of intimidating the population, of extracting information by means of torture, and of evading public scrutiny and responsibility for a multitude of serious violations of human rights, including the rights to personal liberty, integrity and security, to privacy and to recognition as a person before the law, to access to justice and an effective remedy, and ultimately to life. For the victims, the practice of enforced disappearance is a horrifying experience. The disappeared subjected to even more horrendous forms of torture without any outside control or remedy, does not know for how long he or she will be kept in secret detention and is even denied permission to inform the closest family members that he or she is still alive. For the family members, who are also victims, the insecurity around the fate and whereabouts of their loved ones is even worse than the definite knowledge of their death. As long as the families have no proof of their death, they continue to hope and are often torn for many years between hope and despair. Any vague second- or thirdhand information that the missing one might have been seen in some remote place of detention strengthens a family's conviction that his case is exceptional; they keep on hoping, ignoring information that would lead to the conclusion that he has not survived the torture or has been summarily executed.

Many families, not wishing to give up their hopes, are reluctant to agree on a death certificate based on a legal presumption of death. Such reluctance has many further legal effects to the detriment of the families. A widow might receive a pension from the state, but the wife of a disappeared person does not. The same applies to the children, the right to inheritance and similar matters of private and social security law. In other words, in addition to all the emotional suffering, families of disappeared persons are also subject to serious economic hardship and a situation of legal uncertainty. These consequences are usually intended or at least accepted by governments that systematically resort to the practice of enforced disappearances.

The international community has responded to the practice of enforced disappearances by the establishment of the UN Working Group on Enforced or Involuntary Disappearances in 1980, American Convention on the Forced Disappearance of Persons in 1994; by developing respective case law by international and regional treaty monitoring bodies; and by engaging in the process of drafting a binding UN treaty against enforced disappearance. In addition, the systematic or widespread practice of enforced disappearances was recognized as a crime against humanity in the 1998 Statute of the International Criminal Code.

This book by María Fernanda Pérez Solla is the most comprehensive analysis of all the difficult legal questions arising in the context of the phenomenon of enforced disappearances. I express my sincere hope that its publication will contribute to the worldwide efforts to eradicate the practice of enforced disappearances and to bring the perpetrators to justice.

Manfred Nowak is director of the Ludwig Boltzmann Institute of Human Rights at Vienna University and UN Special Rapporteur on Torture. He has served for many years as expert member of the UN Working Group on Enforced Disappearances, as UN expert responsible for the Special Process on Missing Persons in the former Yugoslavia and as UN expert on legal questions regarding enforced disappearances.

Preface

This book constitutes an updated and edited version of my doctoral dissertation at the Law School of the University of Vienna, written under the direction of Professor Manfred Nowak.

The reason for this study is the lack of a comprehensive and coherent framework to protect persons of enforced disappearances. As an Argentinean national, I was a small child during the so-called Proceso de Reorganización Nacional, and later, as law student at the University of Buenos Aires, I could understand the legal issues that have derived from the problem of the *desaparecidos,* disappeared persons. The complexities created by the contradictory policy decisions of subsequent democratic governments encouraged me to study the problem in depth in a comparative framework. Rather than limit the analysis to the Latin American panorama, I have studied the solutions existing in the international arena, at universal and regional levels.

Enforced disappearances should not take place. However, once they are committed, a solid and coherent international and national framework should exist to protect the victims and family members of those disappeared.

I thank Professor Nowak for his guidance, his thorough critique of my work, and his always pertinent comments.

I also thank especially my family for their support and courage to finish my research work.

List of Abbreviations

ACHPR — African Charter on Human and Peoples Rights

ACHR — American Convention on Human Rights

AD — American Declaration on the Rights and Duties of Man

AI — Amnesty International

Annual Report — Annual Report of the Inter-American Commission on Human Rights

AP — Additional Protocol to the Geneva Conventions

Basic Principles — Basic Principles on the Use of Force and Firearms by Law Enforcement Officials

Body of Principles — Body of Principles for the Protection of All Persons under any Form of Detention or Imprisonment

BYIL — British Journal of International Law

CAT — Convention against Torture

CERD — Convention on the Elimination of All Forms of Racial Discrimination

CHR — UN Commission on Human Rights

Code of Conduct — Code of Conduct for Law Enforcement Officials

COE — Council of Europe

CRC — Convention on the Rights of the Child

DAT — Declaration against Torture

Declaration of Basic Principles — Declaration of Basic Principles of Justice for Victims of Crime and Abuse of Power

DED — Declaration on the Protection of Persons from Enforced Disappearances

DERD — Declaration on the Elimination of All Forms of Racial Discrimination

Draft IC — Draft International Convention on the Protection of All Persons from Forced Disappearance

ECHR — European Commission on Human Rights

EcoPT — European Convention for the Prevention of Torture and Inhuman or Degrading Treatment or Punishment

ECPT — European Committee for the Prevention of Torture

ECtHR — European Court of Human Rights

European Convention — European Convention on Human Rights and Fundamental Freedoms

5

FEDEFAM — Federación Latinoamericana de Asociaciones de

Familiares de Detenidos Desaparecidos

GC — Geneva Conventions

GenC — General Comment

Harv. Hum. Rts. J. — Harvard Human Rights Journal

HRC — Human Rights Committee

HRCBH — Human Rights Chamber for Bosnia and Herzegovina

IACAT — Inter-American Convention to Prevent and Punish Torture

IACFD — Inter-American Convention on Forced Disappearances

IACHR — Inter-American Commission on Human Rights

IACtHR — Inter-American Court of Human Rights

ICC — International Criminal Court

ICCPR — International Covenant on Civil and Political Rights

ICESC — International Covenant on Economic, Social and Cultural Rights

ICJ — International Court of Justice

ICRC — International Committee of the Red Cross

ILO — International Labour Organisation

MNC — Multinational Corporation

NGO — Nongovernmental organization

OAS — Organization of American States

OASGA — Organization of American States, General Assembly

OP — Optional Protocol (ICCPR)

POW — Prisoner of War

Principles on Prevention — Principles on the Effective Prevention and Investigation of Extra-legal, Arbitrary, and Summary Executions

Standard Minimum Rules — Standard Minimum Rules for the Treatment of Prisoners

Sub-Commission — Sub-Commission on Prevention and Protection of Human Rights (former Sub-Commission on Prevention of Discrimination and Protection of Minorities)

UDHR — Universal Declaration on Human Rights

U. Miami Inter-Am. L. Rev. — University of Miami Inter-American Law Review

UN — United Nations

UNGA — United Nations General Assembly

WG — UN Working Group on Enforced or Involuntary Disappearances

1

The Notion of Enforced or Involuntary Disappearances

Enforced disappearances have had the attention of the international community for at least 30 years. But the origins of this human rights violation are found in Nazi Germany, 1941.[1] The Inter-American Court of Human Rights (IACtHR) recognized the problem in the leading case *Velásquez Rodríguez:*

> [D]isappearances are not new in the history of human rights violations.
> However, their systematic and repeated nature, and their use not only for
> causing certain individuals to disappear, either briefly or permanently, but also
> as a means of creating a general state of anguish, insecurity and fear, is a
> recent phenomenon. Although this practice exists virtually worldwide, it has
> occurred with exceptional intensity in Latin American in the last few years.[2]

The problem intensified in the 1970s,[3] because of the Latin American dictatorships. This encouraged standard setting. However, the definition is still a pending issue in a binding document of universal character. The exception is the Statute of the International Criminal Court (ICC), concerning disappearance as a crime against humanity.

The phenomenon has not been restricted to Latin America, as the reports of the Working Group on Enforced or Involuntary Disappearances (WG)[4] reveal[5]: Sri Lanka, Iraq and Bosnia and Herzegovina count with unfortunate records. Chechnya, Colombia, Nepal, Pakistan and Algeria alarm the international community with recent cases.

The first question is the definition of enforced disappearance. A comparative analysis follows.

What Is an Enforced or Involuntary Disappearance?

The WG was the first organ to develop a notion of enforced or involuntary disappearances. The group was created as a channel of communication between families of the disappeared persons and the governments concerned, to ensure that sufficiently documented and clearly identified individual cases were investigated and the whereabouts of the disappeared persons clarified. The UN Commission on Human Rights (CHR) expanded the functions of the WG.

Pursuant to the working definition of the WG, any act of enforced disappearances contains, at least, the following three constitutive elements:

(a) Deprivation of liberty against the will of the person concerned;
(b) Involvement of government officials, at least indirectly by acquiescence;
(c) Refusal to acknowledge the detention and to disclose the fate and whereabouts of the person concerned.[6]

The praxis of the WG was recognized in the notion agreed in the *Declaration on the Protection of Persons from Enforced Disappearances* (DED.)[7]

In 1984, the Federación Latinoamericana de Asociaciones de Familiares de Detenidos Desaparecidos (FEDEFAM) submitted a proposal to organs of the UN system for a draft convention on forced disappearances. Article 1 defined forced disappearances as an international crime and a crime against humanity. This was not included later in any of the existing documents. On the other hand, forced disappearances are today crimes against humanity, when they are systematic or widespread and committed against civilian population. Article 2 of the FEDEFAM project characterized enforced disappearance as any action or omission tending to hide the whereabouts of a political opponent or dissident whose fate was unknown by his family, friends or colleagues, to repress, impede or make difficult the opposition or dissidence by those who occupy governmental positions, or public officers of any kind, or by organized groups of individuals that act with the support or tolerance of the others. Article 3 included the following criminal acts:

1. The apprehension or detention of political opponents or dissidents committed with arbitrariness, without giving information on the whereabouts of the victims, or with false information concerning this fact.

2. The denial of information on the whereabouts of any person detained to their family members, friends or colleagues, except if the person was presented before judicial authority within the time frame established by the law.

3. The denial by public authorities or officers of the detention or arrest of a political opponent or dissident.

4. The lack of efficient cooperation of those in governmental functions in relation to the investigation of the fate of a political opponent or dissident whose whereabouts are ignored.

5. The facts enumerated above when they are committed against persons

that are not political opponents or dissidents, but whose disappearance intends to intimidate, cause fear, or condition the performance of the political opposition or dissidence.

The characterization of *the victim as political opposition* was not included in any instrument adopted; the proof of this element would constitute an extraordinary burden for the victims and family members. The history and jurisprudence reveal that not all persons disappeared had political engagement. The elements referred to in 3 and 4 are generally considered alternative: The definition, as such, demands the presence of both requirements. They have been often present in cases of enforced disappearances, but this is not necessary. Finally, point 5 refers to the motivation, but the motivation and its proof are irrelevant.

In the 1980s, Abellán Honrubia defined enforced disappearances as massive and forced disappearances of persons opposing a concrete political regime, performed directly or indirectly by state authorities in office, or by state security forces, out of any legal proceeding, and protected by the denial of the government to recognize that those persons were in custody, or to establish or to allow any efficient proceeding as to investigate.[8] The political activity of the victim was included in the definition, because of the historical context. The example of Srebrenica impedes any demand of this element. The concept underlines the state-link; the lack of effective investigation is also highlighted.

Pasqualacci asserted that a forced disappearance takes place when government agents or those working for the government kidnap and hold a person incommunicado in a clandestine prison. They subject the prisoner to torture and other cruel and inhuman punishment, secretly execute him or her without trial, and destroy or conceal the body, so as to eliminate any material evidence and ensure impunity. In addition, the government refuses to acknowledge that the person has been in custody, and the victims' loved ones live in continual uncertainty, shifting between hope and despair.[9] The author identifies the acts of kidnapping and holding a person incommunicado in a clandestine prison as essential elements. The authors are government agents, or those working for the government, which is somehow vague and imprecise, in particular in comparison with the concept of state organs of the ILC.[10] Further, Pasqualacci makes torture and cruel and inhuman punishment a necessary consequence, as well as secret execution without trial. A similar conception exists in the jurisprudence of the Inter-American Commission on Human Rights (IACHR). Moreover, the destruction or concealment of the body is another necessary element, together with the refusal to acknowledge that the person is held in custody. Consequently, Pasqualacci links enforced disappearances to *concrete human rights violations* and they are integral parts of the notion. The main problem is the descriptive approach. Some cases that are today analyzed as enforced disappearances may not fall within it, for instance, the disappearances of persons legitimately in prison.

Another definition was elaborated by Blanc Altemir, who characterizes enforced disappearances as follows[11]:

• Reasonable grounds to believe that the person was arbitrarily detained by state authorities or their agents, or with their support or tolerance.

• Denial by the authorities of their participation, or the participation of their agents in the detention of the victim, though there is evidence in that respect, or it has even been admitted or confirmed.

• Existence of a persistent and generalized framework of flagrant and systematic human rights violations.

• Inefficacy and lack of impartiality of the judiciary, which causes the futility of domestic remedies.

The requirement of a framework of human rights violations is the most irrelevant issue, as enforced disappearances do not always take place in a context of human rights violations. Moreover, the disappeared person has not always been arbitrarily detained.

The international community agreed on a definition of enforced disappearances in a nonbinding instrument: the DED.[12] In Article 1, paragraph 2, as well as in its preamble, third paragraph, the General Assembly of the United Nations (UNGA) presented a first universal approach, consisting in enumerating the series of acts that constitute a case of enforced disappearances:

> Persons are arrested, detained or abducted against their will or otherwise deprived of their liberty by officials of different branches or levels of Government, or by organized groups or private individuals acting on behalf of, or with the support, direct or indirect, consent or acquiescence of the Government, followed by a refusal to disclose the fate or whereabouts of the persons concerned or a refusal to acknowledge the deprivation of their liberty, which places such persons outside the protection of the law.

The DED is not strictly a binding document, but possesses a strong interpretative value, or expresses *opinio juris*,[13] as this UNGA resolution was adopted unanimously. A resolution of such a character may represent, in some cases, the chronological inversion of the traditional proceeding for the elaboration of international custom: the resolution expresses the *besoin de droit*,[14] and the origin of a practice that leads to the creation of an international customary rule.[15]

In addition, the CHR entrusted the WG to assist states to implement the DED. There are *obligations* for states deriving from the DED that simply embodies rules of international law (cf. Article 1.2 of the DED), in particular, concerning the prosecution and punishment of those responsible of enforced disappearances.[16] As the WG is in charge of monitoring the compliance with the DED, this is only possible if obligations derive from it. The WG has drawn the attention of all governments concerning the need of a full implementation of the DED,[17] which requires an active policy of adapting domestic law to the DED. The WG considers that the DED *obliges* states, for instance, to make all acts of enforced disappearance an offense under domestic criminal law; to investigate promptly, thoroughly and impartially any enforced disappearance; and to bring the perpetrators to justice. Finally, the WG has "strongly urged" states to comply with Article 18 of the DED, which asserts the duty not to benefit perpetrators with amnesty laws or similar measures that exempt them from criminal proceedings or sanctions. Furthermore, the WG has underscored the importance of "effective legislative, administrative and judicial measures aimed at preventing the occurrence of disappearances in the future" (Article 4). The WG receives information about noncompliance by states with the DED. Moreover, the WG has decided recently to issue general comments on provisions of the DED that require further clarification, that are included in its annual report.

According to the DED, enforced disappearances include the following elements:

1. *The arrest, detention or abduction of persons against their will, or deprivation of liberty by officials of different branches or level of governments, or by organized groups or private individuals acting on behalf of, or with the support, direct or indirect, consent or acquiescence of the government.* State participation is necessary under current international human rights law. A concept including nonstate actors would be appropriate, but without relieving the state from the responsibility of preventing enforced disappearances. The enumeration of the acts committed to deprive somebody of the physical freedom is also included: arrest, detention, and abduction. *Abduction* includes placing a person legally detained, or imprisoned in a hidden place, or where the person should not be legally kept.

2. *The subsequent refusal to disclose the fate or whereabouts of the persons concerned, or to acknowledge the deprivation of liberty.* If the state acknowledges the deprivation of liberty, the case falls under the first part of this paragraph: refusal to acknowledge the fate or whereabouts of the victim. This includes the complete lack of response from state authorities, even the act of detention or arrest.

3. The *consequence* is that the victims concerned are placed *outside the protection of the law* (e.g., there is no access to adequate remedies, torture and extrajudicial executions are possible, etc.).

The DED appears to be broad enough as to encompass most cases of enforced disappearances. However, this does not include the action of nonstate actors, particularly those trying to undermine the use of force monopoly by the state (e.g., terrorists, guerrilla groups or organizations), who are able to commit acts that could be characterized as enforced disappearances.[18] However, nothing impedes states, when implementing the DED, to adopt a *broader notion than the definition of the DED,* especially if the state is unable to keep the internal order. States should adopt all measures under due diligence standards as to prevent cases disappearances; if not, the state becomes responsible for acts committed by individuals. A broad definition of enforced disappearances contributes to the prevention and reassertion of the will of the state to prosecute such criminal actions. Two assumptions are made to attribute state responsibility for acts or omissions of nonstate actors: The state has the means to provide protection, and the state had the opportunity to prevent the act, but it failed to do so.[19]

The Inter-American Convention on Forced Disappearances (IACFD) was the first treaty defining the notion, but limited territorially to the Inter-American context.[20] The source is the extensive regional jurisprudence, particularly, since the case of *Velasquez Rodríguez.* The IACHR and the IACtHR apply the treaty:

> Article II
> For the purposes of this Convention, forced disappearance is considered to be the act of depriving a person or persons of his or their freedom, in whatever way, perpetrated by agents of the state or by persons or groups of persons acting with the authorization, support, or acquiescence of the state, followed by an absence of information or a refusal to acknowledge that deprivation of freedom or to give information on the whereabouts of that person, thereby impeding his or her recourse to the applicable legal remedies and procedural guarantees.

The notion presents the following elements.

• Concrete actions performed by human beings. The content consists of the deprivation of a person of the personal freedom, in whatever way. This is the initial stage of a case. The method used is completely irrelevant. This is a clear difference with the DED, which refers to detention, arrest, or abduction.
• The authors of the act must be state agents, or persons or groups acting with the authorization, support, or acquiescence of the state. This leads to the same questions pointed out in previous paragraphs (e.g., the IACFD would not apply to a terrorist organization). State responsibility is clear if the authors are agents or persons or groups acting with authorization (the clearest case of state relation), support (for instance, if authorities of the state express their content with the forced disappearance), or acquiescence of the state. In this last case, the state knows what is happening but does not act, breaching the obligations to ensure the respect of all human rights.

• The last part of the concept deserves serious critiques, for adding extra requirements, hardly useful and restrictive, in comparison to previous practice and jurisprudence. The notion refers to absence of information about the victim, leading to the question of the threshold — which information should be absent to consider a case an enforced disappearance? If the state asserts that the person was detained, does this information exclude state responsibility? The state should still be responsible, because only the information about the fate and whereabouts of the victims is pertinent. The IACFD contains an alternative requirement to the absence of information: the refusal to acknowledge the deprivation of personal freedom. What happens if the authorities acknowledge the deprivation of physical freedom, but they do not give further information about the victim? This is clearly not sufficient. Moreover, the paragraph includes, as alternative to the refusal to acknowledge the deprivation of freedom, the refusal to give information on the whereabouts of the person disappeared. This is the most important element. The other two issues are irrelevant and may lead to confusion, except if they are clearly linked to the fate and whereabouts of the victim, that is, to assert clearly that the absence of information refers to the fate and whereabouts of the victim, and that the lack of acknowledgment of the deprivation of freedom leads to uncertainty about the place where the victim is held.

Finally, the concept contains a very controversial requirement: the lack of access to remedies, mixing enforced disappearance per se and one of their possible consequences. Following the reasoning, if the family members have access to judicial remedies, there is no forced disappearance. The lack of access to judicial remedies (or to due process or law) may happen, but this is not strictly necessary. The text, as adopted, is too restrictive because only an enforced disappearance accompanied by lack of access to domestic remedies is protected. The DED prefers the notion of being "outside the protection of the law," which permits a broader application of the protective rules. A disappeared person is clearly outside the protection of the law. Moreover, a person detained or kept in an isolated or remote place cannot exercise the right to a remedy. However, the IACFD goes further and places a too-restrictive requirement.

The IACFD text, as finally adopted, must be compared with the draft IACFD and the pertaining comments of the IACHR. The draft Article 2 asserted:

Article 2
    For the purposes of this Convention, forced disappearance is understood to be the abduction or detention of any person by an agent of a State or by a person acting with the consent or acquiescence of a State in circumstances

where, after a reasonable period of time there has been made available no information that would permit the determination as of the fate or whereabouts of the person abducted or detained.

The differences are clear: (1) the description of particular acts (instead of the deprivation of physical freedom in whatever way of the IACFD), (2) the requirement of a reasonable period of time after detention (the most doubtful element included, as the jurisprudence has accepted cases of enforced disappearances where the victims have reappeared soon after detention or their bodies have been immediately recovered).[21] The draft contains a broader definition than the version finally adopted, without the final requirements criticized.

The IACHR considered, when commenting on the draft, that for there to be a forced disappearance there should be abduction or an arbitrary arrest. However, some cases of enforced disappearances have originated in legal detentions. The IACHR has added that the abduction or the arrest of the person should be carried out by government agents, either uniformed or in civilian clothing, members of police organizations, or the armed forces, or by paramilitary forces acting under the operational control of the police or armed forces. The IACHR has clearly excluded kidnapping by common criminals. However, the IACHR clarified that in some cases, the perpetrators are members of the paramilitary or parapolice groups. If they act as agents of the state, with its consent or acquiescence, the state responds. This element has been kept in the text finally adopted.[22] The "reasonable amount of time" has been fortunately deleted. This would have constituted an extraordinary burden against the victim and family members. Some disappeared persons have been immediately executed (see *The White Van Case* and *Villagrán Morales,* both decided by the IACtHR, cases considered disappearances, though the victims' bodies appeared soon after their kidnapping or detention).

The finally adopted concept is commonly applied in the Inter-American system, what is evident in the praxis of the IACHR. In the *Report on the Situation of Human Rights in Colombia,*[23] the IACHR defined enforced disappearance as it is spelled out in the IACFD, without stating that the convention was applied. The IACHR only indicated that it was using "the concept of enforced disappearance in the Inter-American system."

For its experience, the praxis and jurisprudence of IACHR are relevant: "[T]he crime of disappearance was typified by the Inter-American Court of Human Rights in the Velásquez Rodríguez Case, and later codified in the Inter-American Convention on Forced Disappearance of Persons."[24] The IACHR has applied the IACFD concept even concerning nonstate parties[25]:

14. Peru is not a State Party to the Convention on Forced Disappearance, but the mere elaboration of a definition of *forced disappearance* by the drafters of the Convention is useful in order to identify the elements of the same. The essential thing is that the individuals are deprived of their liberty by the agents of the State or under the color of law, followed by the negation or incapacity of the State to explain what occurred to the victim or to provide information regarding his whereabouts.

The IACHR does not apply the notion included in the IACFD, but a notion similar to the DED. The IACHR added that

17. The Commission's practice has demonstrated that the main cause of forced disappearances derives from abuse of powers conferred on the armed forces of the State during a state of emergency. Under a state of emergency, the number of arbitrary detentions increases, individuals are detained without charges and kept without trial, deprived of access to judicial remedies, and there is no record of their having been arrested, all of which is flagrantly at variance with the rule of law.[26]

The IACHR emphasized the same crucial elements of enforced disappearances in many other reports.[27]

The European Court of Human Rights (ECtHR) has not elaborated a definition of disappearances until the time of this writing, probably because it dealt only with them in isolated and recent cases. The ECtHR has simply used *disappeared* or *disappearance*. This absence of a definition (even when the ECtHR could pay attention to the DED) has remarkable influence in the methodology employed.[28] In *Kurt v. Turkey* the only reference is found in the submission of Amnesty International (AI)[29] that identified the following elements:

a. A deprivation of liberty;

b. By government agents or with their consent or acquiescence; followed by

c. An absence of information or refusal to acknowledge the deprivation of liberty or refusal to disclose the fate or whereabouts of the person;

d. Thereby placing such persons outside the protection of the law.

This clearly follows the DED.

The DED and the IACFD express what is today recognized as an enforced disappearance. The WG applies the DED and its own practice at the universal level. The IACFD is cited in the Inter-American system. In the European system, the notion has not been defined.[30] In the universal system, the DED is the only instrument applicable today, and a draft International Convention on the Protection of All Persons from Forced Disappearance (Draft IC) is prepared.

In the Draft IC,[31] Article 1 defines forced disappearance as

> The deprivation of a person's liberty, in whatever form, committed by agents of the State or by persons or groups of persons acting with the authorization, support or acquiescence of the State, followed by a refusal to acknowledge the deprivation of liberty or by concealment of the fate or whereabouts of the disappeared person, which places such a person outside the protection of the law.

The draft opts for a broad definition of the initial act ("deprivation of a person's liberty"), without enumerations. This permits a flexible application: The deprivation of liberty may be performed "in whatever form." The purpose is omitted. The state-link is emphasized. The last element is presented as an alternative: nonrecognition of the detention, or concealment about the fate or whereabouts of the victim.

In the work of the Intersessional open-ended Working Group to elaborate a draft legally binding normative instrument for the protection of all persons from enforced disappearance,[32] enforced disappearances require at least the following elements: (a) deprivation of liberty in whatever form; (b) refusal to acknowledge that deprivation of liberty by the authorities, or (c) removal of the disappeared person from the protection of the law. This last element is unnecessary. Concerning perpetrators, many delegations considered that the instrument should refer to agents of the state and related persons, but some delegations preferred to examine nonstate actors. Nevertheless, many delegations recognized that the states should bear the primary responsibility for preventing and punishing forced disappearances.

Additional requirements are necessary to characterize disappearances as crimes against humanity. The Independent Expert charged with examining the existing international criminal and human rights framework for the protection of persons from enforced or involuntary disappearances has included the following elements for "the practice of enforced disappearances" to be a crime against humanity:

(a) It is committed as part of a widespread or systematic attack directed against any civilian population;

(b) The perpetrator knew that the conduct was part of a widespread or systematic attack directed against a civilian population;

(c) The perpetrator was aware that the deprivation of liberty would be followed by a refusal to acknowledge it or to give information on the fate or whereabouts of the person concerned;

(d) The perpetrator intended to remove such person from the protection of the law for a prolonged period of time.[33]

The statute of the ICC contains the most recent definition of enforced disappearance as a crime against humanity with a strict scope of application (individual criminal responsibility) in Article 7.[34] Article 7 requires that enforced disappearances are committed as part of a widespread or systematic attack directed against any civilian population, with knowledge of the attack.

The *Elements of Crimes* are particularly descriptive, for the necessity of a clear definition of the acts that lead to individual criminal responsibility under the ICC statute.[35] They require that the author

a. Had apprehended, detained (it includes maintaining an existent detention, which is particularly important, because in some cases the detention or apprehension could have been originally legal), or abducted one or more persons; or

b. Had refused to recognize the apprehension, detention, or abduction, or to give information on the fate or whereabouts of the person or persons.

Moreover, they include the following requirements:

a. That the apprehension, detention or abduction had been followed or concurred with a denial to recognize the deprivation of physical liberty or to give information on the fate or whereabouts of this person or persons; or

b. That the denial has been preceded or concurred with that deprivation of personal freedom.

To be individually responsible for an enforced disappearance under the ICC statute, the author must have conscience of the following aspects:

a. Such apprehension, detention or abduction would be followed, normally, by a denial to recognize the deprivation of personal freedom or to give information on the fate or whereabouts of this person or persons (if the author maintained a person in detention, he must be conscientious that the denial had taken place); or

b. Previously or simultaneously to such denial, the victim was deprived of his or her personal freedom.

Concerning the author, the elements require that the apprehension, detention, or abduction had been perpetrated by a state or political organization or with its authorization, support, or acquiescence. Moreover, the denial to recognize the deprivation of personal freedom or to give information on the fate or whereabouts should have been perpetrated by a state or political organization or with its authorization or support.

Finally, the author should have had the intention to place that person out of the protection of the law for a long time, his conduct had been performed as part of a generalized or systematic attack against civilian population, and he had knowledge that the conduct was part of a generalized or systematic attack addressed against civil population or had the intention that the conduct were part of such an attack.

The *criminalization* of the maintenance of a person as disappeared (not only the detention and abduction, as in most instruments) is very interesting, covering an essential aspect of the suffering of the victim. In addition, in the intentional aspect, the elements include the intention to place the person out of the protection of the law for a long time. This recalls the Draft IACFD, which has relevance in the context of individual criminal responsibility, as the ICC will only try the most serious crimes.

Furthermore, the elements of crimes remarkably allow not only state involvement but also the participation of a *political organization,* which clearly includes organizations with political purposes, for instance, national liberation movements, guerrilla groups, belligerent communities, and also political parties and even terrorists. Enforced disappearances committed by economic or criminal organizations (e.g., committed by Mafia, cartels, etc.) are outside the application of the definition. However, there is uncertainty in case the criminal or economic organization commits enforced disappearances with political purposes, a problem that is related to the definition of political organization (e.g., Mafia groups not only have economic goals but also try to obtain more power, that is, they also act as a political organization). Can systematic disappearances of members of political parties fighting against corruption committed by Mafia groups be tried by the ICC, as they clearly are committed for political purposes but not by (strictly speaking) political organizations? Many of these organizations with criminal purposes, or groups with economic influence (for instance, some multinational corporations that have been linked with serious human rights violations in developing countries) in reality seek political power and influence. Some state structures are weaker than these organizations and are easily influenced by them.

The notion of the DED is broad enough to maintain its actuality more than 10 years after its adoption. Moreover, its role in the work of the WG, the only organ of the universal system that can potentially deal with disappearances over the globe, because its action is independent of treaty law, has given the DED a key role for the identification of cases of enforced disappearances. Pursuant to the WG and the CHR, the DED is more than a mere declaration, and some obligations for states would emerge from it. However, the main deficit consists in not addressing enforced disappearances committed by nonstate actors. The ICC statute, in a very limited context — for example, enforced disappearances as crime against humanity leading to individual criminal responsibility — includes political organizations as authors, not only states, of enforced disappearances.

The Inter-American system is the only one counting with a definition of enforced disappearances in a treaty, though the notion has been harshly criticized because it includes additional requirements that do not respond to previous practice. The link of the disappearance to the lack of access to legal remedies and procedural guarantees is erroneous. The DED asserts that an enforced disappearance "place such persons outside the protection of the law." This is a broader standard, more acceptable.

In the other systems of protection, there were no intents to define enforced disappearances. Consequently, the notion of the DED is commonly applied; in the Inter-American system, the concept of Article 2 of the IACFD is generally used, even concerning nonstate parties. Moreover, the IACFD, though more restrictive than the provision in the DED, was not applied exactly as written.

The basic elements of the DED have been present explicitly or implicitly in the jurisprudence. However, the Draft IC has the advantage of not enumerating the different forms in which the deprivation of physical freedom takes place. A case does not necessarily start with an illicit deprivation of physical freedom (*see* the cases of *Neira Alegria* and *Durand and Ugarte*).

The perpetrator would constitute the second element. Under current international law, there must be a link to the state, direct or indirect, except in the statute of the ICC, where acts of political organizations may constitute enforced disappearances. An increasing recognition of nonstate actors is very important; however, in domestic law, every state can characterize enforced disappearances with broader notions.

A third element is the absence of information about the victim, in particular his or her fate and whereabouts; or the refusal to acknowledge the deprivation of liberty, committed by state organs, or persons acting under orders, support or acquiescence of the state; or refusal to disclose the fate or whereabouts of the person disappeared. These should be kept as alternative elements.

Finally, to place the victim outside the protection of the law is not a necessary element. It constitutes a possible consequence, but it does not characterize the act. However, this could have particular relevance in case of defining enforced disappearances committed by nonstate actors.

As already asserted, the inclusion of the lack of access to remedies is absolutely unnecessary and does not respond to previous practice and jurisprudence. An enforced disappearance may take place even when the judicial mechanisms of protection work adequately.

Definitions requiring that the victims are political opponents are unacceptable, because members of religious, ethnic or national minorities have also been victims of enforced disappearances.[36]

Enforced disappearances may constitute a crime against humanity, as the Draft IC and the statute of the ICC assert. The crucial element is that the practice is part of a widespread or systematic attack against civilian population. Moreover, the statute of the ICC indicates that these acts are not only committed by state organs but also by organs of political organizations. This question constitutes the more innovative aspect.

The analysis of the different concepts of enforced disappearances reveals the need of an internationally binding instrument defining enforced disappearance to fill up and solve the gaps existing in the practice in the different organs of protection. The Draft IC concept could probably have this role. However, in the meantime, the role of the DED should not be underestimated, because nothing impedes the monitoring organs to apply its definition in cases of enforced disappearances. As a resolution of the GA adopted without a vote, it can express *coutume sauvage,* that is, to advance *opinio juris* to be followed by international practice according to it, originating new customary international law.

Only in the framework of the ICC statute, nonstate actors are considered perpetrators of enforced disappearances in positive international law, that is, when they are members of a political organization. The definition has specific relevance; according to the DED and the regional IACFD, states must define enforced disappearances according to these instruments in domestic criminal law. The *criminalization* contributes to the prevention and provision of remedies. For this reason, authors such as Manfred Nowak insist on the need of including clearly the obligation of defining enforced disappearances as an offence in domestic law, pursuant to international law.[37]

Enforced Disappearance as a Violation of International Customary Law

Only a regional treaty clearly prohibits enforced disappearances, apart from the ICC statute. However, enforced or involuntary disappearances may be considered violations of customary international law. First, the DED could have originated *opinio juris,* inverting the traditional form in which international custom is created, by originating *coutume sauvage:* The practice has followed the recognition of the obligatory character of a course of conduct, in this case, the prohibition of enforced disappearances. The U.S. *Restatement* includes enforced disappearances among human rights violations that constitute violations of international customary law.[38] In addition, Article 1, paragraph 3 of the DED asserts generally that enforced disappearances are violations of rules of international law. The 1998 Draft IC, in its preamble, paragraph four, contained a similar declaration. The WG understands that the DED contain some obligations for states. The CHR has entrusted the WG to monitor the DED, which would not be possible if no obligation were derived from the DED.

Customary law requires the presence of certain elements: a material element, a qualified practice and, finally, *opinio juris,* that is, the conviction that the practice is obligatory. The doctrine has emphasized that the "qualified practice"[39] means a practice that is general, uniform and consistent.[40] There is today a clear *opinio juris,* with its best universal expression in the DED, concerning the prohibition of enforced disappearances. This could constitute *coutume sauvage,* because the *opinio juris* would have preceded the practice. However, the rules prohibiting enforced disappearance would have customary character for additional reasons. The practice could be interpreted in a negative sense: If enforced disappearances are committed, no state can today legitimately argue that they were licit or that the issue is within its exclusive jurisdiction.

However, the definition is still problematic when talking about customary law. There are still gaps and imprecision in the definition and consequences. There is a consistent practice in the WG and Inter-American system, but the characterization is still imprecise, and the monitoring organs appear to recognize an enforced disappearance when they have the case before them, without applying a clear-cut definition, even those derived from the DED and the IACFD.

To support the existence of *opinio juris,* the *Declaration and Programme of Action of Vienna* (1993) called on the governments to abrogate the legislation favoring impunity and to punish human rights violations.[41] In addition, it asserted that states are obliged to investigate disappearances and prosecute those responsible.

However, there is no clear characterization of disappearances after the adoption of the DED. For example, the UNGA, at its 51st session, adopted resolution 51/94 of 12 December 1996 titled *Question of enforced or involuntary disappearances.* It reaffirmed that any act of enforced disappearance is an offense to human dignity and a grave and flagrant violation of the human rights and fundamental freedoms proclaimed in the Universal Declaration of Human Rights (UDHR)[42] and developed in other international instruments, and a violation of international law. Constantly, UN organs have argued for the prevention of enforced disappearances, especially the UN GA,[43] the CHR,[44] and particularly the WG.[45]

Enforced disappearances have been characterized as a grave, serious,[46] and flagrant violation of human rights, coherently with Article 1 of the DED:

> Any act of enforced disappearance is an offence to human dignity. It is condemned as a denial of the purposes of the Charter of the United Nations, and as a grave and flagrant violation of the human rights and fundamental freedoms proclaimed in the Universal Declaration of Human Rights and reaffirmed and developed in international instruments in this field.

The DED refers to any act of enforced disappearances that nevertheless, in the eyes of the UN GA, deserves clear condemnation. Perhaps the DED is the best example to argue that the international community condemns enforced disappearances, but still there is no universal and binding rule, apart from the ICC statute.

In the Inter-American system, the IACFD includes in its preamble:

> CONSIDERING that the forced disappearance of persons in an affront to the conscience of the Hemisphere and a grave and abominable offence against the inherent dignity of the human being, and one that contradicts the principles and purposes enshrined in the Charter of the Organization of American States.

The Draft IC of 1998 asserted that any act of forced disappearance "constitutes an offence to human dignity, is a denial of the purposes of the Charter, and is a gross and flagrant violation of the human rights and fundamental freedoms proclaimed in the Universal Declaration of Human Rights, and reaffirmed and developed in other international instruments in this field."[47] The content is practically identical to above-cited text of the DED. According to the preamble of the Draft IC, enforced or involuntary disappearance is not, if that exists, an *ordinary violation of human rights.* This idea has been supported, for example, by Switzerland, in its comments to the Draft IC.[48]

Consequently, the international community understands enforced disappearances as *qualified* violations of human rights. Their seriousness has even led to its characterization as a crime: The IACHR has referred to an *international crime of enforced disappearance.* One example is the *Report on the Situation of Human Rights in Colombia,* in which the IACHR asserted the following:

> The international crime of enforced disappearance is included under this chapter on the right to life, even though enforced disappearance is a succession of criminal offences. It begins with violation of the right to personal liberty when an individual is either arbitrarily detained or abducted; the enforced disappearance continues with violation of the right to judicial guarantees, due process and violation of the right to humane treatment, because the arrest or abduction are, as a rule, executed by violent means that often leave the victim seriously injured. As a rule, the victim is eventually subjected to abuse or torture in order to extract information or to inflict corporal punishment. Enforced disappearance generally ends with violation of the right to life, since the intent of an enforced disappearance is, from the very outset, to violate the right to life.

The crime of enforced disappearances as *successive offenses* deserves to be emphasized.

Moreover, the IACHR has gone further by asserting that

> 26. Forced disappearance is a crime perpetrated by agents of the State, or by groups of irregulars who act with the state's acquiescence; it is therefore

very difficult to obtain from the authorities an official admission of the arrest. The objective elements of crimes of this kind are that an arrest is made, it goes officially unrecognized, and the prisoner is held in secrecy. If these are the constituent elements of the crime defined as forced disappearance, it is apparent that the legal mechanisms of domestic jurisdiction are ineffective for securing the re-appearance of the victim.[49]

Enforced disappearances are a violation of several internationally recognized human rights including the multiple-rights approach.

The WG has affirmed that this is a particularly odious violation of human rights, and is

a doubly paralyzing form of suffering: for the victims, frequently tortured and in constant fear for their lives, and for their family members, ignorant of the fate of their loved ones, their emotions alternating between hope and despair, wondering and waiting, sometimes for years, for news that may never come. The victims are well aware that their families do not know what has become of them and that the chances are slim that anyone will come to their aid. Having been removed from the protective precinct of the law and "disappeared" from society, they are in fact deprived of all their rights and are at the mercy of their captors. If death is not the final outcome and they are eventually released from the nightmare, the victims may suffer for a long time from the physical and psychological consequences of this form of dehumanization and from the brutality and torture which often accompany it.

The family and friends of disappeared persons experience slow mental torture, not knowing whether the victim is still alive and, if so, where he or she is being held, under what conditions, and in what state of health. Aware, furthermore, that they too are threatened; that they may suffer the same fate themselves, and that to search for the truth may expose them to even greater danger.

The family's distress is frequently compounded by the material consequences resulting from the disappearance. The missing person is often the mainstay of the family's finances. He or she may be the only member of the family able to cultivate the crops or run the family business. The emotional upheaval is thus exacerbated by material deprivation, made more acute by the costs incurred should they decide to undertake a search.

Furthermore, they do not know when — if ever — their loved one is going to return, which makes it difficult for them to adapt to the new situation. In some cases, national legislation may make it impossible to receive pensions or other means of support in the absence of a certificate of death. Economic and social marginalization is frequently the result.[50]

Disappearances are a form of suffering with two faces: the side of the direct victims, and that of the family members. A disappeared person is deprived of all rights, which will have consequences when analyzing the right to juridical personality.

Enforced disappearances as a complex series of acts also leads to the analysis of the ILC work on state responsibility[51]: It begins as a deprivation of personal freedom, and only stops with the discovery of the whereabouts or fate of the victim, and, if possible, with the handing of the body to the family members. It constitutes a *continuing violation of international human rights.*[52] It persists until the fate or whereabouts of the victims are disclosed, and the state is responsible without alleging any statute of limitations, as they should not run until the disclosure or until effective remedies are in force. The DED asserts that

> Article 17
> • Acts constituting enforced disappearance shall be considered a continuing offence as long as the perpetrators continue to conceal the fate and the whereabouts of persons who have disappeared, and these facts remain unclarified.
> • When the remedies provided for in article 2 of the International Covenant on Civil and Political Rights are no longer effective, the statute of limitations relating to acts of enforced disappearance shall be suspended until these remedies are re-established.
> • Statutes of limitations, where they exist, relating to acts of enforced disappearance shall be substantial and commensurate with the extreme seriousness of the offence.

The IACFD contains similar provisions on the continuing character of enforced disappearances in Article 3. Today, enforced disappearances are continuing offenses only in the opinion of some judges. Consequently there is also a need of a clear definition of enforced disappearances as a continuing offense in domestic legislation, to avoid inconsistent interpretations.

Concerning statutes of limitation, Article 7 of the IACFD asserts that the criminal action and the punishment will not be subject to statutes of limitation.[53] The DED, Article 17, asserts that if statutes of limitations exist, they must be substantial and commensurate with the seriousness of the offence.

The Draft IC, Article 2 bis asserts that if enforced disappearance constitutes a crime against humanity it shall attract the consequences provided for under international law. In the other cases, Article 5, the statute of limitation must be substantial and proportional to the seriousness of the offense, starting from the establishment of the fate or whereabouts of the disappeared person. If no effective remedies are available, the term for criminal proceeding must be suspended until they are restored efficiently. This provision, if adopted, would solve most problems just cited. The nonapplicability of statutes of limitation to crimes against humanity is consistent with the ICC statute. However, the Draft IC could prove insufficient because there is no provision on civil actions. Probably the application of the same standard would be the fairest solution.

The approach of enforced disappearances as continuous violations of human rights was not followed by the IACtHR in the *Blake* case.[54] The court understood that the date when the victim was assassinated was key to determining the responsibility to the state. Guatemala had accepted the jurisdiction of the IACtHR after the assassination of Blake. Consequently, the state was not considered responsible for this act, only for the lack of access to domestic remedies and for the harm caused to family members because of the disappearance. A similar approach was used by the HRC in disappearance cases against Argentina and Chile, countries that became party to the International Covenant on Civil and Political Rights (ICCPR) after the initial acts of disappearances had been committed.

In *Matanovic,* the concurring opinion of Manfred Nowak contains an interesting reference to this notion.[55] The fact that the disappearances occurred before the Dayton Peace Agreement took effect should not preclude the Human Rights Chamber for Bosnia and Herzegovina (HRCBH) from considering such cases,[56] as there was evidence that the victims were held in detention after the treaty, by applying Article 17, paragraph 1, of the DED as Article 1 of Annex 6 of the Dayton Agreement provides that the parties "shall secure to all persons within their jurisdiction the highest level of internationally recognized human rights and fundamental freedoms, including the rights and freedoms provided in the European Convention."

In *Blake,* Cançado Trindade included a separate opinion, where the judge understood that the decision was *stricto sensu* legal, but it failed to provide the unity of a system under the American Convention on Human Rights (ACHR). The emphasis should have been placed on the multiple and interrelated human rights violations alleged, which were continuous after Guatemala accepted the IACtHR jurisdiction. Moreover, forced disappearance was defined by the Guatemalan Criminal Code in force (Article 201 ter, as amended) as a continuing crime. Finally, Guatemala was party to the ACHR since 25 May 1978 but accepted the court's jurisdiction on 9 March 1987. Cançado Trindade considered that the IACtHR, led by a rigid interpretation, performed "an artificial fragmentation in the consideration of that crime of forced disappearance," because this is a complex human rights violation; second, a particularly grave violation; and third, a continuing or permanent violation (until the fate or whereabouts of the victims are established). According to the *travaux préparatoires* of the IACFD, the crime was permanent while the person remained disappeared. In *De Becker v. Belgium* case,[57] the ECtHR recognized the concept of a continuing situation.

Another argument refers to the specificity and integrity of human rights treaties. The limitation *ratione temporis* of the court's competence could only affect the competence *ratione materiae,* but it reveals a difference between the law of treaties, and international human rights, where the *voluntarist-*

contractualist spirit of the Vienna Convention on the Law of Treaties (1969) would not apply but superior common values and the notion of collective guarantee would.

Clearly, the characterization of enforced disappearances depends on the good-will of judges, absent clear and binding provisions. The international community has "adopted" the prohibition of enforced disappearances, but the characterization of this notion is far from unanimous. Some characteristics have constantly been present: Enforced disappearances are forbidden and should be investigated (Vienna Declaration, 1993). Moreover, enforced disappearances, according to UN organs, are offenses to the human dignity, and grave and flagrant violations of human rights and fundamental freedoms contained in the Universal Declaration of Human Rights (UDHR) and developed in further instruments. In addition, the DED asserts that they are a denial of the purposes of the UN, even in an isolated case. The IACFD added that enforced disappearances are contrary to the principles and purposes of the charter of the Organization of American States (OAS), a "qualified" violation of human rights. Enforced disappearances are gross violations of human rights, but perhaps the notion of gross violation per se is imprecise in the UN system. The IACHR has even dared to assert that enforced disappearance is an international crime constituted of successive criminal offenses and that any enforced disappearance violates of several internationally recognized human rights. The WG underlined the role of victims and family members that also become victims, for the sufferings undergone and the material losses derived. Finally, enforced disappearances constitute continuous human rights violations. These two instruments differ in their point of view concerning statutes of limitations: Though the IACFD rejects them in all cases, the DED considers that they must be substantial and proportional to the grave character of the offense. The Draft IC opts for differentiating the cases where enforced disappearances constitute crimes against humanity.

This last difference reveals the deepest problem: Even the two existent instruments, the DED and the IACFD, contradict themselves. The need for coherence, the need for a comprehensive system for the protection of all persons from enforced disappearances and the reparation of their consequences through the existing protection frameworks is clear. The characteristics enunciated would constitute "good practice" but are, except in very limited cases, not actually binding. For that reason, inconsistent interpretation of the phenomenon and practice of enforced disappearances has arisen, to the detriment of the victim and his or her next-of-kin. Only more coherence or the development of further binding rules concerning enforced disappearances can solve this problem. International monitoring organs should pay more attention to the expertise developed by other systems.

The DED is extremely important in particular when states define enforced disappearances in domestic law. The characterization of enforced disappearances as gross violations is relevant. Domestic law should expressly include provisions establishing that enforced disappearances are continuing violations, in particular, that statutes of limitation do not start running while the fate and whereabouts of the victim are not known with certainty. Disappearances carry a particular and additional stigma to those next to the victim. This question has concrete consequences in the practice: The due obedience exception, amnesty legislation and similar measures should not apply to cases of enforced disappearances, because the duty to investigate, prosecute, punish and provide for reparation should prevail for the seriousness of this human rights violation.

The definition of enforced disappearances in domestic law as very serious violations of human rights (e.g., giving to these rules constitutional character), as continuing violations of human rights, with substantive statutes of limitations only running from the time the fate or whereabouts of the victim have been established (for the civil and the criminal actions) and only if effective domestic remedies have been in place constitutes necessary measures to adopt. Moreover, the definition of enforced disappearances as crimes against humanity, in this case, without statutes of limitations, is also necessary to prevent new disappearances and to protect adequately the victims and next-of-kin.

Enforced Disappearances as a Practice or as Individual Cases

In *Velasquez Rodriguez,* the IACtHR set out some important guidelines concerning the practice of disappearances. However, disappearances may occur in individual and isolated cases. In the paragraph included below, the IACtHR gives a "special status" to the practice of enforced disappearances, as a radical breach to international human rights law.[58]

> 158. The practice of disappearances, in addition to directly violating many provisions of the Convention ... constitutes a radical breach of the treaty in that it shows a crass abandonment of the values which emanate from the concept of human dignity and of the most basic principles of the inter-American system and the Convention. The existence of this practice, moreover, evinces a disregard of the duty to organize the State in such a manner as to guarantee the rights recognized in the Convention, as set out below.

The concept of radical breach is new proof to remark on the place of this human rights violation. Enforced disappearances represent the crass abandonment of the values emanating from human dignity. Moreover, the passage refers to the basic obligations to ensure the rights protected through the organization of the state system to prevent human rights violations. These obligations were elaborated, for instance, in *Manrique et al. v. Peru,* where the IACHR enumerated the concrete obligations of states concerning a case: to ascertain the whereabouts and situation of the victim, to punish those responsible, and to make reparation to the family members.[59]

Though the IACtHR has declared practices of enforced disappearances in certain Latin American countries, the ECtHR has been reluctant to assert such a thing, in particular, concerning Turkey. One example is *Kaya v. Turkey:* The applicant argued the existence of a practice in Turkey against Articles 2, 3, and 13 of the European Convention, targeting the Kurdish people, allegedly in violation of Article 14. However, the ECtHR considered that it was not necessary to make a determination on this point.[60] In *Timurtaş,* the ECtHR abstained from such declaration,[61] for lack of evidence and similarly in *Taş v. Turkey,*[62] concerning Article 18; in *Ihlan v. Turkey,*[63] an officially tolerated practice in violation of Articles 2, 3 and 13 of the Convention was argued and the ECtHR discarded the analysis. In *Salman v. Turkey,*[64] the applicant insisted and as violations to Articles 2, 3 and 13 were found, the declaration of a practice was considered to be unnecessary.

The assertion of a practice revealed its utility on evidentiary matters: The proof that an individual counts with certain characteristics (e.g., to be member of political organizations, to be religious leader, etc.), and that there is a practice of disappearances against those persons, has permitted the proof of many individual cases of disappearances in the Inter-American system. Moreover, the determination of a practice permits one to qualify the seriousness of a case.

If the ECtHR declares the existence of a practice in a period of time in certain member state, other petitioners would see their evidentiary task alleviated. If the family members can prove that the victim belongs to a group targeted by the mentioned practice in the same area, the burden of the proof shifts to the state that should, in this example, obtain the release or the escape of the victim. The underlying reason is to understand that the state is in a better position than the victim and family members. Perhaps this is the main lesson learned from *Velásquez* Rodríguez and should be imitated by the other systems of protection.

Enforced Disappearances, Crime against Humanity

Enforced disappearance has reached the character of crime against humanity in certain context and circumstances. The IACHR has asserted that enforced disappearance is an international crime and is a crime against humanity included in the statute of the ICC and even in the Draft IC.

The General Assembly of the Organization of American States (OASGA) has declared in several opportunities that the forced disappearance of persons is an affront to the conscience of the hemisphere and constitutes a crime against humanity.[65] The same happened in the framework of the IACHR.[66] Because of this regional practice, the preamble of the IACFD asserts as follows "REAFFIRMING that the systematic practice of the forced disappearance of persons constitutes a crime against humanity." First, the preamble asserts that only the systematic practice of forced disappearance is a crime against humanity, though the previous practice of the Inter-American system was not requiring that threshold.[67] Second, the word *reaffirming* suggests that the characterization as crime against humanity is not due to Article 3 of the IACFD or to the ICC statute, but to previously existent international law rules, in particular the above-mentioned practice of the OASGA and IACHR. The IACtHR in the *Velasquez Rodriguez* case explains this aspect even further[68]: "153. International practice and doctrine have often categorized disappearances as a crime against humanity, although there is no treaty in force which is applicable to the States Parties to the Convention and which uses this terminology." The text of the IACFD characterizes all cases of forced disappearances as crimes engaging the personal responsibility of perpetrators, and state responsibility when its authorities executed or consented to it.

The IACHR has not been consistent. In the *Report on the Situation of Human Rights in Colombia,* the IACHR asserted, "[T]he forced disappearance of persons is considered to be a particularly grave violation of international human rights law. In addition, the systematic practice of the forced disappearance of persons constitutes a crime against humanity."[69]

In *Matanovic,* the concurring opinion of Nowak applies the concept of crime against humanity to the concrete case, by citing the IACFD, Article 3, which asserts that any individual act of forced disappearance is a crime against humanity, though the preamble of the DED only stipulates "that the systematic practice of such acts is of the nature of a crime against humanity." However, in *Matanovic,* there was ample evidence that the disappearance was not an isolated case; the CHR in 1994 established a "Special process on missing persons in the territory of the former Yugoslavia," and both the expert member of the WG, responsible for the special process, and the ICRC estimated that some 20,000 persons were still missing in Bosnia and Herzegovina.[70]

In the ICC statute, the idea of enforced disappearances as a crime against humanity has obtained more strength. However, the ICC is competent only if the case takes place after the entry into force of the ICC statute.

For coherence reasons, enforced disappearance should only be a crime against humanity when it comprises the requirements included in the report of the independent expert, that is, as part of a widespread or systematic attack directed against any civilian population.[71]

Conclusions

Clearly, there are difficulties to finding uniform rules under international human rights law concerning enforced disappearances. The definitions are not uniform; the characterizations address the seriousness of the issue, but they are usually not binding or are too general. They reveal the need of clear and binding rules to be implemented or applied by states in their domestic systems. The only treaty in force devoted specially to enforced disappearances (the IACFD) is applicable among some Inter-American states and it is not a complete set of rules; even the definition of enforced disappearances in this treaty has deserved serious critiques. In the international criminal law arena, the jurisprudence of the ICC would probably play a leading role concerning enforced disappearances as crimes against humanity. A new definition of enforced disappearances as crimes against humanity can be found in the Draft IC, which has the advantage of recognizing the dual character of the phenomenon: Enforced disappearances may amount to crimes against humanity.

The clearest and useful definition is still found in the DED, though it has also its limitations that probably are corrected by the Draft IC and the ICC statute. Because the DED is not binding per se, there are important arguments to assert that the prohibition of enforced disappearances has achieved the status of rule of customary international law, or at least it constitutes *opinio juris,* to be followed by the corresponding practice.

The grave, flagrant and serious character of this human rights violation is generally accepted, but it remains unclear what implies this recognition, in particular, the consequences to follow. Today, thanks to the ICC statute, the conditions under which enforced disappearances may constitute crimes against humanity and lead to individual criminal responsibility before this international tribunal have been clarified. However, in the Inter-American system, the notion of crime against humanity appears linked to every case of enforced disappearances.

This is not the only inconsistency found: Even the two existent treaties apply different standards, for example, concerning statutes of limitations. A clause as that included in the Draft IC constitutes a very intelligent solution to the divergent existing rules.

Moreover, clauses that are similar have received different interpretation in the different monitoring systems, as the notion of enforced disappearance as a continuing human rights violation, as it could be analyzed in the above-cited cases before the IACtHR and the HRCBH.

Only more coherence from the derivative organs when dealing with enforced disappearances, and the development of clear-cut standards in binding instruments, as the Draft IC, can lead to a coherent system of protection for victims and next-of-kin in cases of enforced disappearances. Moreover, the definition of enforced disappearance as a crime under internal law with an adequate and serious penalty and suspension of the statute of limitations (if it exists), while the fate and whereabouts of the victim are unknown, and so on, are essential measures of prevention of cases of enforced disappearances. In addition, the nonapplicability of amnesty legislation, and due obedience exceptions to perpetrators are issues to deal with in the domestic system to guarantee its uniform application by domestic tribunals.

In the following pages, the violations of human rights shall be analyzed to emphasize similar problems among the different systems of protection: the lack of consistency and systematization. In particular, the focus will fall on the lack of comparative analysis of the existence jurisprudence in the field of enforced disappearances. In general, the jurisprudence of the IACHR has been subject to few efforts of systematization. Moreover, the jurisprudence of the ECtHR in the field of disappearances has not received much attention. In addition, the jurisprudence of the HRCBH can provide a new view on these issues as a recently created tribunal with a broad mandate to provide for remedies. Concerning this last aspect, the analysis will fall on the consequences of the human rights violations, for example, the right to a remedy, and the right to restitution in cases of enforced disappearance.

2

The Rights Violated

A state may be responsible for the violation of human rights of persons within its jurisdiction. The IACtHR asserted:

> The international protection of human rights should not be confused with criminal justice. States do not appear before the Court as defendants in a criminal action. The objective of international human rights law is not to punish those individuals who are guilty of violations, but rather to protect the victims and to provide for the reparation of damages resulting from the acts of the States responsible.[1]

Enforced disappearances are multiple violations of human rights.[2] In *Velásquez Rodríguez,*[3] the IACtHR concluded,

> the phenomenon of disappearances is a complex form of human rights violation that must be understood and confronted in an integral fashion...
> The forced disappearance of human beings is a multiple and continuous violation of many rights under the Convention that the States Parties are obligated to respect and guarantee.[4]

In the DED,[5] disappearances constitute a violation of the rights to recognition as a person before the law, to liberty and security of the person, the prohibition of torture, and a violation or a grave threat to the right to life (preamble, paragraph 7).

In the preamble of the IACFD, the multiple-rights approach is adopted without mentioning the rights violated: "The forced disappearance of persons violates numerous non-derogable and essential human rights enshrined in the American Convention on Human Rights, in the American Declaration of the Rights and Duties of Man, and in the Universal Declaration of Human Rights."[6] Nonderogable rights are at stake (Article 4.2 International Covenant on Civil and Political Rights [ICCPR][7]; 27.2, American Convention on Human Rights [ACHR][8]; Article 15.2 European Convention).

If enforced disappearances are multiple violations of human rights, the remaining problem is the determination of which are these rights.

First, the IACtHR considers that in each case, the state not only violates concrete rights but also, at the same time, the general obligations contained in the human rights treaties, concretely, in the ACHR. The framework appears in *Velasquez Rodriguez*.[9] The IACtHR based the analysis on Article 1(1) of the ACHR that "specifies the obligation assumed by the States Parties in relation to each of the rights protected. Each claim alleging that one of those rights has been infringed necessarily implies that Article 1 (1) of the Convention has also been violated."[10] The petitioner does not need to allege this violation, as the IACtHR assumes a determination. Article 1 (1)

> charges the States Parties with the fundamental duty to respect and guarantee the rights recognized in the Convention. Any impairment of those rights which can be attributed under the rules of international law to the action or omission of any public authority constitutes an act imputable to the State, which assumes responsibility in the terms provided by the Convention.[11]

The first obligation derived is to respect the rights and freedoms recognized. Public authority cannot be exercised outside the limits derived from treaty law.

The second obligation is to "ensure" the free and full exercise of the rights to every person within the jurisdiction of the state party:

> This obligation implies the duty of States Parties to organize the governmental apparatus and, in general, all the structures through which public power is exercised, so that they are capable of ensuring the free and full enjoyment of human rights. As a consequence of this obligation, the States must prevent, investigate and punish any violation of the rights recognized by the Convention and, moreover, if possible attempt to restore the right violated and provide compensation as warranted for damages resulting from the violation.[12]

Article 2 of the ACHR adds an extra obligation[13]: to adopt the necessary measures as to comply with the obligations contained in the ACHR.

The Multiple-Rights Approach

Because the only treaty containing a definition of enforced disappearances is the IACFD, the organs of protection have to make recourse to the existing instruments (the ICCPR, the European Convention, etc.) when dealing with enforced disappearances. Enforced disappearances are "translated into" the violation of particular rights. Professor Nowak has recommended the definition, in a universally binding instrument, of a new human right, autonomous and nonderogable — the right not to be subjected to enforced disappearance.[14]

In this sense, the WG also asserts "a number of irrevocable rights are infringed by this form of human rights violation."[15] The IACHR shares this point of view: in *Alarcón,* the IACHR asserted, "forced disappearance involves the violation of multiple rights."[16]

Which rights are included? Switzerland asserted that an enforced disappearance may constitute a violation of the rights to life, the protection against torture, liberty of the person, an effective remedy, equal protection by the law, and the exercise of the other rights protected.[17] The seventh paragraph of the DED enumerates the right to recognition as a person before the law, liberty and security of the person, the prohibition of torture, and the right to life.

The multiple-rights approach appears clearly in the jurisprudence of the IACHR. In *García Franco v. Ecuador,*[18] the IACHR understood that forced disappearance is

> a multiple and continuing violation of the American Convention on Human Rights. The objective of those who perpetrate a disappearance is to operate beyond the margins of the law, to conceal all evidence of their crimes, and to escape any sanction. When a disappearance is carried out, the fundamental protections established by law are circumvented and the victim is left defenseless. For the victim, the consequence of an enforced disappearance is, in essence, to be denied every essential right that — as a matter of law — is deemed to inhere in the very fact of being human.

Enforced disappearance is a denial of "every essential right." In the *Report on the Situation of Human Rights in Chile* (1985), the IACHR asserted:

> This procedure is cruel and inhuman and that, as experience shows, disappearance is not only an arbitrary deprivation of liberty but also an extremely serious threat to personal integrity, safety, and the very life of the victim. In the view of the Commission, disappearance may be a method used to prevent the application of the legal provisions established for the defense of individual freedom, physical integrity, the dignity, and the very life of man. In practice, this procedure renders invalid the legal rules enacted in recent years in some countries to prevent illegal arrest and the use of physical and mental duress against the persons arrested.[19]

In *Tordecilla Trujillo,*[20] the IACHR understood

> 32. The forced disappearance of persons constitutes a multiple and continuing violation of several rights recognized in the Convention that the States Parties are bound to respect and ensure. As expressed by the Inter-American Court, a forced disappearance begins with the abduction of the person, which entails the arbitrary deprivation of liberty, and violates the right of the detainee to be brought before a judge without delay. In most cases it also entails prolonged isolation and coerced incommunication, which constitutes cruel and inhuman treatment, as well as the execution of detainees in secret and without any indictment, followed by hiding the corpse for the purpose of erasing any material trace of the crime, and seeking to ensure impunity for those who committed it. It is, moreover, a continuing or constantly reiterated crime, as it is committed until the

person or his or her remains appear, which makes it all the more abominable, to the point of being considered a crime against humanity. This is so established in the Statute of the International Criminal Court adopted by the Rome Conference on July 17, 1998, at Article 7(1) (i).

After *Velasquez Rodríguez,* the IACtHR supports clearly the multiple rights approach. In *Blake* the court asserted:

66. Forced or involuntary disappearance is one of the most serious and cruel human rights violations, in that it not only produces arbitrary deprivation of freedom but places the physical integrity, security and the very life of the detainee in danger. It also leaves the detainee utterly defenseless, bringing related crimes in its wake. Hence, it is important for the State to take all measures as may be necessary to avoid such acts, to investigate them and to sanction those responsible, as well as to inform the next of kin of the disappeared person's whereabouts and to make reparations where appropriate.

However, the case law is inconsistent, even within the same regional system of protection. In *Caballero Delgado & Santana,*[21] though the IACHR considered that the there was a violation of Articles 4 (right to life), 5 (right to humane treatment), 7 (right to personal liberty), and 25 (right to judicial protection) of the ACHR, the IACtHR added Article 8 (right to a fair trial), without clear argumentation.

Enforced Disappearance as a Violation to the Right to Life, Protection against Torture and Inhuman, Cruel, and Degrading Treatment, and the Right to Personal Freedom

In *Velasquez Rodriguez,* and *Godinez Cruz*[22] *the* IACtHR considered that the state had violated Article 4 (the right to life), 5 (the right not to be tortured or subjected to inhuman treatment), and 7 (the right to personal liberty) of the ACHR. This interpretation is one of the most used formulas in the Inter-American system and easily in the IACtHR. The approach was followed by the IACHR in several cases,[23] and by the European Court in some cases against Turkey;[24] the same has happened in the HRC.[25]

Enforced Disappearance as a Violation to the Rights to Life and Personal Freedom

The IACHR declared simply that enforced disappearances amounted to a violation of Article 4 (right to life) and 7 (right to personal freedom) of the ACHR. There was no explanation about the omission of Article 5, comparing with the foregoing analysis.[26] The HRC has also concluded similarly.[27]

In *Neira Alegría,* the IACtHR reached the same conclusion, but it explained why: lack of evidence concerning Article 5.[28]

Enforced Disappearance as a Violation of the Rights to Life, Prohibition of Torture and Inhuman Treatment, Personal Freedom, and Judicial Guarantees

The IACHR decided at certain point to include, in addition, a violation of the right to judicial guarantees, as protected by Article 8 of the ACHR. This model was used in many cases against Peru.[29] However, there is confusion between the right to a prompt and effective judicial remedy (Article 25) with the guarantees of the due process of law (Article 8).

Enforced Disappearance as a Violation to the Rights to Life, Personal Freedom, and Access to Justice (or Right to a Judicial Remedy)

Another approach of the IACHR was to declare violations to Articles 4, 7, and 25, omitting Articles 5 and 8.[30] This happened in cases against El Salvador at the beginning of the 1990s.

Enforced Disappearance as a Violation to the Right to Life and Access to Justice

This approach asserts that the victim was presumably deprived of the life and had no access to judicial remedies.[31] This is not one of the most common interpretations, but it can be found in IACHR reports.

Enforced Disappearance as a Violation to the Rights to Life, Freedom from Torture and Inhuman Treatment, Personal Freedom, and Access to Justice

The IACHR has also understood disappearances as a violation of Articles 4, 5, 7, and 25 of the ACHR.[32] This is also present in the jurisprudence of the IACtHR since *Castillo Páez*.[33]

Enforced Disappearance as a Violation to the Rights to Life, Freedom from Torture and Inhuman Treatment, Personal Freedom, Fair Trial, and Access to Justice

In subsequent cases, the IACHR added Article 25 of the ACHR (right to judicial protection) to the formula Articles 4, 5, 7, 8.[34] This model has also been used by the IACtHR in *Caballero Delgado & Santana v. Colombia*.[35] Moreover, in *El Caracazo*, Venezuela recognized its international responsibility accepting that it had violated Articles 4, 5, 7, 8.1, and 25.1 and 2 of the ACHR.[36]

In *Amalia Rada et al.*,[37] the IACHR used this framework against Bolivia by applying the American Declaration on the Rights and Duties of Man (AD)[38] as Bolivia was not party to the ACHR. The IACHR decided that Bolivia had violated Articles 1 (right to life, liberty, and personal security), 18 (right to a fair trial), 25 (right to protection from arbitrary arrest), and 26 (right to due process of law) of the AD. The same happened in the *Cases 1702,*[39] against Guatemala.

The Incorporation of the Right to Juridical Personality

The IACHR added the right to juridical personality to the list of rights to life, freedom from torture and inhuman treatment, physical freedom, fair trial and access to justice, for example, in the *Report on the Situation of Human Rights in Colombia*[40]: "The forced disappearance of persons generally entails a violation of the right to life and the right to humane treatment.... A disappearance also violates, at a minimum, the right to juridical personality, the right to personal liberty and the right to due process of law and judicial protection." Another example is *Velasquez Isabela et al.*[41] The IACtHR has shared this point of view in the case of *Bamaca Velasquez v. Guatemala.*[42]

Enforced Disappearance as a Violation to the Rights to Life, Freedom from Torture or Inhuman Treatment, Personal Freedom, and Juridical Personality

In *Matanovic v. the Republika Srpska,* the HRCBH analyzed the forced disappearance of a Roman Catholic priest and his parents, arrested and detained by authorities of the Republika Srpska. After house arrest, the victims were taken to a police station in September 1995 and subsequently disappeared. In two opportunities, the Republika Srpska offered to exchange them for prisoners held by Bosnia and Herzegovina, but this did not happen.

The HRCBH applied Article 1 of Annex 6 of the Dayton Agreement, as the parties "shall secure to all persons within their jurisdiction the highest level of internationally recognized human rights and fundamental freedoms, including the rights and freedoms provided in the European Convention for the Protection of Human Rights and Fundamental Freedoms." The HRCBH understood that they include the right to liberty and security of person, Article 5 of the European Convention, violated by the Republika Srpska. Following *Kurt,* the HRCBH understood there was a fundamental and grave issue under Article 5, and, consequently, a violation of Article 1, Annex 6 of the Dayton Agreement. The HRCBH refrained from analyzing if there were violations of Articles 2 and 3 of the European Convention.

The concurring opinion of Nowak accepted the violation of Article 5 but not the refusal to consider if there were further breaches. Nowak understood that the HRCBH was not restricted by the approach adopted by the ombudsperson who only alleged violations of Article 5. Nowak distinguished the arbitrary deprivation of personal liberty and security from the enforced disappearances, adding that there were also certain indications that one or more of the applicants might have died in detention. The argument was that the DED should be applied together with the European Convention in such cases: "The very act of enforced disappearance is a particularly serious violation of human rights which clearly goes beyond mere arbitrary deprivation of personal liberty and security." Nowak considered that enforced disappearance constitutes a violation of the rules of international law guaranteeing, inter alia, the rights to recognition as a person before the law, liberty, and security, not to be subjected to torture. There is a similar approach to that of the IACHR.[43]

However, in subsequent cases, the HRCBH changed its point of view, with the clear influence of the opinion just cited. In *Palic v. Republika Srpska,*[44] it found violations to Articles 2, 3, and 5 of the European Convention concerning Avdo Palic, an officer of the army of Bosnia Herzegovina, and even violations of Articles 3 and 8 concerning his wife. In the *Srebrenica Cases,*[45] the HRCBH declared a violation of Articles 3 and 8 of the European Convention and the prohibition of discrimination, Article 2 (2) (b) of the Dayton Agreement.

Conclusion: The Necessity of a Multiple-Rights Approach

The insufficiency of existent treaty law has been confronted through the creativity of the different organs of protection: Disappearances violate, at the same time, several provisions of the treaties they are competent to apply. This was due to lack of clear and binding rules as to deal with enforced disappearances.

In the Inter-American system, every case constitutes a violation of several human rights protected in the ACHR and the AD. The HRC has been more cautious: It has not extensively argued or elaborated in favor of the multiplicity of violations. However, the ECtHR counts with the more conservative approach: a case of enforced disappearances *may* constitute a violation of several provisions, but that is strictly not necessary.

Other clear and useful solution was the argumentation of Nowak in *Matanovic:* the application of the DED. In this sense, the organs of protection have been reluctant to refer to this instrument. Concerning the HRCBH, the possibility is clear due to Article 1 of Annex 6 of the Dayton Agreement. In the other cases, treaty law clauses have been the main limitation, as the mandate consist in applying and interpreting a concrete instrument; see, for example, Article 1 of the first Optional Protocol (OP1)[46] to the ICCPR, Articles 44 and 62.1 of the ACHR. However, nothing impedes using the DED as interpretive instrument. The different organs of human rights monitoring and adjudication should be encouraged to apply the DED, as it currently provides for the highest standard of protection in this field (Arg. Article 5.2 of the ICCPR, Article 29 of the ACHR, Article 17 of the European Convention).

The existence of the IACFD in the Inter-American system has more or less solved the problem in that region, as the notion of the convention has been applied even concerning states that are nonparties, without any complaint from the states whose responsibility was analyzed.

Why do we need a multiple-rights approach? Because the derisory organ can consequently deal with this human rights violation with a comprehensive approach, by paying attention to the nature and the different sides of an enforced disappearances case and by granting the monitoring organ a multiple-sided view of the problem, which allows the adoption of the necessary measures to grant full reparation to victims and family members. Moreover, this is the only form to address decisions on efficient and effective preventive measures, as well as the appropriate measures of reparation that should be proportionate to the violations committed.

However, if enforced disappearances are multiple violations of human rights, what are these human rights? The need of coherence is urgent in particular within the Inter-American system. One specific cause of the problem is the internal distribution of work in the IACHR, where the IACHR assigns the cases to different lawyers supporting the work of the commissioners according to the country denounced. Each lawyer deals with two or three countries at the same time; there is some coherence among the countries denounced per year, but not concerning one year and different countries or concerning a country over several years. The IACHR should develop clear guidelines to avoid the impression that enforced disappearances committed in certain countries are less serious (as only imply the violation of some rights), while enforced disappearances in other countries have deserved reports asserting the violation of almost all the nonderogable rights protected by the ACHR.

In this framework, enforced disappearances clearly constitute:

• A violation of a very serious threat to the right to life of the victim (Arg. Article 1, 2nd paragraph, DED; Article 3, UDHR; Article 6.1 of the ICCPR; Article 2, European Convention; Article 1, AD; Article 4, ACHR; Article 4, ACHPR), because the outcome of most cases has been the death of the victim, paying attention to the time elapsed since the disappearance. If the victim survives, the enforced disappearance has put his or her life at extremely high risk.[47]

• As a minimum, they constitute inhuman treatment (Arg. Article 1, 2nd paragraph, DED; Article 5, UDHR; Article 7, ICCPR; Article 3, European Convention; Article 5, ACHR; Articles 4–5, ACHPR), as the victim is held incommunicado, with the anguish of ignoring what would happen to him or her and may reach the highest level of seriousness in cases of torture,[48] as it has been accredited, for example, in the report elaborated by the Argentinean truth commissions, *Nunca Más*.[49]

• Moreover, as the victim is deprived of his or her personal freedom, though the original act of arrest of detention could have been legal, the permanence of the victim, detained in a clandestine place without judicial order based on grounds established by a nonarbitrary and previous law and without presentation before a competent judge as to assess the situation, there is also a violation to the right of personal freedom (Article 1, 2nd paragraph, DED; Article 3, UDHR; Article 9, ICCPR; Article 5, European Convention; Article 1, AD; Article 7, ADHR; Article 6 ACHPR); as well as a violation to the guarantee aiming at the protection of this right, habeas corpus (Arg. Article 10 DED; Article 9.4, ICCPR; Article 5.4, European Convention; Article 25, AD; Article 7.6, ADHR), because the victim is not presented before competent authority that could decide on the illegality of this situation. In this sense, the lack of access of habeas corpus would constitute, in the framework of the Inter-American system, a violation of Article 25 of the ACHR together with Article 7.6.[50]

• In addition, because the effect of enforced disappearance is to place the victim outside the protection of the law, there is also a deprivation of the right to juridical personality (Article 1, 2nd paragraph, DED; Article 6, UDHR; Article 16, ICCPR; Article 17, AD; Article 3, ACHR; Article 5, ACHPR), as the victim is de facto impeded from exercising all the other human rights to which he or she is entitled.[51]

Enforced disappearances require, consequently, a comprehensive analysis and a concrete determination in each case of the existence of these concrete human rights violations to reflect the serious character of this multiple human rights violation, as well as to grant the appropriate reparation of all the damages caused as a consequence of them, as reparation should relate to the violations committed.

In this context, enforced disappearance not only has a victim — the disappeared person — but also the next of kin, who may be considered victims of violations too.

• The right to human treatment for the serious sufferings caused by the disappearance (Arg. Article 1, 2nd paragraph, DED; Article 5, UDHR; Article 7, ICCPR; Article 3, European Convention; Article 5, ACHR; Articles 4–5, ACHPR) (see Chapter 5);

• The right to protection of the family life from arbitrary interferences (Article 11, UDHR; Article 17, ICCPR; Article 8, European Convention; Article 5, AD; Article 11.2, ACHR), as families are destroyed, disrupted, and communication among members of the family turns out to be impossible because of the case of disappearance.[52]

• The right to know the truth, in particular, about the fate and whereabouts of the victim (Arg. Article 13, last paragraph, DED) (see Chapter 7).

• The right to access to justice, when the domestic legal systems grant standing to the victim's family members, to protect the victim's rights and their own rights, and they have been generally impeded to do it in cases of enforced disappearances (Arg. Articles 9 and 13, DED; Article 9, UDHR; Article 2.3, ICCPR; Article 13, European Convention; Article 18, AD; Article 25, ACHR; Article 7, ACHPR).[53]

In the following pages, the jurisprudence of the different organs of protection will be discussed to determine their concrete opinion concerning the human rights violations declared in cases of enforced disappearance in a comparative analysis, to provide for a more or less coherent framework in this regard, and to determine the similarities and differences found among the different systems of protection.

3

The Right to Life

The right to life is the supreme human right, permitting the enjoyment of other human rights. The UDHR simply asserts, in Article 3, that "everyone has the right to life." In treaty law, the ICCPR defines this right as "inherent" (Article 6.1), with natural law origin, with nonrestrictive interpretation.[1] The concept in the CRC, Article 6.1, is similar. The right to life is not negative. States are obliged to adopt measures to protect it,[2] but discretionally,[3] which requires domestic criminal rules.

The DED, in Article 1.3 and Preamble, asserts that enforced disappearance "violates or constitutes a grave threat to the right to life."[4] In the Preamble of the Draft IC of 1998, a "forced disappearance violates the right to life or puts it in grave danger." The language "grave threat" of the DED is replaced by "grave danger."

The link between enforced disappearances and right to life is also recognized by the Human Rights Committee (HRC), General Comment (GenC) No. 6 (§4).

> States parties [to the ICCPR] should also take specific and effective measures to prevent the disappearance of individuals, something which unfortunately has become all too frequent and leads too often to arbitrary deprivation of life. Furthermore, States should establish effective facilities and procedures to investigate thoroughly cases of missing and disappeared persons in circumstances which may involve a violation of the right to life.

In the Americas, the right is framed in Article 4 of the ACHR: "Every person has the right to have his life respected. This right shall be protected by law and, in general, from the moment of conception. No one shall be arbitrarily deprived of his life."

Article 2 of the European Convention recognizes:

1. Everyone's right to life shall be protected by law. No one shall be deprived of his life intentionally save in the execution of a sentence of a court following his conviction of a crime for which this penalty is provided by law.

2. Deprivation of life shall not be regarded as inflicted in contravention of this article when it results from the use of force, which is no more than absolutely necessary:
   a. In defense of any person from unlawful violence;
   b. In order to effect a lawful arrest or to prevent the escape of a person lawfully detained.
   c. In action lawfully taken for the purpose of quelling a riot or insurrection.

The ACHPR asserts in Article 4 that "human beings are inviolable. Every human being shall be entitled to respect for his life and the integrity of his person. No one may be arbitrarily deprived of this right."

A case of enforced disappearances may constitute an arbitrary deprivation of life or a threat to life. The first paragraph of the *Principles on the Effective Prevention and Investigation of Extra-legal, Arbitrary and Summary Executions* (Principles on Prevention),[5] asserts that "governments shall prohibit by law all extra-legal, arbitrary and summary executions and shall ensure that any such executions are recognized as offences under their criminal laws, and are punishable by appropriate penalties which take into account the seriousness of such offences."

An arbitrary execution is the killing of a person perpetrated by an agent of the state or any other person acting under government authority or with its complicity, tolerance, or acquiescence, but without any or due judicial procedure. In some cases, the victim has suffered death threats.

Pursuant to Article 4 of the ICCPR, Article 27.1 of the ACHR and Article 15 of the European Convention, this is a nonderogable right. It cannot be suspended, even in times of emergency. Under international humanitarian law, this right is also protected. Common Article 3 to the four Geneva Conventions (GC) (1949)[6] prohibits "at any time and in any place whatsoever ... violence to life and person, in particular murder of all kinds" against those not taking active part in an armed conflict of noninternational character. Concerning internal armed conflict, Article 4 of Additional Protocol (AP) II also prohibits, regarding persons not taking part of the conflict or that have ceased in their participation, "violence to the life, health and physical or mental well-being of persons ... in particular murder."[7]

In an international armed conflict, willful killings of protected persons under the GC constitute grave breaches of them (I GC Article 50; II GC, Article 51; III GC, Article 130; IV GC, Article 147; AP I, Article 85).[8] In addition, Article 12 of the I and II GC asserts that armed forces and others who are wounded or sick must be treated humanely; attempts on their lives or violence to their persons are prohibited, particularly murder or extermination. Article 13 III GC indicates that prisoners of war (POWs) must be humanely treated at all times; unlawful acts or omissions by the detaining power causing death or serious danger to the health of the POW in custody are prohibited and included as a serious breach. Article 32 of the IV GC outlaws measures causing to civilians in the hands of one party to an international armed conflict "physical suffering or extermination." This includes murder but also brutality applied by civilian or military agents.

The Inter-American Court of Human Rights

In *Velasquez Rodriguez,* the IACtHR explained the link between enforced disappearances and the right to life: "157. The practice of disappearances often involves secret execution without trial, followed by concealment of the body to eliminate any material evidence of the crime and to ensure the impunity of those responsible. This is a flagrant violation of the right to life, recognized in Article 4 of the Convention." The same happened in *Godínez Cruz.*[9]

In *Velasquez Rodriguez,* the IACtHR went further:

> 188. ...The context in which the disappearance of Manfredo Velásquez occurred and the lack of knowledge seven years later about his fate create a reasonable presumption that he was killed. Even if there is a minimal margin of doubt in this respect, it must be presumed that authorities that systematically executed detainees without trial and concealed their bodies in order to avoid punishment decided his fate. This, together with the failure to investigate, is a violation by Honduras of a legal duty under Article 1 (1) of the Convention to ensure the rights recognized by Article 4 (1). That duty is to ensure every person subject to its jurisdiction the inviolability of the right to life and the right not to have one's life taken arbitrarily. These rights imply an obligation on the part of States Parties to take reasonable steps to prevent situations that could result in the violation of that right.

The IACtHR had not seen the body, but the context and the time elapsed (seven years) led to the presumption of an arbitrary execution. Consequently, Honduras had violated Article 4.1. In *Godínez Cruz,*[10] six and a half years had elapsed.[11]

In *Neira Alegria et al. v. Peru,*[12] three persons disappeared in a prison demolished by the security forces to repress a mutiny.[13] The IACtHR emphasized that nobody can be deprived of his or her life arbitrarily. The state can neither exercise its power without limit nor use any mean as to reach its goals.[14] The lack of news for more than eight years and the nonproportional use of force amounted to a violation of Article 4.1 of the ACHR.[15]

In *Caballero Delgado & Santana v. Colombia,* the Colombian army captured the victims in 1989. One was a trade union leader; the other, a member of M19. The detentions were denied, and the procedures had no result. The right to life had been violated, because the Colombian army had detained the victims, and there was no news after six years.

In *Castillo Páez v. Peru,*[16] the IACtHR declared a violation of Article 4. Policemen arbitrarily detained Castillo Páez, the detention was denied, and his whereabouts were unknown for seven years. The state's argument asserting that because the body was missing, there was no violation of the right to life, was rejected.[17]

In *Blake v. Guatemala,*[18] the body of Blake was found after his disappearance but before the acceptance of the jurisdiction of the court by Guatemala, though Guatemala was party to the ACHR when Blake disappeared. The IACtHR understood it had no jurisdiction over Blake's death. This solution has been criticized elsewhere (see Chapter 1).

In *Paniagua Morales v. Guatemala,*[19] five bodies appeared the same day or days later after a kidnapping by state agents. The IACtHR concluded that Article 4 had been violated.

In *Villagrán Morales v. Guatemala,*[20] two police agents kidnapped five young victims and killed them 10–20 hours later, before witnesses.[21] The court asserted that the right to life cannot be understood restrictively, including the right to an existence with dignity. Moreover, the State did not prevent the violations. Article 4 and all the instruments protecting children had been violated.

In *Bámaca Velásquez v. Guatemala,*[22] the victim was executed after secret military detention. States have the obligation to guarantee the right to life of persons detained. According to the circumstances of the detention, the character of the victim (commander of the guerrilla), and the state practice, as well as the time elapsed since detention (eight years and eight months), Bámaca was presumed to be dead. Consequently, Guatemala had violated the right to life.

The European System of Protection

The ECtHR had not always declared violations to the right to life. *Kurt v. Turkey* was the first case of enforced disappearances before the ECtHR, which did not declare a violation of this right. Almost four and a half years had elapsed without information; the court should "carefully scrutinize whether there does in fact exist concrete evidence which would lead it to conclude that her son was, beyond reasonable doubt, killed by the authorities either while in detention in the village or at some subsequent stage."[23] The analysis of "concrete evidence" that would lead "beyond reasonable doubt" to this conclusion constitutes a completely different approach. The ECtHR cited *McCann and Others* and *Kaya v. Turkey,*[24] because there was evidence of a fatal shooting. If this evidence exists, the state should conduct an effective investigation. A case based "entirely on presumptions deduced from the circumstances of her son's initial detention bolstered by more general analyses of an alleged officially tolerated practice of disappearances and associated ill-treatment and extra-judicial killing of detainees in the respondent State" was not sufficient.[25] Consequently, the ECtHR analyzed "the failure to protect the son's life" under Article 5.[26] This approach is hardly justified, because it ignores the phenomenon of enforced disappearances and the situation in Turkey. The decision imposes an impossible burden on the family members and the victim. Enforced disappearances are just a violation to the right of personal freedom (e.g., the only relevant information is that the victim was arbitrarily detained).

In *Kurt v. Turkey,* AI made a submission to the ECtHR considering that disappearances often include secret execution without trial and concealment of the body.[27]

In *Ertak v. Turkey,*[28] the victim's father alleged that his son had disappeared in Turkey and had been subjected to severe ill treatment, dying in custody. The ECtHR differentiated the case from *Kurt,* because there was evidence of mistreatment, and the fate of the victim.[29] For that reason, there was a violation of the right to life.

The ECtHR differentiated the substantive violation of the right to life from the procedural violation. The substantive aspect has just been analyzed. The procedural aspect is the "obligation for agents of the State to account for their use of lethal force by subjecting their actions to some form of independent and public scrutiny capable of determining whether the force used was or was not justified in a particular set of circumstances."[30] There was no adequate or effective investigation, so the procedural aspect of Article 2 had also been violated. Under "right to life," the ECtHR analyzes at the same time the concrete violation, as well as the judicial guarantees (see, e.g., the analysis concerning Article 8 and Article 25 of the ACHR).

In *Çakici v. Turkey,*[31] the applicant's brother disappeared in 1994 after detention by security forces. The victim was severely beaten and received electric shocks. The authorities claimed that Çakici had been killed in a clash, as his identification card was found. The ECtHR asserted that the identity card could lead to a strong inference on the dead, as there were "sufficient circumstantial evidence, based on concrete elements, on which it may be concluded beyond reasonable doubt that Ahmet Çakici died following his apprehension and detention by the security forces." The case was also distinguished from *Kurt,*[32] Article 2 not only applies to "intentional killing from the use of force by agents of the State" but also to a "positive obligation on States that the right to life be protected by law,"[33] that is, some effective official investigation.[34]

In *Mahmut Kaya v. Turkey,* the applicant's brother was a medical doctor who treated members of PKK. He received threats several times. One day, Kaya assisted a member of the PKK, together with a human rights lawyer, but they never returned. The bodies were found five days later. They had been shot, and the lawyer's body presented signs of torture. The perpetrators were undercover state agents or persons acting under its instructions or implied instructions with state equipment and support.[35] The ECtHR asserted that

> not every claimed risk to life therefore can entail for the authorities a Convention requirement to take operational measures to prevent that risk from materializing. For a positive obligation to arise, it must be established that the authorities knew or ought to have known at the time of the existence of a real and immediate risk to the life of an identified individual or individuals from the criminal acts of a third party and that they failed to take measures within the scope of their powers which, judged reasonably, might have been expected to avoid that risk.[36]

There was no evidence that state agents had committed the murder; however, the perpetrators were known by the authorities,[37] because the victims were transported through several checkpoints, and one of the suspects was seen when receiving official assistance. Moreover, Kaya was suspected of cooperating with PKK; he was at real and immediate risk,[38] and the authorities were too permissive concerning violence against certain persons and groups.[39] The investigation was defective,[40] the criminal law protection of the right to life was not adequate — there was a violation to Article 2.[41]

In *Timurtaş v. Turkey,* the father of the disappeared Abdulvahap received an anonymous phone call in 1993 indicating that soldiers had detained him with a friend. They were shown to the villagers to be recognized. Another son of the applicant had died in custody two years before. The applicant could know the place of detention and that his son did not want to talk. Prison workers asserted that the victim was there, so the prosecutor accepted the father's declaration. In 1995, the father met scared witnesses, who had been mistreated during interrogation. More than six and a half years had passed without further news.[42] If a person was healthy when entering into custody, the state should determine how the physical integrity would have deteriorated. In absence of the body, Article 2 was at stake again, depending on circumstantial evidence and based on concrete evidence that supported the presumption that the person died.[43] The time in custody was relevant.[44] To apply Article 2 instead of Article 5, the court enumerated denial of information, concealing of reports about the person in custody, etc.[45]

The court distinguished the case from *Kurt:* The time elapsed was longer (six and a half years versus four and a half years), and in *Timurtaş* there was evidence of detention of the victim, which was absent in *Kurt.* Moreover, in *Timurtaş,* the applicant's son was detained for alleged PKK activities, which was life threatening. The death of the applicant's son was presumed because of the unacknowledged detention by security officers.[46] There was a procedural violation of Article 2 because the investigation was "dilatory, perfunctory, superficial and not constituting a serious attempt to find out what had happened to the applicant's son."[47]

In *Orhan v. Turkey*,[48] the violation of Article 2 was declared for the lack of information about the Orhans for almost eight years after unacknowledged detention and a deficient investigation.

In *Taş v. Turkey*, in an area with terrorist activity, during a police operation Taş was shot in the knee and taken into custody. He was in the hospital, and his whereabouts were later unknown. According to security officers, he had escaped. The prosecutor did not investigate the case, though there were requests for information.[49] The absence of a body (e.g., the application of Article 2) and the time elapsed since detention were relevant,[50] along with the lack of records of detention and medical treatment. The court made "very strong inference" that the victim should be presumed dead,[51] Turkey was responsible because "the authorities have not accounted for what happened during Muhsin Taş's detention and that they do not rely on any ground of justification in respect of any use of lethal force by their agents."

The ECtHR linked Article 2 to the general duty of Article 1. The approach was similar to the one of the Inter-American system: "Some form of effective official investigation when individuals have been killed as a result of the use of force."[52] The lack of reaction to the "loss" of a detained person was "incompatible with this obligation."[53] The court understood that

> it has already found in a number of cases that the use of provincial administrative councils to investigate allegations of unlawful killings did not comply with the requirement that the investigation be carried out by an independent body in a process accessible to the alleged victim's close relatives, in particular since these councils were composed of officials under the authority of the Governor who was administratively in charge of the security forces under investigation.[54]

The investigation was not prompt, adequate, or effective; Article 2 (procedural obligation) was breached.

In *Salman v. Turkey*, the applicant's husband, a taxi driver, 45 years old without ill health or heart problems, was taken into custody by anti-terror police officers in 1992. He was released the same day after beatings and immersion in cold water. He was sick for two days. Police officers detained him again days later. The apprehension was never recorded. Salman was interrogated, and his heartbeat, breathing, and other vital functions stopped; cyanosis developed. Salman was dead on arrival to hospital. The body presented several injuries. The ECtHR cited the ECPT and its visits to Turkey. The ECPT asserted that torture and ill treatment happened during police custody and concluded: "The practice of torture and other forms of severe ill-treatment of persons in police custody remains widespread in Turkey."[55]

Article 2 covers not only intentional killing but also permitted use of force, which may result in the deprivation of life as an unintended outcome,[56]so the ECtHR indicated

> the deliberate or intended use of lethal force is only one factor however to be taken into account in assessing its necessity. Any use of force must be no more than "absolutely necessary" for the achievement of one or more of the purposes set out in sub-paragraphs (a) to (c). This term indicates that a stricter and more compelling test of necessity must be employed when determining whether State action is "necessary in a democratic society" under paragraphs 2 of Articles 8 to 11 of the Convention. Consequently, the force used must be strictly proportionate to the achievement of the permitted aims.[57]

Persons in custody are vulnerable and authorities should protect them.[58] There was no explanation concerning the injuries and subsequent death. Turkey had violated Article 2.[59] The court again related Article 2 to Article 1,[60] including the performance of an autopsy, that no effective investigation had taken place.

In *Çiçek v. Turkey,*[61] the applicant's sons and her grandson, who were visually impaired, had disappeared. About 100 soldiers surrounded the village in 1994, woke up the villagers, asked for identification, and sent them to the mosque. The victims were detained, but no record was reliable.[62] A difference concerning *Kurt* was that the sons were not released, in contrast with other villagers.[63] The ECtHR for the first time asserted that southeast Turkey was life-threatening.[64] After six and a half years, the victims should be presumed dead.[65] The procedural obligation (Article 2) had also been violated.[66]

In *Akdeniz v. Turkey,* the ECtHR concluded that 11 disappeared persons should be presumed dead. The authorities did not account for them, violating Articles 2 and 1. The prosecutors did not investigate the case: "There was a failure to provide an effective investigation into the *disappearance* of the applicants' relatives and there has accordingly been a violation of Article 2 of the Convention on this account also" (emphasis added).

In *Cyprus v. Turkey,*[67] Cyprus alleged that Turkey newly violated the convention though there were previous commission reports (10 July 1976 and 4 October 1983) and reports from the Committee of Ministers of the Council of Europe. Cyprus presented the problem of Greek-Cypriot missing persons and their relatives after military operations in northern Cyprus in 1974 and the division of Cyprus. In 1981 the United Nations Committee on Missing Persons (CMP) was set up to "look into cases of persons reported missing in the inter-communal fighting as well as in the events of July 1974 and afterwards" and "to draw up comprehensive lists of missing persons of both communities, specifying as appropriate whether they are still alive or dead, and in the latter case approximate times of death." On 10 July 1976, the commission asserted that Turkey had violated Articles 2, 3, 5, 8, 13, and 14 of the convention and Article 1 of Protocol No. 1. In the 1983 report, the commission included breaches of Articles 5 and 8 of the convention and Article 1 of Protocol No. 1.

For the first time, the disappearances in Cyprus reached the ECtHR. Cyprus requested that the court "decide and declare that the respondent State is responsible for continuing violations and other violations of Articles 1, 2, 3, 4, 5, 6, 8, 9, 10, 11, 13, 14, 17 and 18 of the Convention and of Articles 1 and 2 of Protocol No. 1"; 1,491 Greek Cypriots were still missing after 20 years. They were last seen alive in Turkish custody.

Turkey questioned the number of missing persons and argued that they were still alive. Cyprus contended it because the head of the TRNC, Mr. Denktaş, had broadcasted a statement in 1996 admitting that the Turkish army had handed over Greek-Cypriot prisoners to Turkish-Cypriot fighters under Turkish command and that these prisoners had been killed. In 1998, Professor Küçük, a Turkish officer in 1974, asserted that the Turkish army had committed widespread killings of civilians.

The ECtHR recognized the weight of these statements, but they were insufficient for Turkey to be responsible. A period outside the time frame of the case was at stake. There was no proof of unlawful killings, though there was a climate of risk and fear. The authorities had never investigated Mr. Denktaş's statement, identified those released from Turkish custody to the Turkish-Cypriot paramilitaries, or inquired where the bodies were. The obligation of Turkey was not discharged by cooperating with the CMP, there was a "continuing violation of Article 2 on account of the failure of the authorities of the respondent State to conduct an effective investigation aimed at clarifying the whereabouts and fate of Greek-Cypriot missing persons who disappeared in life-threatening circumstances."[68]

The disappearance in life-threatening circumstances obliges the state to investigate and find out the fate of the victims, a procedural obligation according to Article 2.

In *Bilgin v. Turkey*,[69] the victim was detained in Ankara; he never reappeared. The victim's brother alleged death in custody.[70] More than six and a half years had elapsed: The state was obliged to respond for their health.[71] The ECtHR required evidence to apply Article 2, and the time elapsed was relevant. Witnesses accredited that Bilgin was held in very poor state of health.[72] The ECtHR concluded that Bilgin should be presumed dead and that Turkey was internationally responsible.[73] As to the inadequacy of the investigation, the ECtHR found also a procedural violation of Article 2.

The Human Rights Committee

The HRC, monitoring the ICCPR, may receive individual communications against state parties. As in the jurisprudence of the IACtHR, enforced disappearance is directly linked to the violation of the right to life (Article 6 of the ICCPR).

In *Bleier,* the HRC assumed that Uruguay violated Article 6: The victim was member of the Communist Party, arrested in 1975, held a long period as incommunicado, and tortured because of his Jewish origin.[74]

In *Sanjuán Arévalo,*[75] the victims disappeared in Colombia on 8 March 1982. Both of them were students. Agents of the police had watched their house and inquired about them. No investigation had success; a high authority of the security forces assured the victim's father that his sons would soon reappear. The HRC found a violation of the right to life.[76]

In *Rafael Mojica,*[77] the victim disappeared in 1990 in the Dominican Republic. He boarded a taxi with unidentified men. He had received death threats from the military for presumed communist inclinations. The case was not investigated. The HRC applied the GCom 6.[78] The right to life had not been effectively protected, because no measure of prevention was adopted.[79]

In *Bautista de Arellana,*[80] Nydia Bautista, a Colombian citizen, disappeared in 1987, and her body was subsequently recovered. She belonged to M-19 and was detained by a military unit. She was kept incommunicado and allegedly tortured. On signing a statement that she had been well treated, she was released. Later she was abducted again from the family home. Finally, her body appeared in 1987, but the family could identify her only in 1990. In 1991, a member of the intelligence testified that Nydia had been abducted by members of his brigade, acting either with the consent or order of a colonel, and he revealed the names of the perpetrators. No measure was taken against them. The HRC applied again the GCom 6,[81] and concluded that the state was directly responsible.

In *Villafañe Chaparro,*[82] three members of a Colombian indigenous group boarded a bus in 1988 to Bogotá to interview government officials. Members of the community were arrested, accused of belonging to the ELN (Ejército de Liberación Nacional or Army of National Liberation) and of storing weapons. They were later released. The leaders on the bus never reached their destination. The bus driver claimed that four armed men had forced them to board a car; the police did not investigate the case. Days later the three corpses were recovered; no attempt was made to identify them. The death certificates established that the victims were tortured and shot in the head. One person offered money in exchange for information, but later the same person threatened that if there were no confessions about the kidnapping of a landowner, they would kill more indigenous people. The HRC asserted that the state was directly responsible.[83]

In *Ana Rosario Celis Laureano*,[84] her grandfather denounced that in 1992, Ana, 16 years old, was abducted by armed men, presumably from Sendero Luminoso (Shining Path). She returned and asserted that the guerrillas would kill her if she refused to join them, that she had to carry their baggage and cook for them, but she could finally escape. In May 1992, the guerrillas again abducted her, but she escaped. In June 1992, Ana was detained by the military for collaboration with Sendero Luminoso. She was held incommunicado and, during a transfer, she suffered a fractured hip. Afterward a judge ordered her release because she was a minor. However, masked men abducted her from her grandfather's house with military uniform and official weapons. On GCom 6, the HRC asserted a violation of Article 6 together with Article 2.1 of the ICCPR: There was neither prevention nor investigation.[85]

The Inter-American Commission on Human Rights

The IACHR issues recommendations to state members of the OAS concerning violations of the AD. If the state is party to the ACHR, this instrument is applied. If the state has accepted the jurisdiction of the IACtHR, the IACHR must submit the case to this judicial organ, except when there is a majority decision to the contrary, on limited grounds,[86] or to issue a final report. Most of the jurisprudence concerns cases that the IACHR has issued the final decision. In any case, the IACHR can only issue recommendations.

The right to life was always present in disappearance cases. In the *Report on the Situation of Human Rights in Ecuador*,[87] the IACHR asserted: "The right to life is a peremptory norm under international law, and, as set forth in Article 27 of the Convention, may not be derogated from under any circumstance."

In the *State Report on Dominican Republic,* the IACHR asserted the same concept and analyzed disappearances of political opponents to Trujillo.[88]

The IACHR dealt extensively with disappearances in Argentina, Chile, Guatemala, and later Peru. In the *Report on the Situation of Human Rights in Chile* (1985),[89] the IACHR explained the disappearances' methodology and referred to torture against the victims. The IACHR underlined the serious violations to the right to life.[90]

Most disappearances in Argentina took place before being party to the ACHR. Consequently, the IACHR declared a very serious violation to the right to life, Article 1 of the AD.[91]

Disappearances in Colombia are related to the internal armed conflict and repression by the armed forces and paramilitary. In *Bernal Dueñas*[92] and

García Villamizar,[93] the IACHR decided that Colombia had violated Article 4 of the ACHR. In *Tordecilla Trujillo,*[94] the IACHR declared that

> 32. The forced disappearance of persons constitutes a multiple and continuing violation of several rights recognized in the Convention that the States Parties are bound to respect and ensure.... The execution of detainees in secret and without any indictment, followed by hiding the corpse for the purpose of erasing any material trace of the crime, and seeking to ensure impunity for those who committed it. It is, moreover, a continuing or constantly reiterated crime, as it is committed until the person or his or her remains appear.

The multiple violations included the right to life, because 10 years passed without information about the victim's whereabouts.

In *Medina Charry,*[95] the victim was detained for not carrying identification; he disappeared. Nine years elapsed, and the IACHR presumed his death.[96]

Chile was not party to the ACHR when most of the disappearance cases took place. In *París Roa,*[97] the day of the coup (11 September 1973), the victim was at the presidential palace as officer and advisor to the government. He announced to his family he would remain with Allende. After Allende's death, he was arrested and publicly tortured. The authorities officially acknowledged the place of detention; after 17 September there was no information about him. Foreign publications and radio broadcasts reported his alleged death, though this was never acknowledged or denied. The IACHR asserted a very serious violation of the right to life and personal security, Article 1 of the AD.

In *García Franco v. Ecuador,*[98] the IACHR asserted that states are legally required to take steps to respect and ensure the right to life; "a 'disappearance' not only constitutes an arbitrary deprivation of liberty but also a serious danger to the personal integrity and safety and even the very life of the victim"; over eight years had passed since García was last seen or heard from.

Concerning El Salvador, several disappearances of young students took place; the IACHR declared serious violations to the right to life, Article 4 of the ACHR.[99]

In Guatemala, the IACHR has found violations to the right to life. Many years had elapsed — even 18 to 20 — since the disappearance.[100]

In *Vladimir David,*[101] the victim, 17 years of age, disappeared in 1986 in Haiti after a demonstration protesting against the disappearance of Charlot Jacquelin. The IACHR declared the violation to the right to life.

In the *Report on the Situation of Human Rights in Mexico,*[102] the IACHR expressed concern for enforced disappearances, which started in the 1960s in Guerrero, against dissident armed movements. Some cases were carried out by private parties tolerated by the state or directly by state agents. The recent cases concerned the fight against guerrillas, drug trafficking, and common crime. Concerning Chiapas, disappearances took place against indigenous people, peasants, and members of political organizations mostly in 1994.

In Nicaragua, in *Carrero Roque,*[103] the victim was arrested, imprisoned, and since then missing. Nicaragua had violated Article 4.

Peru has originated the most extensive jurisprudence on disappearances.[104]

The IACHR has declared the violation of the right to life in all cases.

Conclusion

All the organs of protection have declared violations to the right to life, because an enforced disappearance may derive to an extrajudicial execution or a serious risk that such execution takes place. The only exception is the European system of protection, where the jurisprudence is more conservative and reticent, except if there is concrete evidence that should lead to the conclusion beyond reasonable doubt that the victim has been killed.[105] The ECtHR has given particular importance to evidence on mistreatment.[106]

The DED clearly recognizes that an enforced disappearance constitutes a violation of the right to life or a serious threat to it. In most cases, the victim is extrajudicially executed. The serious threat is linked to the exposition of the victim, who is likely to be executed.

The international organs of protection face the problem of the absence of the body, which is solved by paying attention to the time elapsed since the absence of news. In most cases, the tribunal has paid attention to years elapsed since the disappearance. However, another circumstance should be also considered. Previous threats against the victim and the participation of the victim in groups likely to suffer enforced disappearances (e.g., militants of parties of leftist ideology, students, persons participating actively in demonstrations, social workers, university professors, etc.) are relevant.

How many years are necessary to wait to consider an enforced disappearance a violation of the right to life? In *Kurt,* the ECtHR asserted that four and a half years is not enough. In *Timurtas,* the court compared the cases, asserting that six and a half years was enough. The HRC and the organs of the Inter-American system have paid special attention to the circumstances of the deprivation of physical freedom and the lack of further news in a certain context (e.g., a "practice" of disappearances or police violence, e.g., see *Garrido and Baigorria*). The ECtHR has recognized life-threatening circumstances (e.g., to be member of a proscribed political party, to live in a region where violent repression against terrorist activities has taken place, etc.), but this is not a "rule" in the jurisprudence. The kidnapping of a person without further news and without signs of violence in the Inter-American system and before the HRC leads to a declaration of a violation of the right to life. The ECtHR requires something more: the proof that the victim was subject to certain levels of violence, witnesses of the conditions of detention, and proof that the authors belong to the security forces or persons acting with their acquiescence or protection. In the other two systems, the response is more realistic and contextual: The perpetrators have acted clandestinely.

The idea a priori that a case of enforced disappearance constitutes a violation to the right to life — except, for instance, when the same victim that reappeared is submitting the case — is extremely useful and necessary. It relieves the victim's family, and it reflects the seriousness of the human rights violation. It reveals the reality of many enforced disappearances: In many cases, the victim is extrajudicially executed and the body hidden in a place unknown for the relatives and friends.

The ECtHR makes resource to Article 2 to address "procedural violations" to the right to the life. This approach is unique; this problem is treated normally applying the general treaty obligations (Article 1.1 in the ACHR; Article 2.3 in the ICCPR). The ECtHR asserts that states are accountable for the use of force, and these acts should be submitted to public scrutiny. Consequently, if a person was healthy in custody, the state has to determine how the health could deteriorate. This procedural violation leads to a change in the burden of the proof. In absence of a body, the state has the obligation to investigate what had happened.[107] Moreover, the ECtHR has linked this procedural violations to the duty contained in Article 1: The state has the obligation to protect life, consequently, the lack of reaction violates these provisions.[108] A procedural violation reveals the lack of investigation.[109]

However, the duty to prevent and investigate has been also asserted clearly in the other systems of protection.[110] However, the ECtHR does not follow the same approach concerning further human rights violations, for example, violations to Article 3 of the European Convention. There is no justification to refer to procedural violations concerning the right to life and not understand that there is a general duty to investigate human rights violations.

4

The Right to Liberty and Security of the Person

The "liberty of the person" protects the freedom of body movement in the narrowest sense.[1] The GenC 8/16 interprets it broadly, prohibiting the deprivation of liberty beyond the permitted cases of arrest or detention. Any deprivation of liberty should be legal and not arbitrary.[2] Arbitrary detention includes holding a person in custody because of political views, without specific charges, or incommunicado detention. Habeas corpus is specially protected for guaranteeing and permitting the judicial protection of this right. The right to security of the person calls on states to protect the persons under its jurisdiction through reasonable and appropriate measures.[3]

Enforced disappearances start as an arbitrary deprivation of physical freedom: The victim is detained without judicial order and on arbitrary grounds, only known by the authorities in charge. The case continues with arbitrary execution or subjection to torture as to obtain information.

The UDHR includes in Article 3 the right to liberty and security of the person and, in Article 9, the right not to be subjected to arbitrary arrest. In treaty law, the right is protected by Article 9 of the ICCPR (paragraph 1), which conditions the deprivation of liberty to the grounds and procedure previously established by law. Paragraph 1 applies to all kinds of deprivation of physical freedom.[4] The following paragraphs contain parameters of protection: right to information of the reasons and charges for detention (paragraph 2), prompt presentation before a competent judge (paragraph 3), and judicial challenge to the deprivation of liberty (paragraph 4).

Article 37.b of the CRC includes the obligation not to deprive children of the liberty unlawfully or arbitrarily. Habeas corpus appears in Article 37.d.

Article 5 of the ECHR protects this right. The basic principle is that no one shall be deprived of the liberty, save in the cases enumerated, and in accordance with a procedure established by law. Guarantees protect the persons detained: prompt information of the reasons of arrest and the charges;

in case of prosecution, right to be brought promptly before a judge; and to challenge the lawfulness of the detention. The right to be brought promptly before a judge is included only in case of prosecution; the ICCPR includes it in all cases.

In the AD, the right to liberty and security of the person is protected in Article I; the right to protection against arbitrary arrest, in Article 25: The deprivation of personal freedom can only be carried out according to procedures and cases established previously by law; it includes the right to challenge the deprivation of physical liberty. The ACHR protects this right in Article 7, particularly in paragraph 1. The prohibition of arbitrary arrest or detention is in paragraph 3 and habeas corpus in paragraph 6.

The ACHPR includes the right to personal freedom in Article 6, prohibiting arbitrary arrest or detention.

In international humanitarian law, safeguards protect these rights, depending on the categories of persons in an armed conflict.[5]

The DED Preamble asserts:[6]

Deeply concerned that in many countries, often in a persistent manner, enforced disappearances occur, in the sense that persons are arrested, detained or abducted against their will or otherwise deprived of their liberty by officials of different branches or levels of Government, or by organized groups or private individuals acting on behalf of, or with the support, direct or indirect, consent or acquiescence of the Government, followed by a refusal to disclose the fate or whereabouts of the persons concerned or a refusal to acknowledge the deprivation of their liberty, which places such persons outside the protection of the law.

The UNGA recalled that the UDHR and the ICCPR protect "the right to liberty and security of the person." The same is asserted in the Preamble to the Draft IC of 1998.[7]

The DED, Article 1, paragraph 3, asserts that the right to liberty and security of the person is violated by any act of enforced disappearance. Article 10 of the same declaration includes some guarantees: Persons deprived of liberty must be held only in official places of detention, and, according to internal law, they must be brought promptly before a judicial authority. Accurate information on the detention and place of detention, including transfers, should be included, which should be available to family members, counsel, or persons with legitimate interest, unless that is against the wish of the interested people. The state must keep an updated register of the persons deprived of their liberty in every place of detention. Moreover, the state must keep a centralized register, available to the persons mentioned above, as well as to any judicial or independent national authority and any other independent authority legally (or through a treaty) entitled to trace the whereabouts of the victim. The WG has asserted that the DED provides for no exceptions to Article 10,[8] not even state of emergency. States should respect Article 9.3 of the ICCPR and other relevant UN standards concerning administrative detention.

Article 11 of the DED indicates that a person deprived of liberty must be released as to permit the verification of that event. Article 12 includes the obligation of states to establish the officials authorized to deprive the liberty and the requisites of such orders and penalties against officials that do not inform a detention without justification. The state must ensure strict supervision, including a clear chain of command of law enforcement officials in charge of apprehensions, detentions, arrests, custody, transfers, imprisonment, and so on.

The IACFD recognizes the link between disappearances and deprivation of liberty, establishing obligations of prevention:

> Article XI
> Every person deprived of liberty shall be held in an officially recognized place of detention and be brought before a competent judicial authority without delay, in accordance with applicable domestic law.
> The States Parties shall establish and maintain official up-to-date registries of their detainees and, according to domestic law, shall make them available to relatives, judges, attorneys, any other person having a legitimate interest, and other authorities.[9]

The following measures contribute to prevention:

- Holding detainees in officially recognized places of detention.
- Bringing the detainee without delay before the competent judicial authority.
- Maintaining official and updated registries of detainees, accessible to interested actors and authorities.

There are further provisions in soft law useful for prevention and protection. The Body of Principles for the Protection of All Persons under Any Form of Detention or Imprisonment (Body of Principles)[10] applies to all persons under any form of detention or imprisonment, which includes victims of enforced disappearances, which would be included in the concept of "arrest": "apprehending a person ... by the action of an authority." "Detained person" means any person deprived of personal liberty, excluding "imprisoned person," where the deprivation of personal liberty is a consequence of conviction for an offense. However, this does not mean that enforced disappearances may not take place concerning these persons.[11] The emphasis is on the notion of a judicial or other authority, that is, the authority (judicial included) under the law whose status and tenure should afford the strongest possible guarantees of competence, impartiality, or independence. Principle 2 asserts that "arrest, detention or imprisonment shall only be carried out strictly in accordance with the provisions of the law and by competent officials or persons authorized for that purpose." Principle 4 requires order by judicial or other authority as defined or effective control of judicial or other competent authority. Principle 9 establishes that authorities can only exercise the powers granted by law; their exercise is subject to judicial or authority control. Principle 10 recognizes the right to be informed on detention of the reason and charges. Principle 11 requires effective opportunity to be heard by a judicial or other authority (paragraph 1), full and prompt communication of any order of detention with grounds to the detained person and his or her counsel (paragraph 2), and judicial review (paragraph 3) or habeas corpus.

The Body of Principles requires the record of the reasons and time of the arrest, first appearance to judicial or other authority, the identity of the officials, and the place of custody (Principle 12). The right to communication with the outside world (family or counsel) can only be denied as a matter of days (Principle 15). This opposes to prolonged incommunicado detention. Family members should be notified of transfers (Principle 16).

Principle 29 indicates that places of detention must be visited regularly by qualified and experienced persons; the detained person has the right to communicate with them. Principle 32 asserts the right to proceedings before a judicial or other authority to challenge the lawfulness of a detention to be released without delay if the detention is unlawful (paragraph 1). This proceeding must be simple and expeditious and at no cost for needy persons (paragraph 2). A special provision concerns the death or disappearance of a detained or imprisoned person: An inquiry into the causes must be held by judicial or other authority, either on its own motion or at the insistence of a member of the family or any person with knowledge of the case (Principle 34). This instrument increases the protection provided by treaty law.

In the Principles on Prevention, the following provisions are emphasized.

6. Governments shall ensure that persons deprived of their liberty are held in officially recognized places of custody, and that accurate information on their custody and whereabouts, including transfers, is made promptly available to their relatives and lawyer or other persons of confidence.
7. Qualified inspectors, including medical personnel, or an equivalent independent authority, shall conduct inspections in places of custody on a regular basis, and be empowered to undertake unannounced inspections on their own initiative, with full guarantees of independence in the exercise of this function. The inspectors shall have unrestricted access to all persons in such places of custody, as well as to all their records.

There is preoccupation about officially recognized places of custody, "accurate" information, availability to relatives and counsel, and inspections to monitor that the custody is carried out pursuant to internationally recognized human rights standards.

The Standard Minimum Rules for the Treatment of Prisoners (Standard Minimum Rules)[12] include special paragraphs on register of persons imprisoned (paragraph 7.1) and characteristics of the registration book (bound, with numbered pages, obligation to register every person received — identity, grounds, day and hour of admission and release). No person should be received without a "valid commitment order" (paragraph 7.2).

All the instruments contain the main concern: arbitrary or illegal arrest or detention; a public official or any other person acting in an official capacity or with official instigation, consent or acquiescence deprives a person without order based on legal grounds and of a competent authority of his or her liberty and confines the victim to a detention facility or compels the victim to stay in an assigned residence. Legality is essential, as the deprivation of liberty is only permissible when the grounds and the proceeding are established by law and are not arbitrary. This principle of legality is breached when somebody is arrested or detained on grounds not established by law or contrary to such law. The law and the enforcement must not be arbitrary. Arbitrariness is broader than legality, containing elements of injustice, unreasonableness and lack of proportionality. Arrests should not be discriminatory and should be appropriate and proportional according to the case.

Another aspect is freedom of movement and residence and the nonrefoulement principle. The UDHR, Article 13, recognizes the right to freedom of movement and residence within a state in paragraph 1 and the right to leave a country (including the country of the own nationality) and return in paragraph 2. According to Article 12.3 of the ICCPR, the rights can only be restricted by law; the restrictions must be necessary to protect national security, public order, public health or morals or the rights and freedoms of others; and the rights must be consistent with the other rights recognized in the ICCPR. In the European system, these rights are protected by Protocol 4 to the European Convention, Article 2 and 3, and by Protocol 7, Article 1. In the Inter-American system, the AD protects the right to residence and movement in Article 8. The ACHR contains these provisions in Article 22.

In *Cabrera v. Argentina*,[13] two Paraguayan legal residents in Argentina and the Argentinean wife of one of them were handed over by Argentina to the Paraguayan police to be detained in a kind of concentration camp. They disappeared. The right to residence and movement (Article 8 of the AD) had been violated.

Article 8 of the DED contains the principle of nonrefoulement: No state "shall expel, return (refouler) or extradite a person to another State where there are substantial grounds to believe that he would be in danger of enforced disappearance." The considerations to take into account include a consistent pattern of gross, flagrant, or mass violations of human rights. When commenting on the Draft IC, the WG asserted the nonrefoulement in Article 15 went beyond existing international law. The formula was amended, and the draft in 2004 contained the prohibition of refoulement if there are substantial grounds for believing that the person would be in danger of being subjected to enforced disappearance. Among the grounds, a consistent pattern of gross, flagrant or mass violations of human rights or humanitarian law was relevant (Article 15 bis).[14] In the above-mentioned case, the IACHR applied the AD, which does not contain the principle of nonrefoulement, though customary international law, codified in Article 22.8 of the ACHR, recognizes it when the person is at risk of a violation of the right to life and personal liberty.

The Inter-American Court of Human Rights

In *Velásquez Rodríguez v. Honduras,* the IACtHR asserted, concerning Article 7 of the ACHR:

155. ...The kidnapping of a person is an arbitrary deprivation of liberty, an infringement of a detainee's right to be taken without delay before a judge and to invoke the appropriate procedures to review the legality of the arrest, all in violation of Article 7 of the Convention which recognizes the right to personal liberty.

186. As a result of the disappearance, Manfredo Velásquez was the victim of an arbitrary detention, which deprived him of his physical liberty without legal cause and without a determination of the lawfulness of his detention by a judge or competent tribunal. Those acts directly violate the right to personal liberty recognized by Article 7 of the Convention (supra 155) and are a violation imputable to Honduras of the duties to respect and ensure that right under Article 1 (1).

Velasquez Rodríguez has been cited in all the subsequent jurisprudence. In *Godínez Cruz,*[15] similar arguments are found.[16]

The right to liberty of the person is linked to the guarantee of habeas corpus that requires the presentation before a judge, also when conditions of detention have deteriorated or for investigation of the fate of a person detained. In *Neira Alegría v. Peru,* the IACtHR analyzed the violation to Article 7.6 of the ACHR (habeas corpus), concerning two persons in prison that disappeared after the state demolished the facility.[17] Habeas corpus was the adequate proceeding to investigate and disclose the whereabouts of the victims. As it was ineffective, the right had been violated.

In *Caballero Delgado and Santana v. Colombia,*[18] the IACtHR asserted a violation of the right to personal liberty because of the illegal detention leading to disappearance. The IACtHR concluded similarly in *Castillo Páez v. Peru*[19]: the police detained the victim without cause, in violation of Article 7 paragraphs 2 and 3 of the ACHR, and did not bring him before a competent court, in breach of Article 7, paragraph 5, ACHR.

In *Bamaca Velasquez*,[20] the IACtHR asserted that Guatemala had violated the right to personal liberty in the subject matter (arrest only on causes and cases established by law) and procedural aspect (formal aspect). If a person is deprived of the freedom without judicial review of the arrest, that person must be released or presented immediately before a judge. The IACtHR followed the ECtHR when interpreting "without delay" or "immediately": Under no circumstance could the authorities unduly delay the detention without breaching the ACHR, which would constitute a complete denial of Article 7 of the ACHR and a very serious violation of this provision. Bamaca remained detained clandestinely for at least four months.

In *Villagrán Morales*,[21] four children were deprived illegitimately and arbitrarily of their physical freedom by police agents, who never presented them before a competent judge so they could execute them extrajudicially. Article 7 of the ACHR was violated.

In *Paniagua Morales v. Guatemala,* security forces abducted, arbitrarily detained, inhumanely treated, tortured, and murdered five persons (the "white van case" because of the vehicle used as modus operandi). Some bodies were found the same day or some days later. Article 7 had been breached.[22]

The European Court of Human Rights

The first disappearance case reaching the ECtHR was considered a violation to Article 5 of the ECHR. In *Kurt v. Turkey,* the victim's mother complained against Turkey, alleging her son's disappearance. In 1993, security forces carried out an antiterrorism operation.[23] The victim was seen by his mother surrounded by soldiers with "bruises and swelling on his face as though he had been beaten."[24] There was no further news about him; the government alleged a kidnapping by the PKK. The ECtHR concluded that Article 5 had been violated:[25] "the unacknowledged detention of an individual is a complete negation of these guarantees and a most grave violation of Article 5."[26] The control over the individual implied the responsibility for the whereabouts. The authorities should "take effective measures to safeguard against the risk of disappearance and to conduct a prompt and effective investigation into an arguable claim that a person has been taken into custody and has not been seen since."[27] The court stated that "the absence of holding data recording such matters as the date, time and location of detention, the name of the detainee as well as the reasons for the detention and the name of the person effecting it must be seen as incompatible with the very purpose of Article 5 of the Convention."[28] The authorities did not offer any "credible and substantiated explanation" about the victim's fate, and no meaningful investigation was conducted: "unacknowledged detention in the complete absence of the safeguards contained in Article 5."[29]

In *Çakici v. Turkey*, the ECtHR concluded that Çakici was arbitrarily deprived of his physical freedom by security forces, and subsequently no credible or substantial explanation was given.[30] The ECtHR recalled that no steps were taken to investigate the disappearance.[31]

In *Timurtaş v. Turkey*, the applicant's son had disappeared. Timurtaş was detained; there was no record of the detention and no investigation. Turkey had violated Article 5 because it had not provided a plausible explanation on the victim's fate and, in addition, no investigation. There was an arbitrary deprivation of physical freedom.[32]

In *Orhan v. Turkey*,[33] the court concluded that the three victims had been held in unacknowledged detention "in the complete absence of the most fundamental of safeguards required by Article 5 of the Convention."

In *Taş v. Turkey*,[34] the case had the peculiar twist that the public prosecutor had authorized the detention for 30 days, though there was a legal limit. The applicant alleged a violation of Article 5.3 (excessive length of pretrial detention before the son was brought to a judicial authority), Article 5.4 (inability for having a prompt decision on this illegal detention) and Article 5.5 (lack of compensation.) The court concluded that 30-days incommunicado detention violated both Articles 5.3 and 5.4; the lack of compensation breached Article 5.5.[35]

In *Çiçek v. Turkey*, the lack of record of the detention of the applicant's sons was important: "the gendarmes had set up a practice according to which there was a difference between detaining suspected persons and putting them into custody." An "unofficial" period of detention was not allowed.[36] There was a violation of Article 5.

In *Akdeniz v. Turkey*, the court repeated *Kurt* and *Çakici*, concluding that there was a violation of Article 5: 11 victims were held incommunicado by security forces for at least a week during an operation, after which they disappeared. The authorities did not inform on their whereabouts and fate, and the investigation was neither prompt nor effective. There were no entries in official custody records. Consequently, the ECtHR concluded the detention lacked the safeguards contained in Article 5.

In *Cyprus v. Turkey*, Cyprus asserted that Turkey had an administrative practice of breaching Article 5 of the ECtHR, because Turkey did not carry out a prompt and effective investigation of the detention and disappearance of Greek-Cypriot missing persons, in violation of the procedural obligations of Article 5. Turkey had not kept any accurate or reliable records of detention and agents or taken any other effective measures to safeguard against disappearances. Article 5 had been breached, and there was no time limitation for the duty to investigate and inform. Most serious crimes, including war crimes or crimes against humanity, could have taken place. However, there was no violation of Article 5 concerning the detention of Greek-Cypriot missing persons, because there was no evidence that they were still detained.

The ECtHR repeated that the unacknowledged detention is a complete denial of Article 5, and a most grave violation of that article: "Having assumed control over a given individual, it is incumbent on the authorities to account for his or her whereabouts." Turkey should have prevented disappearances and conducted a prompt and effective investigation. There was irrefutable evidence that Turkish or Turkish-Cypriot forces held Greek-Cypriots, but no records on the identities or the dates or location of detention. Article 5 could not be discharged by only cooperating with the CMP. There had been a continuing violation of Article 5 for the failure to conduct an effective investigation into the whereabouts and fate of the missing Greek-Cypriot persons. The court found that it was not proved that Greek-Cypriot missing persons were still detained.

In *Bilgin v. Turkey*,[37] the ECtHR repeated the need of substantive and procedural guarantees for a detention, but also respect for Article 5, in particular, nonarbitrariness. Article 5 provides a corpus of substantive rights to ensure independent judicial scrutiny and accountability of the authorities. There was a violation of Article 5: The detention was not recorded, the whereabouts or fate were unknown, and the authorities had given no plausible explanation.[38]

The Human Rights Committee

The HRC decided violations of Article 9 of the ICCPR when persons were kidnapped by Uruguayan secret service agents in Argentina and Brazil and taken back to Uruguay, which was characterized as arbitrary arrests.[39] The same conclusions were reached against Uruguay and Colombia.[40]

In *Rafael Mojica*,[41] the victim disappeared in the Dominican Republic. The HRC asserted that the right to liberty and security of the person may be invoked not only in the context of arrest and detention but also disappearances. The Dominican Republic had failed to ensure the victim's right to liberty and security of the person, in violation of Article 9, paragraph 1 of the ICCPR. A similar conclusion was reached in *Bautista de Arellana*.[42]

In *Villafañe et al. v. Colombia*, three indigenous leaders were illegally abducted and detained without arrest warrant or formal charges. There was a violation of Article 9.[43]

In *Bleier v. Uruguay*,[44] the victim was arrested without court order in 1975. The authorities did not acknowledge the arrest; the victim was held incommunicado at an unknown place. His name appeared on a list of prisoners read out once a week at an army unit in Montevideo, where his family delivered clothing for him and received his dirty clothing. On 11 August 1976, Communiqué No. 1334 of the Armed Forces Press Office was printed in all newspapers requesting public help to capture 14 persons, among them the victim, "known to be associated with the banned Communist Party." There was a violation of Article 9.

In *Quinteros v. Uruguay*,[45] the victim was arrested in Montevideo on 24 June 1976. She was held incommunicado and taken by military personnel where she was to meet somebody they wanted to arrest. Elena escaped and entered the embassy of Venezuela. Military personnel entered the premises, beat the Secretary of the Embassy and members of the staff, and dragged the woman off the premises. She never reappeared. Uruguay had violated Article 9 of the ICCPR.

In *Ana Celis Laureano*,[46] the victim was kidnapped by state agents in 1992 without arrest warrant. A judge ordered her release under the custody of her grandfather. Peru had violated Article 9, paragraph 1 and Article 2, paragraph 1 of the ICCPR.

The jurisprudence has been clear: violation of the right to personal freedom, even without evidence of the arrest or the abduction but only the disappearance (see *Rafael Mojica*).

The Inter-American Commission on Human Rights

The IACHR has repeatedly asserted very grave violations of Article 7 of the ACHR.[47]

In the *Report on the Situation of Human Rights in Chile* (1974),[48] the IACHR discussed cases where persons were found in prisons and detention camps without charges or presentation to a judge. Persons of 16 years of age were detained for over 10 months just for "endangering the maintenance of order"; Chile attempted to justify the prolonged detention by stating possible tax violations. In petitions against Argentina in 1976–83, the IACHR asserted violations of Article I of the AD, right to liberty and security of the person, as well as the right to protection from arbitrary arrest (Article 25).[49]

In other cases,[50] the IACHR asserted that "the right to petition for a determination of the legality of detention is the fundamental guarantee of a detainee's constitutional and human rights in the case of deprivation of liberty by state agents. This right may not be suspended under any circumstances, and its importance cannot be overestimated."[51] Victims were illegally abducted without judicial order, by state agents without legal authority to take such actions, and held incommunicado clandestinely. They were prevented from exercising habeas corpus in violation of Article 7 (5) and (6). The IACHR added, "detention incommunicado describes the situation of a person in custody who is cut off from communication with the outside world. Those responsible for the detention thus have exclusive control over the detainee."[52] Defining disappearances, the IACHR understood "a detention is arbitrary and illegal when it is practiced for reasons not validly envisaged by law, when it is carried out without observing legal standards, and when powers to detain have been abused, i.e. when a detention is carried out for reasons other than those contemplated and required by law."[53] The IACHR underlined that disappearances not only violate Article 7.1 but also Articles 7.5 and 7.6 of the ACHR. Anyone deprived of liberty must be kept in officially recognized detention centers and brought promptly before a judge, pursuant to domestic legislation. In case of failure, the state had to guarantee the detainee the possibility of an effective judicial recourse, to judicially control the legality of the detention: "the right to be brought before a competent judge is a fundamental guarantee of the rights of every detainee."[54] Moreover,[55] "any lawful deprivation of liberty must be issued from and be executed by a competent authority, and must be effectuated in accordance with the substantive and procedural requirements of domestic law as well as of the American Convention. A disappearance stands in direct opposition to such requirements, and outside the boundaries of the rule of law."[56] The IACHR added, "an individual who is disappeared is also deprived of the right to be taken without delay before a judge and to invoke the appropriate procedures to obtain a review of the legality of the detention, in further violation of the provisions of Article 7 of the American Convention."

Recently,[57] the IACHR asserted that

> 32. The forced disappearance of persons constitutes a multiple and continuing violation of several rights recognized in the Convention that the States Parties are bound to respect and ensure. As expressed by the Inter-American Court, a forced disappearance begins with the abduction of the person, which entails the arbitrary deprivation of liberty, and violates the right of the detainee to be brought before a judge without delay.

Conclusion

The right to personal freedom is the only case where there is unanimity in all the systems of protection: Enforced disappearances constitute violations to this right in its different aspects, that is, not only regarding the illegality or arbitrariness of the initial arrest, abduction or detention, but also the subsequent questions: lack of presentation before a judge, prolonged incommunicado detention, lack of charges, absence of register of the detention, and so on. Linked to this right, the guarantee of habeas corpus should be effective and efficient to protect the right of personal freedom.

The right to personal freedom is broadly interpreted in all the cases; if an enforced disappearance has not started with an illegal or arbitrary detention, incommunicado detention is a clear denial of this right, as the person should have been submitted to a competent and impartial judge.

In the Inter-American system, emphasis has been placed on arbitrary detention (in the formal or substantial aspect: form or reasons of the detention). In the European system the focus is placed on incommunicado detention. The role of habeas corpus is more important in the jurisprudence of the Inter-American system. The institution is not only understood as the presentation of the person before a competent judge to analyze the legality of the deprivation of personal freedom but also as a remedy as to know the fate and whereabouts of the victim, which is reasserted in the Draft IC, Article 17.

Preventive measures are essential. Some provisions exist in treaty law, linked to the protection of the right of personal freedom, but the elaboration of a binding document dealing with enforced disappearances must reassert them, together with concrete measures tending to create a culture contrary to enforced disappearances in the security forces. Among them, the existence of inquiry proceedings, as included in the Body of Principles, acquires particular relevance. Ex officio or at the request of the next of kin, an investigation should be performed to determine the facts and responsibilities in cases of enforced disappearances. These proceedings should permit the participation of the victim's next of kin, in particular, the presentation of evidence and the control of the acts of the authorities in the course of the proceedings. Though the Draft IC refers to the right to complain and to have that complaint investigated (Article 12), the participation of the victim's next of kin should have a clearer role in the project. The control of detention facilities and prisons through periodic visits by independent monitoring organs is important (Article 16 1.d) to prevent and detect irregularities. A binding document in the field of enforced disappearances should be adopted containing clear preventive measures.

Unfortunately, the coincidence among the systems of protection will have no parallel as in the case of violations of the right to personal freedom.

5

The Right to Humane Treatment

The Right Not to Be Subjected to Torture or Other Cruel, Inhumane, or Degrading Treatment

The prohibition of torture is one of the clearest rules of human rights with international customary law character. The right to physical, mental and moral integrity is considered inalienable at all times and circumstances.[1] The UDHR asserts in Article 5 that "no one shall be subjected to torture or to cruel, inhuman or degrading treatment or punishment." The first line of Article 7 of the ICCPR is similar. Children are especially protected by the CRC, Article 37, paragraph a.

The CAT contains a more complete definition of torture, Article 1.1:

> Any act by which severe pain or suffering, whether physical or mental, is intentionally inflicted on a person for such purposes as obtaining from him or a third person information or a confession, punishing him for an act he or a third person has committed or is suspected of having committed, or intimidating or coercing him or a third person, or for any reason based on discrimination of any kind, when such pain or suffering is inflicted by or at the instigation of or with the consent or acquiescence of a public official or other person acting in an official capacity. It does not include pain or suffering arising only from, inherent in or incidental to lawful sanctions.

This definition is not applied if another instrument provides for broader protection, Article 1.2 of the CAT. The prohibition goes from the mere degrading treatment or punishment, to what is inhuman and cruel treatment, up to torture, the most serious violation.[2]

The CAT contains several obligations for state parties concerning prevention: the systematic review of interrogation rules, instructions, methods and practices, arrangements for the custody and treatment of persons subjected to "any form" of arrest, detention or imprisonment within its jurisdiction (Article 11); a prompt and impartial investigation of acts of torture (Article 12); right to complain with due guarantees (Article 13); right to reparation (Article 14), and so on. Concerning cruel, inhuman, or degrading treatment or punishment, the CAT contains the obligation of prevention, if acts are committed by public officials or persons acting in an official capacity (Article 16).

Defining an act as torture rather than cruel, inhuman, or degrading treatment has important consequences: Article 4 of the CAT requires each state party to ensure that all acts of torture are offences under its criminal law; victims of torture have an enforceable right to fair and adequate compensation (Article 14); any statement induced by torture cannot be invoked as evidence except against a person accused of torture (Article 15). These provisions do not apply to cruel, inhuman, or degrading treatment or punishment.

The ICCPR, Article 7, includes the worry on nonvoluntarily medical or scientific experimentation. The European Convention includes a simple formula, similar to the UDHR, but omitting the word *cruel* (Article 3).

The ACHR asserts the right to humane treatment in Article 5.1: "the right to have his physical, mental and moral integrity respected." Article 5.2 is similar to the UDHR and ICCPR adding the right of the persons deprived of their liberty to a treatment respectful for his human dignity.

The ACHPR, Article 4, asserts that "human beings are inviolable," and Article 5 indicates that "every individual shall have the right to the respect of the dignity inherent in a human being." It contains the prohibition of torture, cruel, inhuman, or degrading punishment or treatment.

In international humanitarian law, the prohibition of torture and other cruel, degrading and inhuman treatment is also included. [3]

In regional instruments, the IACAT obliges states to prevent and punish torture (Article 1), to criminalize torture with severe punishment (Article 6), and guarantee victim's access to jurisdiction (Article 8). In the ECPT, the European Committee for the Prevention of Torture was created.

The preamble of the DED recognizes the right not to be subjected to torture. The preamble of the 1998 Draft IC is similar. The DED, also in the preamble, refers to the CAT. The second paragraph of Article 1 of the DED asserts "any act" of enforced disappearance "inflicts severe suffering on [the disappeared persons] and their families." The victim is not only the person disappeared but also family members. Any act of enforced disappearance violates this right. Article 11 of the Declaration emphasizes that if a person is released, physical integrity and ability to fully exercise human rights must be guaranteed.

In the Body of Principles, the prohibition of torture or cruel, inhuman, or degrading treatment or punishment is in Principle 6, concerning persons under any form of detention or imprisonment; no circumstance may be invoked as justification. Principle 7 includes the interpretation of cruel, inhuman or degrading treatment or punishment, "including any abuse, physical or mental, as for instance, holding a detained person depriving him temporarily or permanently of the use of any of his senses or his awareness of place or time." Principle 21 prohibits taking undue advantage of a person imprisoned or detained as to compel a confession, self-incrimination, or to testify against somebody. Principle 23 refers to duration of interrogations and intervals between them and identity of the officials conducting them, which must be recorded and legally certified; this information must be accessible to the person detained or imprisoned and counsel. Principle 24 provides for proper medical examination after detention, and thereafter medical treatment and care, when necessary. Principle 33 recognizes the right of the detained or imprisoned person, his or her counsel, or a family member to complain particularly in cases of torture, or other cruel, inhuman or degrading treatment.

The Code of Conduct[4] recognizes the right discussed by imposing limits to the conduct of law enforcement officials: Article 6 asserts they must ensure the health of the persons in their custody.

In all the 1949 GC and both the 1977 APs, torture and other cruel, inhuman, or degrading treatment or punishment are forbidden. Torture is forbidden concerning those wounded and sick on land (I GC, Article 12); wounded, sick, and shipwrecked at sea (II GC, Article 12); POWs (III GC, Articles 17 and 87); and civilians (IV GC, Article 32; AP I, Article 75; AP II Article 4). Concerning humane treatment, civilians confined are protected by Article 37, IV GC. The same convention, in Article 118, forbids imprisonment "in premises without daylight and, in general, all forms of cruelty" against internees. Article 11, AP I, prohibits endangering the "physical or mental health and integrity of persons who are in the power of the adverse party, or who are interned, detained or otherwise deprived of liberty." Article 75 forbids "outrages upon personal dignity, in particular humiliating and degrading treatment."

In noninternational armed conflicts, Article 3 common to the four GCs forbids "cruel treatment and torture" to persons taking no active part in the hostilities, as well as "outrages upon personal dignity, in particular, humiliating and degrading treatment," "mutilation, cruel treatment and torture." Article 4 of AP II prohibits at any time and in any place whatsoever:

> (a) violence to the life, health and physical or mental well-being of persons, in particular murder as well as cruel treatment such as torture, mutilation or any form of corporal punishment ... (c) outrages upon personal dignity, in particular, humiliating and degrading treatment, rape, enforced prostitution and any form of indecent assault ... (h) threats to commit any of the foregoing acts.

The Inter-American Court of Human Rights

In *Velasquez Rodriguez v. Honduras,* the IACtHR found a violation to Article 5 of the ACHR[5]:

156. ...Prolonged isolation and deprivation of communication are in themselves cruel and inhuman treatment, harmful to the psychological and moral integrity of the person and a violation of the right of any detainee to respect for his inherent dignity as a human being. Such treatment, therefore, violates Article 5 of the Convention, which recognizes the right to the integrity of the person...

187. The disappearance of Manfredo Velásquez violates the right to personal integrity recognized by Article 5 of the Convention (supra 156). First, the mere subjection of an individual to prolonged isolation and deprivation of communication is in itself cruel and inhuman treatment which harms the psychological and moral integrity of the person, and violates the right of every detainee under Article 5 (1) and 5 (2) to treatment respectful of his dignity. Second, although it has not been directly shown that Manfredo Velásquez was physically tortured, his kidnapping and imprisonment by governmental authorities, who have been shown to subject detainees to indignities, cruelty and torture, constitute a failure of Honduras to fulfill the duty imposed by Article 1 (1) to ensure the rights under Article 5 (1) and 5 (2) of the Convention. The guarantee of physical integrity and the right of detainees to treatment respectful of their human dignity require States Parties to take reasonable steps to prevent situations which are truly harmful to the rights protected.

Enforced disappearance included cruel, inhuman, or degrading treatment, and not torture due to the prolonged isolation and incommunication (see §156). However, the language is imprecise in §187: The IACtHR reasserts that, but indicates that though there is no direct evidence on torture, there was cruel, inhuman and degrading treatment, the kidnapping and imprisonment together with the practice of subjection of detainees to "indignities, cruelty, and torture," which reveals a violation of the duty to guarantee (Article 1.1) concerning the rights protected by Articles 5.1 and 5.2 of the ACHR. Enforced disappearance breaches Articles 5.1 and 5.2 (inhuman, cruel or degrading treatment); however, the IACtHR found also a breach of the duty to prevent torture (duty to ensure, Article 1.1.), protected by Articles 5.1 and 5.2, for the practice of torturing detainees. In *Godínez Cruz,* the IACtHR followed the same interpretation.[6]

In *Caballero Delgado & Santana v. Colombia,* there was no violation of Article 5 for lack of evidence.[7] Prolonged isolation and incommunication was not per se cruel, inhuman or degrading treatment. There was no violation of the obligation to prevent torture.

In *Castillo Páez v. Peru,* Peru violated Article 5.[8] The victim, after detention by the police, was placed in the trunk of the official vehicle, which constituted inhumane treatment.[9] The method used to kidnap was a key element.

In *Neira Alegría v. Peru*,[10] Article 5.2 guarantees the right to live in conditions of detention compatible with the personal dignity; the state must guarantee the right to life and personal integrity, and be responsible for centers of detention. However, the IACtHR considered that Peru had not violated Article 5 because though it is possible that a person deprived of life is also deprived of physical integrity, that is not the sense of the ACHR. There was no evidence on mistreatment.[11]

In *Paniagua Morales v. Guatemala*,[12] the IACtHR applied Article 5 and the IACAT (Articles 1, 6, and 8) and found torture committed against the young victims. In four out of the five cases, the victims' bodies had signs of torture (tying, beating, etc.). The victims were killed by stab wounds, and some were even decapitated. Other victims at the disposal of the judiciary presented injuries, grazes, and bruises, attesting cruel, inhuman or degrading treatment. The court found violations of Articles 5(1) and 5(2) of the ACHR and Articles 1, 6 and 8 of the IACAT.

In *Blake v. Guatemala,* the IACtHR for the first time decided that Guatemala had violated Article 5 concerning the victims' relatives. The forced disappearance directly impaired their physical and mental integrity, as they had to travel to Guatemala without cooperation from the authorities.[13] The victim's brother suffered a serious depression, needing psychiatric treatment.[14] The violation of the family members' moral and mental integrity was direct consequence of the forced disappearance.[15] The cultural values prevailing in Guatemala were analyzed to analyze the suffering of Blake's relatives,[16] though they were U.S. citizens, living in the United States. The IACtHR asserted that burning mortal remains opposes the prevailing values in Guatemala, affecting the moral integrity of Blake's family.[17] From this case on, the IACtHR considered family members as victims per se.

In *Villagrán Morales*,[18] the IACHR argued a violation of Article 5 for the kidnapping of five street children by state agents under custody. The victims were detained and held incommunicado, with great anxiety and suffering for their age (two were 15 and 17 years old). The IACHR also claimed a violation of the families' rights. The IACtHR first analyzed if there was a violation of Articles 5.1 and 5.2. During detention, the children suffered mistreatment and physical and psychological torture, with signs of serious physical violence and bites by animals. AI reported horrendous mutilations when the victims were still alive, which was the typical treatment against those who reported against the police.

The victims' mothers knew only extraofficially about the deaths. The authorities did not identify the victims, who were considered of unknown identity, though some had criminal records. The families could bury the victims days later. Some family members suffered serious health disorders and even received threats and feared for their lives. The IACtHR considered that Guatemala had violated Articles 5.1 and 5.2 with Article 1.1 (torture), and Article 5.2/Article 1.1 concerning parents and grandparents. The IACtHR also applied the IACAT.[19] Guatemala had violated Articles 1 (torture), 6 (duties of prevention and sanction), and 8 (impartial investigation ex officio). The IACHR had argued the lack of investigation, prosecution, or sanction (Article 7/12, CAT; the DAT Articles 9 and 10; and the Body of Principles).[20]

The IACtHR reasserted the competence to decide about the IACAT if the state party accepted the court's jurisdiction. Article 8 of the IACAT obliges states to act ex officio and immediately in cases of torture; Articles 1, 6, and 8 of the IACAT had been breached.

In *Bámaca Velasquez,*[21] the IACtHR decided that Article 5 of the ACHR should be analyzed from two perspectives: If there was a violation of Articles 5.1 and 5.2 concerning Bámaca Velásquez; second, if family members were victims of a violation of the right to personal integrity.[22] *Blake* was again introduced. A person illegally detained is vulnerable to violation of other rights.[23] Prolonged isolation and coercive incommunication per se constitute cruel or inhuman treatment. The IACtHR considered that incommunication produces moral sufferings and psychical anomalies and should be exceptional. *Velasquez Rodríguez* was reintroduced, though in the case, state agents had tortured Bámaca Velásquez.[24] The IACtHR asserted that internal unrest couldn't lead to restrictions to the physical integrity. Any use of force not strictly necessary attacks the human dignity, violating Article 5 ACHR.

The IACtHR cited the IACAT, Article 2, defining torture. The acts were committed as to obtain information from Bamaca.[25] The victim suffered physical and psychological torture.

The IACHR requested the IACtHR to declare that the victim's family members had suffered a violation to Article 5 of the ACHR.[26] The IACtHR asserted that when fundamental rights are violated, those close to the victim are also victims. The body was hidden, and exhumation was impeded. The victim's wife suffered inhuman, degrading, and cruel treatment (Articles 5.1 and 5.2). For the lack of information, family members were also victims (Articles 5.1 and 5.2 of the ACHR).

Velasquez Rodriguez was revitalized: Enforced disappearances are per se inhuman, cruel and degrading treatment, because of the uncertainty and sufferings of the victim, held in isolated places, with anguish about his or her destiny. The characteristics of the "abduction" or "kidnapping" led the IACtHR to assert that there is also inhuman, cruel or degrading treatment. If there is evidence, the IACtHR decided that there was torture.

Finally, family members are also victims (Article 5 of the ACHR) since *Blake*. Since *Bámaca Velásquez*, serious violations to the right to life or physical integrity are per se violations of Article 5 concerning them. The anguish for prolonged periods and the lack of cooperation of the authorities are relevant.

European Court of Human Rights

AI presented this issue in *Kurt v. Turkey*,[27] by asserting that prolonged isolation and incommunication are in themselves cruel and inhuman treatment, harmful to the victim's psychological and moral integrity — following the IACtHR in *Velasquez Rodríguez*, violating Article 3 of the European Convention. AI added that "disappearances" gravely violate the rights of the "disappeared" person's family, who suffer severe mental anguish, prolonged for years until the fate is disclosed, which follows the approach of the HRC in *Quinteros v. Uruguay*.[28] But the applicant did not present "specific" evidence that her son suffered ill treatment or an officially tolerated practice of disappearances and ill treatment of detainees.[29] For the ECtHR, enforced disappearances do not constitute violations per se to Article 3. Concerning the victim's mother, the ECtHR declared the violation of Article 3: The prosecutor ignored her claims, she saw her son while he was beaten and suffered anguish for ignoring his fate. There was no official information about him.

The high standard applied to the victim, in comparison with the low one concerning family members, is not justified.

In *Çakici v. Turkey*, the ECtHR analyzed whether Article 3 was breached regarding the disappeared person and his brother. Witnesses knew of the detention and ill treatment, including beatings and electric shocks. The ECtHR found a violation of Article 3 (torture).[30]

Concerning the victim's brother, the court cited *Kurt* and distinguished the cases: Kurt created no principle in favor of a family member concerning Article 3.[31] Some factors were necessary as to assert that a family member is victim of a violation to Article 3:

> a dimension and character distinct from the emotional distress which may be regarded as inevitably caused to relatives of a victim of a serious human rights violation. Relevant elements will include the proximity of the family tie — in that context, a certain weight will attach to the parent-child bond — the particular circumstances of the relationship, the extent to which the family member witnessed the events in question, the involvement of the family member in the attempts to obtain information about the disappeared person and the way in which the authorities responded to those enquiries. The Court would further emphasize that the essence of such a violation does not so much lie in the fact of the "disappearance" of the family member but rather concerns the

authorities' reactions and attitudes to the situation when it is brought to their attention. It is especially in respect of the latter that a relative may claim directly to be a victim of the authorities' conduct.

The applicant was the brother; he was not present when the victim was arrested. The applicant lived with his own family in another town — though making petitions and inquiries to the authorities; he did not bear all the investigation, as his father had the initiative. There were not aggravating features deriving from the authorities' response. Consequently, Article 3 was not violated.

The partly dissenting opinion of Judge Thomassen, joined by Jungwiert and Fischbach, considered that a brother could also deeply suffer. The absence of the applicant when the security forces took his brother was not convincing. Though the man was living with his own family, he formulated petitions and inquiries. The uncertainty for more than five and a half years disregarded feelings and efforts.

In *Mahmut Kaya v. Turkey*, the ECtHR analyzed whether concrete ill treatment is torture. Article 3 of the European Convention includes this notion and inhuman or degrading treatment. The convention attaches a special stigma to deliberate inhuman treatment causing very serious and cruel suffering. The court requested a purposive element (CAT): torture is "intentional infliction of severe pain or suffering with the aim, inter alia, of obtaining information, inflicting punishment or intimidating" according to Article 1 of the mentioned Convention.[32] The marks in Kaya's body (the binding of the wrists with wire cutting the skin; prolonged exposure of the feet to water or snow) inflict inhuman and degrading treatment (Article 3). The provision was breached, but there was not torture.[33]

The court asserted that

> the obligation imposed on High Contracting Parties under Article 1 of the Convention to secure to everyone within their jurisdiction the rights and freedoms defined in the Convention, taken together with Article 3, requires States to take measures designed to ensure that individuals within their jurisdiction are not subjected to torture or inhuman or degrading treatment, including such ill-treatment administered by private individuals.

There was state responsibility: The law framework does not provide adequate protection if the authorities do not avoid ill treatment.[34] The authorities knew or ought to have known the risk suffered for helping PKK members. Turkey was responsible.[35]

In *Timurtaş*, the ECtHR asserted: "the uncertainty, doubt and apprehension suffered by the applicant over a prolonged and continuing period of time caused him severe mental distress and anguish."[36] Consequently, the applicant, father of the disappeared, suffered inhuman and degrading treatment, Article 3. The court recalled *Çakici:* "special factors" were present; the reparation for family members is exceptional.[37] The applicant was the victim's father. His son had left his house two years before disappearing, but this should not relieve him from knowing his son's fate,[38] plus the lack of response by Turkish authorities. Article 3 was violated concerning the applicant.[39]

In *Orhan v. Turkey,*[40] the court, not recognizing the victim's rights under Article 3 of the European Convention for lack of evidence, found that the uncertainty and apprehension suffered by the applicant for eight years had caused him severe mental distress and anguish, which constituted inhuman treatment contrary to Article 3.

In *Taş v. Turkey,* the applicant alleged a violation of Article 3,[41] as his son did not receive medical treatment concerning his injuries, and was 15–26 days in incommunicado detention. However, there was no evidence about the first point; the ECtHR does not see disappearances per se as inhuman, cruel, or degrading treatment. The applicant requested a declaration of violation of Article 3 concerning him, but the court repeated that there was no right for family members derived from it depending only on "special factors."[42] The rights violation was not due to the disappearance but to government reactions. The applicant was the victim's father, who had made requests to the authorities. Due to their indifference, the court asserted that he was victim of a violation of Article 3.[43]

In *Ilhan v. Turkey,* the applicant alleged torture, inhuman and degrading treatment against the victim and that these crimes were not adequately or effectively investigated. The court recalled that ill treatment must attain a minimum level of severity, depending on the case: duration, physical and/or mental effects, sex, age, and state of health. The court differentiated between torture and inhuman or degrading treatment, and underscored the need of a special stigma to deliberate inhuman treatment causing very serious and cruel suffering and the purposive element. The victim was beaten on the head with a rifle, which resulted in severe bruising and two injuries, brain damage and long-term impairment of function. In addition, there was a delay of 36 hours in bringing him to hospital. In the view of the court, there was torture without analysis of the purposive element.

The court added that to find a procedural breach of Article 3, the circumstances of the case should be analyzed: The lack of effective investigation falls under Article 13 and not Article 3. The different treatment given to "procedural violations" is inadequate; either they fall under Article 13 and the procedural violations of substantive rules do not exist, or every substantive violation that is investigated is a procedural violation of the substantive provision. The double standards just bring confusion.

In *Salman v. Turkey,* the applicant complained that her husband had been tortured before dying. The government had explained why the body presented marks and injuries. The bruising and swelling on the left foot and the grazes on the left ankle constituted "falaka," which the ECPT reported as ill treatment, inter alia, in the Adana Security Directorate. The victim presented a bruise to the chest overlying a fracture in the sternum, due to a blow to the chest — all injuries attributable to ill treatment.

The court remembered the need of a special stigma to deliberate inhuman treatment: and a purposive element (CAT). There had been torture and no procedural finding on Article 3.

In *Çiçek v. Turkey,* the applicant alleged a violation of Article 3 concerning the persons disappeared and argued that family members suffered psychological torture,[44] as the victim's mother was told that his sons were ill treated during detention. Concerning the persons disappeared, the court understood that Article 3 is very strict, that mistreatment should surpass a certain level and should be proved beyond reasonable doubt. The court was not satisfied with the evidence presented:[45] "where an apparent forced disappearance is characterized by a total lack of information, whether the person is alive or dead or the treatment which he or she may have suffered can only be a matter of speculation." [46] Consequently, enforced disappearance was not per se a violation of Article 3.

Regarding family members, the court referred to "special factors":[47] the fate of the sons was unknown "over a prolonged and continuing period of time has undoubtedly caused her severe mental distress and anguish." [48] She was the victim of a violation of Article 3.[49]

In *Akdeniz v. Turkey,* Article 3 was breached, as 11 relatives of the applicants were detained at least for a week and were kept bound, which amounted to inhuman and degrading treatment. The court followed previous jurisprudence and did not grant reparation.

In *Cyprus v. Turkey,* Cyprus alleged the violation of Article 3 against the victims' relatives because of their continuous suffering. There was a continuing violation of Article 3: The victims became inaccessible to the relatives, which led to uncertainty and anxiety. There was inhuman treatment and no investigation or information about the fate of the victims. As Greek-Cypriots had to seek refuge in the south after the division of Cyprus, this was a very serious obstacle as to obtain information, and Turkey was responsible.

The ECtHR is extremely conservative: A violation of Article 3 requires evidence of inhuman treatment or even of torture. Concerning family members, the proof of "special factors" (Çakici) is linked to the lack of cooperation, not paying attention to the drama of enforced disappearances and the suffering of victims and family members.

The Human Rights Chamber for Bosnia and Herzegovina

The HRCBH, applying the European Convention in *Unkovic v. Federation of Bosnia and Herzegovina*,[50] declared that Article 3 was violated against a person whose daughter's family had been kidnapped and killed in 1992, but the applicant did not receive information until 1999. The mental suffering was the main argument. However, in *Decision on Request for Review Case no. CH/99/2150, Dordo Unkovic v. the Federation of Bosnia Herzegovina*,[51] the HRCBH reconsidered the decision, as Bosnia had investigated the case and there was no cruelty.

In *Palic v. Republika Srpska,* the HRCBH found violations of Article 3 against the victim for prolonged incommunicado detention. Moreover, the chamber found a violation of the wife's rights: The duty to respect her family life, for the arbitrary withholding of information concerning the fate of her husband, including his body, Article 8. The Inter-American Court in *Velasquez Rodriguez* asserted that incommunication is inhuman or degrading treatment; the HRCBH asserted a violation of Article 8 of the ECHR.

In the *Srebrenica Cases,*[52] the HRCBH found violations to Article 3 of the European Convention, following *Cyprus v. Turkey* (continuous violation against family members). The disappeared persons were missing since 10–19 July 1995, documented by the International Criminal Tribunal for the Former Yugoslavia.[53] There was "inhuman treatment" against family members. The Republika Srpska should clarify the fate and whereabouts of the missing persons or provide relief to the families and "contribute to the process of reconciliation in Bosnia and Herzegovina." The lack of investigation of mass killings, location of mass gravesites, absences of interrogations to officers, lack of prosecution and public disclosure and of cooperation were relevant factors. After seven years, the family members had not received relevant information about the fate and whereabouts of the relatives. The situation was "a particularly egregious violation of the rights of the applicants protected under Article 3 of the European Convention." The chamber declared a violation of Article 8 of the European Convention,[54] for the lack of access to information. The provision was read together with AP I, Article 32, that "reinforces, in the context of the aftermath of an armed conflict, the positive obligation arising under Article 8 of the European Convention for the Republika Srpska to search for and to share all relevant information with the families about their relatives who have been reported missing from Srebrenica since July 1995" (§175, in fine), in an "exceptionally high" level of trauma.

The Human Rights Committee

The HRC clearly declared that enforced disappearances violate Article 7 of the ICCPR.

In *Bleier v. Uruguay*,[55] the HRC asserted a violation to Article 7. The victim had suffered special mistreatment because he was Jewish.

In *Quinteros v. Uruguay*,[56] the HRC found a violation to Article 7 against the disappeared woman. The mother also alleged to be a victim.[57] The anguish and stress and the continuing uncertainty constituted violations of the ICCPR. This was the first time a family member was recognized as victim of an enforced disappearance, but the HRC did not follow this approach later.

In *Mojica v. Dominican Republic*, the HRC understood that disappearances place victims at risk of ill treatment.[58] There was "a strong inference" that the victim was tortured or subjected to cruel and inhuman treatment, in particular "aware of the nature of enforced or involuntary disappearances in many countries"; disappearances were "inseparably linked" to Article 7.[59]

In *Celis Laureano*,[60] the grandfather alleged a violation of Article 7 for lack of contact with Ana. This was cruel and inhuman treatment, breaching Article 7, with Article 2, paragraph 1, of the ICCPR. In *Bautista de Arellana v. Colombia*, the HRC asserted that Nydia suffered torture before assassination.[61] In *Villafañe et al. v. Colombia*,[62] the autopsies and the death certificates revealed that indigenous leaders were tortured before being shot in the head; there was also lack of information. The HRC concluded that the victims were tortured. The brothers suffered ill treatment, including being blindfolded and dunked in a canal, which amounted to torture.[63]

The HRC links disappearances with violations to Article 7 of the ICCPR. Disappearances per se breach the provision. If there is additional evidence, there is torture. Second, family members can be victims of disappearances, in particular, in Article 7. However, after *Quinteros* there were no further cases.

The Inter-American Commission on Human Rights

The IACHR has changed jurisprudence concerning violations to Article 5 of the ACHR, without explaining the different approaches. Different criteria of the rapporteur may be the main cause.

Concerning family members, in the first *Report on the Situation of Human Rights in Chile*, the IACHR asserted that disappearances caused Chilean families great anxiety and distress.[64]

In *Riván Hernández v. El Salvador*,[65] the IACHR recalled *Velásquez Rodriguez* and asserted that enforced disappearances, including prolonged isolation and incommunication, are per se cruel and inhuman treatment.

In many cases, the IACHR declared simply that a disappearance violates Article 5,[66] and in others just recalled this jurisprudence.[67] In *Cruz Gomez v. Guatemala*,[68] the IACHR analyzed the right to be treated humanely. The IACHR asserted that a disappearance constitutes an implicit violation of Article 5 due to the nature of the crime. The victim is forcibly abducted, detained under clandestine conditions, and held incommunicado, cut off from contact with the outside world and any form of aid or protection. This alone would necessarily produce great anxiety and suffering.

The victim was forced from home by heavily armed men in the early morning hours. The kidnappers threatened other family members and beat the victim's brother and sister. They tied the victim's hands and took him on foot. Article 5 was breached.

The IACHR asserted,[69]

In addition to the harm posed to the victim's physical and mental integrity, a disappearance by its nature causes great anxiety and suffering for the victim's loved ones. The victim's family is unable to come to his aid, unable to clarify his fate, and unable to find any sense of closure with respect to the victim's fate. The passage of time gives rise to a presumption that the victim was killed, but family members have no means to locate the remains or to provide a proper burial.

Guarcas Cipriano v. Guatemala followed it.[70]

Sometimes the violation of Article 5 is the consequence of a disappearance, defined as multiple violation of human rights. [71]

In other cases, the IACHR dealt with disappearances where the victim, released, denounced the state. In *Martínez Francisco v. El Salvador,*[72] the victim was kidnapped in 1988 by two men, who drove him in a car and put him in an underground jail because of presumed links with guerrilla groups. The victim denied it and asserted he was beaten and tortured, including electric shocks. He was released with the recommendation to leave the country. Article 5 (inhuman treatment) was breached. In *Lovato Rivera,*[73] the victim was arrested in 1990 by El Salvador's army and accused of guerrilla participation. During detention, he was tortured but released three weeks later, with threats of disappearance. The IACHR found a violation of Article 5.

In recent cases, the IACHR always finds violations of Article 5. In *Orellana Stormont v. Guatemala,*[74] the IACHR found torture because she was caused to suffer asthmatic attacks. In *García Franco v. Ecuador,*[75] the victim was forced into a gray Trooper by five marines, with his eyes taped. He was hit with sticks and interrogated about a missing vehicle. He was subjected to beatings and electric shocks, with scalding water on his feet. His whereabouts were unknown. The marines had Mr. García hanging from a tree and had beaten him. The IACHR asserted, "the state necessarily bears a certain responsibility for any individual who has been detained by its agents. This is particularly so where an individual has been illegally and arbitrarily detained by state agents, and where there are prima facie indications that he or she may have been tortured while under their control."[76] The state could not prove the contrary case; consequently, García suffered torture. In *Tordecilla Trujillo v. Colombia*,[77] Tordecilla Trujillo disappeared in Colombia after detention by state agents in Bogotá:

> 32. The forced disappearance of persons constitutes a multiple and continuing violation of several rights recognized in the Convention that the States Parties are bound to respect and ensure.... . In most cases it also entails prolonged isolation and coerced incommunication, which constitutes cruel and inhuman treatment.

The IACHR repeated in *Velásquez Isabela v. Guatemala* that a disappearance violates implicitly Article 5:[78] The victim was forcibly abducted, detained under clandestine conditions, and held incommunicado: "While it is impossible to verify precisely how long the victims may have been held by their captors, it may be presumed under the circumstances that the treatment they were accorded contravened the standards of Article 5 of the Convention." The family could not come to the victim's aid or clarify the fate: The remains could not be located, and there was no burial.

In *Sandoval Flores v. Peru*,[79] the victims were tortured during detention. Similar conclusions were found in further cases against Peru.[80]

In *Solares Castillo v. Guatemala*,[81] the IACHR declared that Guatemala had violated the right to human treatment against three young women that were abducted by government officials:

> Prolonged isolation and deprivation of communication are in themselves cruel and inhuman treatment, harmful to the psychological and moral integrity of the [disappeared] person and a violation of the right of any detainee to respect for his inherent dignity as a human being. Such treatment, therefore, violates Article 5 of the Convention, which recognizes the right to the integrity of the person.[82]

The IACHR considers that disappearances violate the right to be free from inhuman, cruel or degrading treatment, and this also concerns family members. With additional evidence, the existence of torture was declared.

The Specific Problem of Conditions of Detention

In some cases, the problem of conditions of detention was present, but the HRC, because of Article 10, ICCPR, has developed clear jurisprudence. Some violations of Article 10 of the ICCPR per se do not violate Article 7 of the ICCPR, for example, incommunicado detention.[83]

The right of detainees to be treated respecting their dignity is especially protected by the ICCPR. Further instruments concern this delicate issue. The

Body of Principles asserts (in Principle 1) that all persons under any form of detention or imprisonment shall be treated in a humane manner and with respect for the inherent dignity of the human person. The Standard Minimum Rules refers to "Persons Arrested or Detained without Charge," who must receive the same protection of part I and part II, section C of the rules, as they benefit from the provisions of part II, section A of them, where they may be conducive to the benefit of this group. The Standard Minimum Rules, Paragraph 8, assert that different categories of prisoners must be kept in separate institutions; there must be a record, legal reason, and necessity of this treatment. Concerning sleeping accommodation, paragraph 9(1) refers to individual cells or rooms and that one person must occupy one cell or room by himself. Paragraph 10 refers to sleeping accommodations, with due regard to health, climatic conditions and cubic content of air, minimum floor space, lighting, heating and ventilation. Pursuant to Paragraph 11, if prisoners must live or work in a facility, windows should allow natural light and fresh air; sufficient artificial light is required. Concerning sanitary installations, Paragraph 12 asserts they must be adequate to enable to comply with the needs of nature, when necessary, and in a clean and decent manner. The Rules provide in Paragraph 13 for adequate bathing and shower installations, to have a bath or shower at a suitable temperature, as frequent as necessary, but at least once a week. They also include safeguards on personal hygiene (§15–16), clothing and bedding (§17–19), food (§20), exercise and sport (§21), and medical services (§22–26). Concerning discipline and punishment, Paragraph 31 prohibits corporal punishment by placing in a dark cell and all cruel, inhuman or degrading punishments as punishments for disciplinary offenses, as well as instruments of restraint such as handcuffs, chains, irons and straitjackets (§33). The Standard Minimum Rules provide for information and complaints by prisoners about treatment (§35–36). The Rules understand that prisoners should contact the outside world, for example, regular communication with family and friends by correspondence and visits (§37). In case of death, illness, or transfer the nearest relative must be notified by the director of the detention center (§44). The Rules provide for regular inspection of detention institutions (§55).

In addition, the Basic Principles establish respect for prisoners according to their dignity (§1),[84] no discrimination (§2), respect for religious beliefs and cultural precepts (§3) and sets that the purpose of custody should be the well-being and development of all members of society (§4). The Basic Principles assert that except in cases "demonstrably necessitated by the fact of incarceration" (§5), prisoners enjoy the rights contained in the UDHR, the ICCPR with the OP1, and the ICESC. The Basic Principles address the progressive abolishment of solitary confinement or its restriction (§7), as well as access to health services (§9).

In *Weismann and Lanza Perdomo v. Uruguay*,[85] Ana García Lanza complained to the HRC on behalf of her aunt and uncle, Beatriz Weismann and Alcides Lanza Perdomo, alleging that both had been arbitrarily arrested and detained in Uruguay. The cases were not disappearances, but they reveal the practices used against victims in a context of disappearances.

Alcides was arrested in 1976 in Montevideo by an army vehicle; afterward his whereabouts were unknown. He was admitted four times to a hospital for mistreatment; he lost his memory and was probably unconscious for two months. His hearing was impaired, and he had movement difficulties from injuries in one hip. He was housed in a railway wagon with 16 other prisoners and forced to work in fields. Finally, he was accused before a military court.

Beatriz was arrested shortly after by army personnel, who took her with her two small sons and handed them over to their grandmother. Due to torture, she had no feeling from the waist down and could not move without help. Beatriz was nevertheless obliged to work. She was released and traveled to Sweden, where she submitted a communication on behalf of her husband and later cosponsored and coauthored the communication of her niece. Her husband was kept in different military quarters and prisons, held incommunicado for nine months and subjected to torture (electric shocks, hanging by his hands, immersion in dirty water nearly to asphyxia, submarino seco). He suffered from several serious health problems (hypertension, permanent trembling in his right arm and sometimes in his whole body and loss of memory due to brain damage). Alcides was sentenced in 1976 to three years' imprisonment by a military court, and he continued to be kept in detention after that.

Beatriz had been kept in barracks of the armed forces "El infierno" (hell), blindfolded, with her hands tied, subject to torture. Later in 1976, she was transferred to another unit, to a dirty cell in miserable hygienic conditions, without adequate clothes against the cold and most of the time blindfolded. She complained to the military judge, and he advised her not to do it as to avoid El infierno. She was transferred to an individual cell 2 × 1.5 m. Daily prisoners remained seated without speaking. Later she was transferred to another prison, where she shared a cell for 4 prisoners with 11 prisoners. Female prisoners were forced to perform hard work.

She was charged in 1976 with "assisting a subversive association," and condemned in 1978 to 24 months, but her detention continued afterward under the "prompt security measures."

Alcides was expelled from Uruguay and obtained asylum in Sweden. His health was poor, and he had scars his legs for cigarette burns, hearing problems, tremor of his right hand and inability to use it properly and symptoms of mental depression.

The HRC asserted that, among others, Uruguay had violated Article 10(1). The same happened in enforced disappearances cases, for example, *Bleier v. Uruguay* and *Quinteros v. Uruguay*.[86]

In *Martínez Machado v. Uruguay*,[87] the victim's brother complained against Uruguay, because the victim was arrested and submitted to military courts and suffered incommunicado detention. The HRC found a violation of Article 10(1) because Raul Martinez was held incommunicado for more than five months.

Conclusion

Enforced disappearances include the isolation of the person, held in unknown places, far from his or her relatives and friends, incommunicado, fearful for his or her fate, which is cruel, inhuman or degrading treatment, but this is not so clear for the organs of protection. The IACtHR and the HRC are more sensitive, in particular since *Velasquez Rodriguez*. The IACHR considered enforced disappearances as a violation of the right to humane treatment; however, without explanation, the violation of this right is omitted in some jurisprudence. The ECtHR was the most reticent organ, with a very high standard of proof. All of them declared the existence of torture when additional evidence was presented to prove this question. Concerning conditions of detention, due to the clear provision of Article 10 of the ICCPR, the HRC was the organ clearly raising the concern in disappearances, independently from Article 7 of the ICCPR.

Considering humane treatment to family members, the HRC counts with the leading case, *Quinteros v. Uruguay,* followed by the IACtHR only since *Blake.* However, the HRC has never repeated this jurisprudence, mainly followed in the Inter-American system and with important restrictions in the European Court. The characteristics of disappearances violate the right to humane treatment of family members. The ECtHR, in *Kurt,* declared the violation of Article 3 concerning the victim's mother, but later, in *Çakici,* a detailed standard was developed, requiring the proof of "special factors," with emphasis in the lack of cooperation of state authorities in the investigation of the fate or whereabouts of the victim. The victims' parents have been favored in comparison with other relatives. The focus of the ECtHR on the state attitude is hardly acceptable, as it denies the pain that a disappearance causes.

An enforced disappearance always constitutes at least inhuman treatment. Moreover, the act of detention can derive in further violations, as well as the analysis of the treatment during detention, which can amount to torture. The body of the victim is the best evidence to determine if there was torture.

The parameter applied by the IACtHR concerning family members in recent cases (fundamentally, *Bámaca Velasquez*)[88] asserting that the violation of fundamental rights always amounts to inhuman and cruel treatment once the relation was accredited is very important for recognizing the anguish and distress caused by such violations. Once this link is accredited, the presumption of inhuman and cruel treatment should enter into place. The parameters applied by the ECtHR are too restrictive and demanding. Following the argument of the court, if judicial authorities nicely help the family members, the anguish and distress caused by the disappearance should have been erased. The ECtHR emphasizes the wrong side. The next of kin of a disappeared have a very big problem: They cannot help the victim, and the time elapsed indicates that he or she must be dead, but they cannot locate the corpse and prepare a proper burial.

The incommunication of the victim is considered a violation to the right to physical integrity; the HRCBH has understood that it can constitute a violation to Article 8 of the ECHR, the right to privacy and family life. This approach is not common, and it permits to apply to disappearances the rich jurisprudence of the European system. The objection is that in context of disappearances, states of emergency have been declared and derogations of Article 8 are permissible. Only in the Inter-American system, the right to family (Article 17) cannot be suspended, but the right to privacy (Article 11), the provision that is similar to Article 8 of the ECHR, can be subject to suspension. Though this approach brings a rich insight, the approach asserting violations of the right to integrity, a nonderogable right, should be preferred.

The problem analyzed requires concrete preventive measures, some of them included in the CAT or in the IACAT. In the framework of enforced disappearances, efficient and adequate legislation on investigative procedures ex officio or at request of the next of kin are necessary where the next of kin have the possibilities of participation and presentation of evidence and the follow-up of the proceedings. If an official knows that there is a monitoring proceeding, this is an important deterrent factor. In addition, periodic monitoring visits to places of detention by independent organs are essential, as well as the necessary education of security forces in human rights to avoid abuses of power.

6

The Right to Recognition as a Person before the Law

The right to recognition "everywhere" as a person before the law is found in the UDHR in Article 6, which is linked to the first sentence of Article 1: "All human beings are born free and equal in dignity and rights." In treaty law, Article 16 of the ICCPR is similar to Article 6 of the UDHR.

In the regional systems, only the Inter-American protects this right, in both the AD and the ACHR. The AD, Article 17, asserts the right to be recognized everywhere as a person "having rights and obligations, and to enjoy the basic civil rights." The formula is clear and goes further, distinguishing between the entitlement and the enjoyment of rights. In the ACHR, Article 3 includes it as the first right recognized, even before the right to life: The right to life can only be enjoyed if recognition as a person exists. The formula is similar to those analyzed, but omitting "everywhere." Perhaps the most correct solution is presented in the ACHR; the obligations extend "within the jurisdiction of the State party."

The DED establishes in Article 1, paragraph 2 and in the preamble that this right may be breached in enforced disappearances. The 10th paragraph of the preamble of the 1998 Draft IC is similar.

The Jurisprudence in the Inter-American System of Protection

The IACtHR, in *Bámaca Velásquez* alleged that Guatemala had violated Article 3 of the ACHR,[1] as the disappearance caused the exclusion of the legal and institutional order of the state, denying his existence as human being. The IACHR argued that forced disappearances, pursuant to Article 1, paragraph 2, of the DED, violate international rules that guarantee inter alia the right to juridical personality.

The IACtHR interpreted Article 3 of the ACHR with Article 17 of the AD: This right implies the capacity to be entitled to rights to enjoy and bear duties, and its violation supposes an absolute denial of the possibility to have rights entitlement.[2] The IACtHR cited the IACFD that does not refer to juridical personality. Consequently, though the deprivation of life suppresses the human person, the right to juridical personality is not breached. Article 3 has own content (e.g., the deprivation of the capacity to enjoy rights and obligations). Consequently, Guatemala had not violated Article 3.

The IACHR adopts a different approach: Enforced disappearances constitute violations to the right to juridical personality. In *Cruz Sosa v. Guatemala*,[3] a disappearance took place in 1990 by the intelligence unit of the Guatemalan army. The perpetrators were identified, but no investigation was conducted. The IACHR considered that there was a general picture: the disappearance, the lack of information, the failure to prosecute and investigate. Among others, the disappearance constituted a violation of Article 3 of the ACHR because the victim was necessarily placed outside and excluded from the juridical and institutional order of the state, which factually denied the recognition of the very existence of Mr. Cruz as a human being. This jurisprudence was followed in cases against Guatemala, as *Pratdesaba Barillas*,[4] *Marroquín*,[5] *Lemus Garcia*,[6] and *Orellana Stormont*.[7]

In 1997, in a case against Ecuador, the IACHR asserted that

> for the victim, the consequence of an enforced disappearance is, in essence, to be denied every essential right that — as a matter of law — is deemed to inhere in the very fact of being human. In this sense, the act of enforced disappearance violates the right of the individual under Article 3 of the American Convention "to recognition as a person before the law."[8]

In *Medina Charry*, the IACHR explained that the jurisprudence had evolved since *Velásquez Rodríguez*. At least since 1992, the UN characterized forced disappearances as a violation of the right to recognition as a person before the law. The IACHR clarified also that forced disappearances violate the right to juridical personality.[9]

In *Cruz Gomez v. Guatemala*,[10] the IACHR argued:

> The objective of those who perpetrate a disappearance is to operate beyond the margins of the law, to conceal all evidence of their crimes, and to escape any sanction. When a disappearance is carried out, the fundamental protections established by law are circumvented, and the victim is left defenseless. For the victim, the consequence of an enforced disappearance is to be denied every essential right deemed to inhere in the very fact of being human.

The jurisprudence was followed in subsequent cases.[11]

The Human Rights Committee

Though the HRC has never declared a violation of Article 16 of the ICCPR in a disappearance case, in one case the commission recognized that this provision was at stake but preferred to consider the issue under another provision of the ICCPR. This happened in a communication against Argentina dealing with a minor child claimed by her grandmother after kidnapping and separation from her real family during the dirty war in Argentina.[12]

On one hand, the HRC found that the provision was not breached because the courts had endeavored in establishing her identity, issuing identity papers accordingly. However, from the reasoning, it can be derived that Article 16 would have been violated if the state had not endeavored in establishing the child's identity. In the same case, concerning the grandmother, the HRC asserted that though she had been denied standing to represent her granddaughter in the guardianship proceeding, the courts had recognized her standing to represent her granddaughter in other proceedings, for instance, to declare the invalidity of the adoption, and she was the minor's guardian. Consequently, the HRC understood that there was no issue under Article 16. However, the initial denial of Mrs. Monaco's standing left the minor without adequate representation, depriving her of protection as a minor. There was a question under Article 24 of the ICCPR. Probably if the grandmother had been denied standing in all cases, Article 16 would have been violated.

Other cases against Chile also raised questions under Article 16. The HRC applied the reservation entered by Chile on ratification of the OP1 in 1992: The events took place before 11 March 1990; they were not within the HRC's competence. Consequently, the communication was inadmissible.[13] However, Solari Yrigoyen submitted a dissenting opinion, asserting that the breach of Article 16 was a consequence of the lack of investigation of the whereabouts or location of the victim's body, a fundamental right to which anyone is entitled, even after death, and the right should be protected. Consequently, Yrigoyen asserted that the HRC was not precluded ratione temporis from examining the author's communication. Moreover, in an individual opinion of Christine Chanet concerning Communications Nos. 717/1996 and 718/1996, the conclusion was that the case had long-term consequences. Chanet interpreted Article 16 by indicating that although this right is extinguished on the death of the individual, the effects last beyond death (e.g., wills, organ donation). The right would survive when the absence is surrounded by uncertainty; the victim may reappear and, even if not present, does not cease to exist under the law; civil death cannot be substituted for confirmed natural death. This right is not unlimited in time: Either the body's identification is incontestable and a death's certificate is made, or uncertainty remains and the state must lay down rules applicable to all cases. Chanet expressed the same opinion in *Vargas Vargas*,[14] with the support of Fausto Pocar.

Conclusion

Though the DED clearly recognizes the link between enforced disappearances and the right to recognition of a person before the law, only the IACHR has adopted this point of view. The IACtHR has explicitly rejected the declaration of the violation of this right. The HRC has never declared a violation of Article 16.

The *travaux préparatoires* and academic work on the ICCPR both reinforce that Article 16 of the ICCPR is aimed at preventing a state from denying individuals the ability to enjoy and enforce their legal rights, rather than dealing with an individual's capacity to act.[15] Accordingly, Article 16 could not be understood to confer an entitlement to acquire rights on any particular legal status or to act in a particular way.[16] However, though originally the instruments of protection only referred to the purpose to prevent states to issue rules denying the character of subject of law to human beings, enforced disappearances could not have been previewed when elaborating these instruments, as the practice acquired strength years later as a complex and sophisticated human rights violation that in fact deprives a human being of all his or her rights. As Cassesse argued concerning the dictatorship in Argentina in the 1970s,[17] a paradigm of the phenomenon of enforced disappearances, the situation caused by disappearances was as to be back in time about 300 years. In a Western and civilized modern state, every individual has a name and a place of residence and can be identified because of his or her movements. If he or she has a problem, family and friends can help, and the authorities start an investigation. In theory, the individual is not alone or isolated from the society. Though he or she can be sent to prison, the family and public authorities have evidence of his or her existence and acts. Moreover, the death is proved through a formal and external element: the death certificate after the presence of a body, a subsequent burial and a tomb, which permits one to prove that a person existed in time and space. According to Cassesse, this was eliminated in Argentina and in every case of enforced disappearance.

The approach of the IACHR and the dissident opinions of the HRC are correct, as they are consistent with the DED, concerning a right expressly included in the ACHR and ICCPR, which acquires a dynamic expression if recognized as an element of the multiple rights violation. The position of the IACtHR is unacceptable, because it ignores the DED. Moreover, the IACtHR in *Bámaca Velásquez* cited the IACFD not to recognize this right. As Article 29 of the ACHR asserts, no treaty can be cited to deny the existence of rights derived from other instruments of protection. The omission of a right in an instrument of protection, right expressly recognized in further instruments, does not imply its denial: The other instruments enrich the meaning of the ACHR, according to Article 29 of the ACHR.

Treaty law provisions protecting the right to juridical personality should be read with the DED, that is, the only specific and universal instrument, up to the moment of writing these lines that enumerates the human rights that could suffer a violation in a case of enforced disappearance. The DED gives the right a clear application and dimension of protection.

Moreover, as the IACHR has indicated, a person that has disappeared has been brought to this situation to impede him or her the exercise of all rights, to exclude him or her from the juridical system.

Though the corresponding *travaux préparatoires* may assert that the right refers to legal entitlement, these treaties must be interpreted according to own rules, that is, nothing can be read as implying the right to engage in any activity or perform any right aimed at the destruction of any of the rights and freedoms recognized (Arg. Article 5 ICCPR, Article 29.a, ACHR). Consequently, this right clearly forbids the state to deny personality through legislation, but that does not imply that the state can do it de facto. Moreover, the Vienna Convention on the Law of Treaties (1969) has given the preparatory work only a subsidiary role when interpreting a treaty (Article 32), by privileging other interpretation methods,[18] in particular, good faith, ordinary meaning, contextual method, and the object and purpose of the instrument (Article 31.1). Together with the context, the same Article 31, in paragraph 3.b refers to "any subsequent practice in the application of the treaty which establishes the agreement of the parties regarding its interpretation." The DED, adopted without a vote by the UN General Assembly, could be considered a subsequent interpretation of the right to juridical personality contained in previous treaty law that has received new life, through a dynamic interpretation of the human rights rules.

The multiple-rights approach deserves to be supported, and the recognition of a violation of this right is the element that gives the whole complex of human rights violations full unity, as the effect and intention of the perpetrators is to place the victim outside the protection of the law, that is, to impede the exercise of all rights, as the preamble of the 1998 Draft IC also recognizes.

Better coordination among the systems of protection is required, and clear binding rules leading the task of the interpreters.

7

The Right to Know the Truth

The right to know the truth is one of the most problematic issues in enforced disappearances cases. Some domestic tribunals have accepted it, and some practitioners and scholars claim the need of recognition. However, no instrument recognizes it, except the AP I, Article 32.

The first recognition of this issue took place in *Elena Quinteros v. Uruguay,* decided by the HRC. Uruguay had violated Article 7 of the ICCPR toward the mother of the disappeared woman, as "the author has the right to know what has happened to her daughter."[1]

Historically, the recognition of this right has been encouraged as a reaction against the amnesty and, in general, impunity legislation in some Latin American countries for the lack of determination of the whereabouts and fate of the victims of enforced disappearances. The lack of criminal prosecutions had the unfortunate consequence of the inexistence of concrete state activity to disclose the destiny of the "disappeared." Consequently, the jurisprudence and the scholars attempted to solve this problem by developing this right as an individual right of victims and family members in disappearances cases. Truth commissions also served as a new incentive to the development of this question.[2]

Those who argue for the right to the truth, indicate that it must be complete, official, public and impartial,[3] comprehensive and representative of the repressive reality to investigate. A limited truth should be valid if it was obtained impartially and without hindrances.[4] A moral duty toward the victims and family members is claimed, aiming at the investigation and punishment of those responsible, to reassert democracy and citizen control on public institutions, and as a guarantee of nonrepetition. Professor Méndez refers to the right to the truth as an "emerging principle" in international law,[5] and understands it as a wider right to justice of the victims of all crimes against humanity, which would create four types of obligations: the obligation to investigate and to make public the results (truth), the obligation to prosecute and punish (justice), the obligation of full reparation (reparation), and the obligation to purge the security forces of those who committed, ordered, or tolerated these abuses (creation of security forces appropriate to a democratic state).

Finally, the right to the truth contributes to forgiveness and reconciliation and the future respect of international law. This is also part of the reparation (analyzed later) due by the state to the victims and the society as a whole, a component of the right to remedy.

The NGO Latin American Federation of Relatives of Disappeared Persons, when commenting on the 1998 Draft IC, asserted the need of specific protection.[6] The International Commission of Jurists, Human Rights Watch, and the International Federation of Human Rights have also expressed their support to this right.[7]

The Rules of International Law Applicable to the Problem

No treaty in force today, apart from the AP I, includes explicitly the right to the truth; this can be derived from specific instruments dealing with enforced disappearances, particularly the DED. The organs of protection did not apply the Declaration but further treaty law provisions to justify the existence of this right, in particular the IACHR.

In Article 9 of the DED, a "right" to a "prompt and effective judicial remedy" is defined, which objective is evidently the content of "the right to the truth": "determining the whereabouts or state of health of persons deprived of their liberty and/or identifying the authority ordering or carry out the deprivation of liberty" that is required "to prevent enforced disappearances under all circumstances." The WG considered that the lack of investigation of disappearances breached Article 9 of the DED.[8] Article 9 must be read together with Article 13 of the DED, which leads to clear recognition of the right to the truth. Article 13 provides for the state obligation to ensure that any person having knowledge or a legitimate interest who alleges that a person was subjected to enforced disappearance has the right to complain to a competent and independent state authority and to have that complaint promptly, thoroughly and impartially investigated. Investigation should take place *sua sponte,* even if there is no formal complaint. Apart from the characteristics of the investigation, paragraph 4 of Article 13 asserts that "the findings of such an investigation shall be made available upon request to all persons concerned." These findings are the aim of the right to the truth: to know what happened to the person disappeared. The last paragraph of Article 13 asserts that the investigation must be conducted "for as long as the fate of the victim of enforced disappearance remains unclarified." The purpose of the investigation is to find out the whereabouts or fate of the victim, not the criminal responsibility. The WG recalled the obligation of states to continue investigations as long as the fate and whereabouts of the victims are unknown.[9]

The Draft IC Preamble,[10] affirms the right of victims to know the truth about the fate and whereabouts. Article 16 bis paragraph 1 guarantees the access to information about the victim, legal representative, counsel or person authorized concerning the authority to which the person has been handed over; that ordered the deprivation of liberty; in charge of supervision, whereabouts and transfer; date and place of release; state of health; and in case of death, circumstances and causes. To this end, Article 17 guarantees the right to a prompt and effective remedy.

In international humanitarian law, AP I, Article 32 provides for the right of the families to know the fate of their relatives. The independent expert charged with examining the existing framework of international criminal and human rights applicable to enforced disappearances asserted the existence of the same right, as derived from international customary law, in noninternational armed conflicts.[11]

In the Principles on Prevention,[12] paragraph 17, a written report must be made within reasonable time on the method and findings of investigations concerning extrajudicial executions. The report has to be immediately public and must include the scope of the inquiry, procedures and methods used to evaluate evidence, conclusions and recommendations based on findings of fact and on applicable law. The report additionally must describe in detail the specific events and evidence on which the findings are based.

The Practice of the Working Group on Enforced or Involuntary Disappearances and the Commission on Human Rights

The WG recognizes "the truth" as a necessary outcome of the investigation of a disappearance case. Since its creation, the WG acted with the purpose of "finding a solution to the problem of enforced or involuntary disappearances and of determining the whereabouts or fate of persons reported missing or disappeared."[13] Moreover, it constantly criticized countries that had not performed the necessary investigations as to find out the truth in disappearances cases:

> The true objective of the Working Group, which is to achieve a clarification of each case of disappearance, is not being achieved with sufficient speed. This is because, generally speaking, the Governments involved tend to undertake their part of the process with a slowness which, in the opinion of the Working Group, is undesirable. They should consider it unacceptable that some of their own citizens should be subjected to untold pain and pressure — made all the more intolerable when news about the fate of the disappeared is not

forthcoming to their families. In addition, all Governments should make a special point of employing whatever time, effort and resources it takes, using all available legal and other means, to achieve speedy and truthful clarification of such cases.[14]

The expert member of the WG in charge of the Special Process on Missing Persons in the territory of former Yugoslavia, Manfred Nowak, clearly asserted that "in particular, the relatives of some 30,000 missing persons have the right to know the truth and to be properly informed about the fate and the whereabouts of their husbands, sons and other family members unaccounted for."[15]

The WG referred to an *amicus curiae* presented before an Argentinean tribunal, citing details, by indicating "the right to the truth is said to belong not only to the relatives, but to society as a whole."[16]

More clearly, in a subsequent report,[17] concerning the activities of the expert member of the WG in charge of the Special Process, the WG asserted this right clearly: "The expert facilitated, in particular, a programme of excavation of mass graves and exhumation of mortal remains for the purpose of identifying deceased missing persons, returning the remains to the families concerned and, thereby, responding to the right of the families to know the truth about the fate of their loved ones."

In the corresponding report of the expert member of the WG, the idea is clearly present: "The full truth about the horrible crimes against humanity committed between 1991 and 1995 can no longer be concealed."[18]

The expert asserted the "legitimate right" of the families of missing persons to know the truth and to get their loved ones back, alive or dead.[19]

In a new report, the WG assessed the situation of the cases in Chile and expressed concern on amnesty legislation because "as a result of the restrictions imposed by the military regime, [the laws] are affecting the judicial system and are preventing the progress made in establishing the truth from leading to any possibility of punishing those responsible for enforced disappearances."[20] Concerning Argentina, the WG received information that "the rights to truth and justice of the families of the disappeared persons and victims of human rights violations continue to be ignored."[21] In the same report, the concern about Peru, where "the right to justice, truth and social and financial redress for the relatives of victims of enforced or involuntary disappearances committed in the campaign against the organizations calling themselves the Communist Party of Peru, Shining Path and the Túpac Amaru Revolutionary Movement" was at stake.[22]

The WG referred to the situation in Chile by asserting that "much remained to be done to establish the truth regarding the fate and whereabouts of the disappeared persons."[23]

In some opinions, reparation should include the determination of the truth,[24] as component of the duty to guarantee and not as an alternative: complementary and interdependent obligations, all of them mandatory. The CHR expressed that impunity affects all sectors of the society; public knowledge of the victims' suffering and the truth are essential steps toward rehabilitation and reconciliation. All necessary and possible steps to hold accountable perpetrators should be adopted. The CHR urged governments with long-unresolved cases to continue efforts to disclose the fate of the victims and to set appropriate settlement machinery, reminding them that all acts of enforced disappearances are crimes punishable by appropriate penalties adequate to their extreme seriousness in criminal law.[25]

The Approach of the HRCBH: The Violation of Article 8 of the European Convention, Comparative Analysis of the Right to Protection of Family Life

The right to privacy and protection of family life was linked to the right to the truth by the HRCBH. In the European system, Article 8 of the European Convention asserts this right with a positive formula: respect for the private and family life, home and correspondence (Article 8.1). The European treaty protects against interference against "public authority." Some restrictions are permitted (Article 8.2): interference in the exercise of this right is allowed "in accordance with the law ... necessary in a democratic society in the interests of national security, public safety or the economic well being of the country, for the prevention of disorder or crime, for the protection of health or morals, or for the protection of the rights and freedoms of others."

This right is protected in all human rights instruments (Article 12 of the UDHR, Article 17 of the ICCPR; in the AD, Article 9 protects the right to inviolability of the home; Article 10, the right to inviolability and transmission of correspondence; Article 5 concerns protection of the law against "abusive attacks" on the honor, reputation, private and family life in a separate provision; Article 11 of the ACHR). The different human rights instruments contain specific provisions for the protection of the family (Article 16.3 of the UDHR, Article 23.1 of the ICCPR, Article 6 of the AD, Article 17.1 of the ACHR, Article 18.1 of the ACHPR). The right contains a negative dimension: the prohibition of interference in the privacy, family, home, and correspondence; the honor and reputation are also covered, but against attacks. The second aspect is to have a remedy to protect the right, evidently through the judicial system. Enforced disappearances constitute an arbitrary and unlawful interference in family life.

This right has not been commonly alleged in enforced disappearances. The important exception is the HRCBH, which cited Article 8 concerning the wife of the person disappeared in *Palic v. Republika Srpska,* for the arbitrary lack of information about the whereabouts of her husband and the fate of his body.[26]

In *Unkovic,*[27] the chamber had declared a violation to Article 3 of the European Convention and considered that to make a declaration under Article 8 was not necessary. In the decision on review, the chamber understood that the Federation of Bosnia and Herzegovina had violated this right as

> that information concerning the fate and whereabouts of a family member falls within "the right to respect for his private and family life," protected by Article 8 of the Convention. When such information exists within the possession or control of the respondent Party and the respondent Party arbitrarily and without justification refuses to disclose it to the family member, upon his or her request, properly submitted to a competent organ of the respondent Party or the [ICRC], then the respondent Party has failed to fulfill its positive obligation to secure the family member's right protected by Article 8."[28]

In the *Srebrenica Cases,*[29] the chamber repeated and enriched the position of *Palic* and *Unkovic.* From Article 8 of the European Convention derives the right to access to information of the family members; the chamber asserted that the Republika Srpska had Article 8, read together with Articles 32 and 33 of the AP 1, provisions that reinforce the obligations contained in Article 8, that is, "to search for and to share all relevant information with the families about their relatives who have been reported missing from Srebrenica since July 1995" (§175). The chamber asserted that the Republika Srpska had within its possession or control information about the missing persons, which was destroyed or denied, and did not conduct any meaningful investigation of the events of July 1995. The chamber concluded that there was a "catastrophic" impact of the events in the right to respect for private and family life, as the fate of the missing persons was not officially known with traumatic consequences to pursuing a normal life.

In the Inter-American system, the violation of the right to family life in enforced disappearances is very rare. In *Julio Solalinde et al.,*[30] the petitioners denounced deaths, disappearances, illegal detentions, and torture, especially of women and children, at the hands of Paraguayan authorities. Among the victims, four adults and unborn children died because of torture. The commission resolved that Paraguay, among other provisions of the AD, had violated Articles 6 (right to a family and to the protection thereof) and 7 (right to protection for mothers and children) of the AD. The focus is on the protection of the family and not on arbitrary or illicit interference in family life.

In *Castillo Páez v. Peru,* the IACtHR analyzed an aspect presented by IACHR[31]: the violation of Article 17 of the ACHR concerning the family, because the IACHR asserted that Castillo Páez's family disintegrated because of his disappearance. The IACtHR concluded that this was consequence of the disappearance that "this Court deems to have been proven, in violation of the American Convention, with all its legal consequences."

In the European system, in the case of *Cyprus v. Turkey,*[32] Cyprus alleged a violation of Article 8 for the persistent failure of Turkey to account for the families of missing persons, which would constitute a grave disregard for their right to respect for family life. The ECHR asserted these issues had to do with the treatment received by the family members from Turkey, analyzed *ut supra* as a violation to Article 3. The ECtHR agreed. Consequently, the ECtHR prefers to apply Article 3, what implies the application of the high standard of "special factors" (*Çakici v. Turkey.*) The ECtHR did not argue on Article 8.

The possibility that an enforced disappearance violates the right to privacy and family life cannot be denied a priori. This would require evidence of the disruption of the family life caused by the enforced disappearance. Moreover, the confusion with the issues arising from a violation of the right to humane treatment should be avoided to impede an interpretation of the ECtHR in *Cyprus v. Turkey.* In the Inter-American system, the notion was related to the protection of family life per se; in the only case before the European Court, the analysis under Article 8 was rejected and considered as a violation of Article 3. Consequently, the HRCBH is the only organ of protection that links the truth to Article 8 of the European Convention.

The Practice in the Inter-American System

There is a contradictory interpretation between the IACHR and the IACtHR. The IACHR recognizes this right; the IACtHR considers that this does not exist independently, as the truth is an aspect of the duty to investigate.

The basic interpretation is included in *Velasquez Rodríguez,*[33] where the IACtHR asserted that "an investigation must have an objective and be assumed by the State as its own legal duty, not as a step taken by private interests that depends upon the initiative of the victim or his family or upon their offer of proof, without an effective search for the truth by the government." This was repeated in *Godínez Cruz,*[34] and *Caballero Delgado & Santana.*[35]

The jurisprudence of the IACHR is clear in the opposite sense: It derives a right to know the truth that exists additionally to the duty of the state to investigate. The victim's family is given special empowerment to be able to claim, before domestic and international instances, specific activity from the state organs, directed to disclose the fate and whereabouts of the victims of enforced disappearances. This is clear jurisprudence since 1985.[36] In the *Report on the Situation of Human Rights in Chile,* 1985, the IACHR insisted on the need of information about the fate of disappeared persons.[37]

In *García Franco v. Ecuador,*[38] the IACHR analyzed the right to know the truth: "The State of Ecuador failed to honor its obligation to provide simple, swift and effective legal recourse to the Garcia family, so that they could know the full truth about what happened to Manuel, including the circumstances of his torture and death."

The commission asserted that the obligation, derived from Article 1.1 of the ACHR, consists in the "use [of] all the means at its disposal to carry out a serious investigation of violations committed within its jurisdiction [in order] to identify those responsible," as asserted in *Velásquez Rodríguez.*[39] Moreover

> family members are entitled to information as to what happened to their relative (...) this right to know the truth about what happened is also based on the need for information to vindicate another right. In the case of a disappearance, family members have the right to know the exact fate of the victim, not only for the purpose of learning exactly how his or her rights were violated, but also in order to enforce their own right to compensation from the State. Under Ecuadorian law, the right to civil compensation cannot be pursued in the absence of a judicial determination of criminal responsibility.

In *Guarcas Cipriano v. Guatemala,* the IACHR recognized the victims and/or relatives' rights to a judicial investigation by a criminal court to establish and sanction responsibility for human rights violations. This derives from the obligation to "use all the means at its disposal to carry out a serious investigation of violations committed within its jurisdiction to identify those responsible, pursuant to Article 25 and Article 8.1 of the ACHR."[40] The victim's family had a right to know the truth about the victim's fate and to use that information to vindicate their right as heirs to reparation.

In *Palomino Morales et al v. Peru,* the IACHR asserted "in the event of a 'forced disappearance,' the State is obligated to ascertain the whereabouts and situation of the victim, punish the responsible, and grant reparation to family members."[41]

In *Velasquez Isabela v. Guatemala,* the IACHR asserted "the victims' families have a right to know the truth about what happened to them."[42] Because the state failed to respond for the disappearance, the family had been denied justice, as they had right to know and seek reparation.[43]

In 1997, the IACHR tried to obtain a concrete declaration on the right to the truth by the IACtHR. In *Castillo Páez v. Peru,*[44] the IACtHR analyzed the alleged violation of the "the right to truth and information, in the light of the State's lack of interest in investigating the events that gave rise to this case."

The IACtHR asserted that the

> argument refers to the formulation of a right that does not exist in the American Convention, although it may correspond to a concept that is being developed in doctrine and case law, which has already been disposed of in this case through the Court's decision to establish Peru's obligation to investigate the events that produced the violations of the American Convention.

The IACtHR solved the issue by asserting that the state has the duty to investigate the facts of the case, derived from Articles 8 and 25 of the ACHR. Moreover, the IACtHR underlined that the right to the truth does not exist in the American Convention.

In *Bámaca Velásquez,*[45] the IACHR insisted and alleged that because of the enforced disappearance, the state had violated the right to the truth of the family and the society. The IACHR asserted that the right to the truth is a collective right: the right of the society to have access to essential information, which is at the same time an individual right, as the right of the family members of the victims to know what happened to the loved ones, which is a kind of reparation. The IACHR argued on the duty to investigate and went further, asserting that this is a right of the society based on international law according to a dynamic interpretation of the human rights treaties, particularly Articles 1.1, 8, 25, and 13 of the ACHR.

The IACtHR repeated its point of view: It was out of question that the wife and family members had a right to know the truth. However, "in the circumstances of the case," the right to the truth is subsumed in the right to obtain from the competent organs the determination of the facts through investigation and trial, as asserted in Articles 8 and 25 of the ACHR.[46] In *Barrios Altos,* this opinion was re-asserted.[47]

Argentinean Jurisprudence Concerning the Right to the Truth

In Argentina, the enactment of amnesty legislation stopped all criminal prosecutions and consequent investigation for human rights violations between 1976–1983, which encouraged practitioners and judges to recognize this right and overcome amnesty legislation to pursue judicial investigation. The Supreme Court asserted that the amnesty legislation was constitutional. The right to know the truth constituted a creative possibility for challenging that decision in the facts. Without questioning the amnesty legislation, the right to know the truth was aiming at finding out the fate and whereabouts of the victims, and not at punishing the perpetrators, protected by the legislation and the jurisprudence of the highest Argentinean tribunal.

The Federal Chamber for Criminal Affairs (FCCA) of the City of Buenos Aires investigated the whereabouts of the victims during the last dictatorship in Argentina.[48] Though the FCCA was competent to investigate and prosecute federal crimes, its jurisdiction to determine the truth was asserted because the right to the truth is one of the immediate aims of a criminal case, because there was a state obligation to use all mechanisms available to determine the fate and whereabouts of the disappeared persons.

The interpretation of the Supreme Court in *Urteaga*[49] and *Ganora*,[50] contributed to this view. The Argentinean Supreme Court asserted that the lack of legislation could not impede the exercise of *habeas data,* a new constitutional guarantee (Article 43, Argentinean constitution, as amended in 1994). In *Urteaga,* the Supreme Court authorized habeas data as to request information about a person allegedly killed during the dirty war to penetrate public records. The Supreme Court asserted that eventual harm to security, national defense, and so on could not be alleged against habeas data; if any of these questions existed, the state should invoke it, and the tribunals should analyze its reasonability on a case-by-case basis.

In La Plata, the FCCA started hearing a trial for the truth, pursuing only the determination of the truth and not criminal punishment. The Permanent Assembly for Human Rights presented a petition requesting the remission from Buenos Aires and San Martín of all the cases initiated in La Plata but that were finally incorporated to the famous cases investigated in 1985 and 1986 in Buenos Aires, which were the only criminal cases finished before the Argentinean courts concerning individual criminal responsibility for human rights violations during the dirty war. The argument was that the prosecutors in 1985–86 chose only some of the cases. Later, the Full Stop and Due Obedience Laws impeded further investigation, and many crimes remained unpunished.

In Mar del Plata, the FCCA started a trial for the truth in 2001, and the same happened in Salta: The judge admitted the case by asserting that the right to truth is inalienable and not subject to statutes of limitation.[51]

These achievements overcame the *Lapacó* case, decided by the Argentinean Supreme Court, where only Justice Fayt, in a dissident opinion,[52] asserted that Argentina violated the right to know the truth, to respect the victims' corpse and to mourn, as well as the right to know the identity of the children born in captivity.

Conclusion

The right to know the truth is not a clear-cut right in the instruments of protection. However, the DED, the jurisprudence of the IACHR, the

HRCBH, and the jurisprudence of some domestic tribunals in Argentina recognize it. However, imprecision exists, for instance, when debating who is entitled to the truth: the family members, the society, and so on.

Probably, the right to the truth is one of the most dynamic issues in the field of enforced disappearances, as Méndez asserts — an emerging principle, not only as a right but also as content of the reparation, deserving specific remedies.[53]

The debate on the truth has been present in the Inter-American system as a consequence of the amnesty legislation that impeded the full investigation of many cases. The truth is a necessary consequence of any criminal case, and the characteristics of enforced disappearances convert the question in a central issue to satisfy the most basic needs of family members: to know what happened to the victim and the fate and whereabouts, which is linked with the possibility of a burial.

The lack of investigation is considered a procedural violation of Article 2 of the European Convention by the ECtHR, and the truth is a necessary outcome, but not a right. The HRC recognized in *Quinteros* the need of the victim's mother to know the truth, but the question did not receive much analysis, as most cases were rejected for incompetence *ratione temporis*. The HRCBH derived the right from Article 8 of the European Convention of Human Rights. The approach is a new dimension concerning enforced disappearances.

As to avoid these interpretations and to adequately protect the victims, the right should be consecrated in a binding instrument. The Draft IC includes different remedies that would lead to the truth, the need of recognition of this right of family members in a text clearer than the Draft IC, and the recognition of a remedy addressed at the exercise by asserting the right to access to state databases containing data regarding the victims and families. Together with the obligation of authorities to cooperate and the duty to reply to the requests, this would afford a more satisfactory standard of protection.

8

Specific Questions Related to Children's Rights

Cases of enforced disappearances may constitute human rights violations concerning children[1]: the right to personal identity (Article 8.1 of the CRC), as some children of disappeared persons have been abducted and "adopted" in the context of systematic disappearances, as an additional violation to the CRC; a child may lose one or both parents because of a case of enforced disappearances (Article 9 CRC; Article 20 CRC), and so on. Following the CRC, Article 1, children are persons less than 18 years of age. In the ICCPR, Article 24.1 provides for the right of every child to "measures of protection as are required by his status as a minor, on the part of his family, society and the State." The formula of Article 19 of the ACHR is similar.

In enforced disappearances instruments, specific provisions recognize the historical problems of children in cases of enforced disappearances, in particular, in Argentina between 1976 and 1983.

Both the UN system and OAS addressed the question through studies over the impact of disappearances on children.[2]

Some children were kidnapped to punish their parents or grandparents: They were kidnapped with their parents or born during captivity. Hundreds of cases happened in Argentina. Some cases affected Uruguayan children during their parents' exile in Argentina, with responsibility of both the Argentinean and Uruguayan authorities.

The kidnapping was committed sometimes with the complicity of security forces of more than one country, either through clandestine transportation of the minor across borders, or in the irregular and unlawful protection afforded in other countries to those who took the children away to evade justice.

In some cases, the final fate was the extrajudicial execution and the attempt to hide the corpses. In other cases, the minor was returned to the natural family, often after being held in clandestine detention or in orphanages or hospitals for abandoned infants. The families endured offensive treatment, long waits, and uncertainty.

In other cases, the children were taken away to be given in irregular adoption to other families. In some cases, the family receiving the child ignored the child's origin; in other cases, the adopting family was that of a captor or a member of the police or armed forces who knew the child's origin.

There was ideological motivation — in particular, the fear that the children of the disappeared would grow up hating the Argentine army, motivating a new generation of "subversive" or "potentially subversive elements."

When the adoptive family was innocent, the policy of Abuelas de Plaza de Mayo in Argentina was to accept the new family's custody if (1) the family environment was appropriate for the child's welfare, (2) visiting rights were established for natural grandparents and other relatives, (3) the child was informed, at an appropriate time, of his or her real identity.

Some children were born in concentration camps and delivered to acquaintances of the repressors. Many pregnant mothers were seen alive until giving birth and then were never seen again. In some cases, the security forces caused the disappearance and presumably the murder of nurses and midwives who tried to give information to the relatives after assisting deliveries.

According to the opinion of the IACHR and Prof. Van Boven, removing children of disappeared persons violates fundamental norms of international law, in particular, the right of direct victims, in this case, to the identity and name of children (Article 18, ACHR), liberty and security of the person, not to be subjected to inhuman or degrading treatment, to be recognized legally as persons (Article 3, ACHR; Article 17 AD), and enjoy special measures of protection, attention, and assistance (Article 19 ACHR and Article 7 AD), by the real family and the state. Moreover, the IACHR declared that these actions abuse international law standards protecting the family (Articles 11 and 17 ACHR and Articles 5 and 6 AD). In addition, the IACHR asserted that these acts constituted also criminal offences in domestic law.

The IACHR concluded that the children's relatives have the right to insist on knowing the whereabouts of the children and to participate in their education and upbringing, as is most conducive to the child's development and welfare. The children victimized have a fundamental right to their identity as persons and to know that identity, as well as to recover the memory of their natural parents, to know that they never abandoned them, and to be in contact with their natural family.

Concerning custody, the IACHR considered that judges must have discretion to determine an appropriate custody arrangement and, where applicable, regularize adoptions if the best familial environment is the adoptive home. However, judges should respect the exercise of the natural relatives to visits and contacts with the child.

Where the adoptive parent participated in the abduction, torture, or execution of the parents or was accomplice, the IACHR recommended the immediate separation from the family group.

Moreover, the IACHR solicited the GA of the OAS a recommendation concerning the increase of penalties for suppression and misrepresentation of civil status and abduction of minors; the review of procedural standards to include scientific evidence to speed the proceedings and to grant injunctive relief to prevent the flight of persons, the hiding of children, or the destruction of evidence; and the review of the rules concerning adoption.

In *Reggiardo Tolosa,*[3] the IACtHR ordered preliminary measures at the request of the IACHR to protect the children abducted during the dirty war in Argentina and not living with their biological family, who was claiming for them. The children had not been handed over to the biological family. After several remedies of Abuelas de Plaza de Mayo, a judge decided that minors should be placed in a "substitute home." The IACtHR decided that Argentina should adopt the necessary measures to protect the physical integrity of the children and to present a report to the court about those measures.

This unfortunate practice of abductions led to the recognition of the problem in international instruments. In the universal system, the DED, Article 20 asserts the obligation of states to prevent and suppress the abduction of children from parents subjected to disappearances and of children born during the mother's enforced disappearance. Moreover, the provision includes the obligation to "devote their efforts to the search for and identification of such children and to the restitution of the children to their families of origin." The families of origin cannot derive a right this provision. Perhaps only a case-by-case answer is possible, as the health and welfare of the children should be especially protected.

As for children adopted during the disappearance of their parents, the DED asserts the "need to protect the best interests of children," so states must provide an opportunity to declare void the adoption. The DED conditions the continuance of the adoption to the consent of the child's closest relatives. This system has not worked out, though some children have been recovered; the children (now adults) are the persons deciding their own destiny. Moreover, some of them have preferred to stay with their adoptive family, even knowing that they had some kind of participation in the disappearance of their parents.

Related to this issue, the DED asserts the obligation of states to criminalize as "an extremely serious offence" the abduction of children of parents disappeared or of children born during the captivity of the mother and the act of altering or suppressing documents attesting the identity of these persons.

Finally, the DED refers to the conclusion of bilateral or multilateral agreements, which has not taken place until the moment of writing these lines.

In the IACFD, only Article 12 refers to this delicate issue, including the duty of assistance between states parties in the search for, identification, location, and return of minors removed to another state or detained as a consequence of the forced disappearance of parents or guardians. Consequently, "domestic" abduction is left out of the IACFD, which only deals with "international" disappearances. This is the result of the policy of status quo in Latin America concerning enforced disappearances. Unfortunately, today the disclosure of the real identity of children separated from their families through these mechanisms depends on the private efforts of NGOs, as the Mothers or Grandmothers of Plaza de Mayo. In other Latin American countries, children were direct victims of disappearances, but in Argentina the suppression of identity and abduction of children of disappeared persons is the most important question.

The Draft IC[4] includes in Article 18 the obligation of states to prevent and punish the abduction of children whose parents are victims of disappearances and children born during their mother's forced disappearance. Moreover, the obligation to search for and identify such children is included. The general rule is that the child will be returned to the family of origin, and the best interests of the child are taken into account, as well as the child's views according to age and maturity. Consequently, the provision attends to the reality analyzed in Argentina. The project includes international assistance and the possibility of reviewing adoptions, taking into account the child's views. Moreover, the provision requires punishment for abductions, as well as for falsification or suppression of documents attesting to the child's identity. The WG specially welcomed Article 18 and the principle of the best interest of the child of the CRC.[5]

In *Ximena Vicario,* the HRC has found violations to Article 24 of the ICCPR, because Argentina did not protect a daughter of disappeared persons. Ximena was daughter of disappeared parents, and the domestic courts denied her grandmother standing to participate in legal proceedings concerning her custody. Moreover, Ximena could not obtain new documents according to her real identity, which, in addition, constituted a violation to Article 24.2.[6]

Apart from these cases, the HRC has analyzed cases on disappearances of children. In *Celis Laureano,*[7] the grandfather alleged a violation of Article 24, paragraph 1 of the ICCPR, as the state failed to protect her as a minor.

Shining Path kidnapped her for forced labor. Later, the Peruvian security forces abducted her, presuming her "collaboration" with terrorists. The HRC noted that before she disappeared, a civil court ordered her provisional release *because* she was a minor. Subsequently, the state did not adopt any particular measures to investigate the disappearance and locate her or to ensure her security and welfare. Ana did not benefit from special measures of protection deserved for being a minor: Article 24, paragraph 1 was breached.

In *Villagrán Morales v. Guatemala,*[8] the IACtHR considered that Guatemala did not adopt adequate measures of protection and prevention concerning the victims, who disappeared and whose bodies appeared later with signs of torture, abandoned. Some of the victims were under 18 years of age. There was a practice of violence in the state party against children in risk situation, known as children of the street. The children were victims of a double aggression: First, states did not protect them against misery, depriving them of the minimum conditions for a life with dignity, and impeding them the full and harmonious development of their personality, though every child is entitled to a project of life that must be cared for and encouraged by the public organs, and in the benefit of the society. Second, some states attempted against the child's physical, psychical, and moral integrity, even against the child's life. The IACtHR resorted to the CRC as a very comprehensive international *corpus juris* for the protection of children as to determine the content and scope of Article 19 of the ACHR. The IACtHR referred to Article 2 (nondiscrimination; measures of protection against discrimination); Article 3.2 (protection and care of children according to their welfare and the rights and duties of their parents, through legislative and administrative measures), Article 6 (right to life and development of the children), Article 20 (special protection to children deprived of their family environment), Article 27 (right to an adequate standard of living; assistance from the state), and Article 37 (prohibition of torture and other cruel, inhuman or degrading treatment or punishment, prohibition of illegal detention, as last recourse and during a brief period; human treatment to children in detention, right to counsel when deprived of physical freedom).

The IACtHR interpreted these measures of Article 19 of the ACHR as including the above-mentioned rights, even the guarantee of survival and development of the child, right to an adequate standard of living, and right to social reinsertion of any child victim of abandonment or exploitation. The state must deepen the measures to prevent the crimes against children and to guarantee the rehabilitation of juvenile criminals. Consequently, Article 19 of the ACHR had been breached.

In *Velasquez Isabela v. Guatemala,* the IACHR interpreted Article 19 asserting that it establishes special measures of protection for children corresponding to their vulnerability as minors, which were violated in disappearances cases.

In *Lopez Rivera v. Guatemala,*[9] two persons (one of them 11 years of age) were illegally and arbitrarily detained by the security forces after leaving their house. The commission declared that Guatemala had violated Articles 4 (right to life) and 7 (right to personal liberty), further aggravated by the fact that one victim was a minor. The IACHR reached the same conclusion in *Del Cid v. Guatemala,*[10] where the victim, Laura, 12 years of age, was illegally and arbitrarily detained by security forces, and in *Chirico Ortiz v. Guatemala*[11] and *Garcia Guzman v. Guatemala,*[12] where the victims, both 15 years of age, were illegally and arbitrarily detained by security forces. In *Giron Ruano v. Guatemala,*[13] the victim was 17 years of age.

Children are direct or indirect victims; the problem received special attention within the Inter-American system and before the HRC, concerning Latin American issues. An approach that includes the protection of the children in cases of enforced disappearances would contribute to a better paradigm, especially concerning one of the most vulnerable groups in our societies.

In general, the organs of protection have been sensitive to the problem and have declared the violation of children's rights.

As the CRC indicates, the interest of the children should always be the guideline for the opportune adoption of preventive measures by states. In particular, apart from the necessary education in human rights for security forces, the abduction of children puts at the stake the role of the professionals in health services. Without their participation, the abduction of children immediately after their birth could have never taken place.

9

The Right to a Remedy (I):
Access to Justice

*The Van Boven/Bassiouni Projects and the Victim's Right to a
Remedy or to Restitution under Human Rights Law*

The reparation of human rights violations is a pending problem. The question is extremely difficult, for its complexity and lack of political will.[1] Though in some regional systems the victims can request a tribunal to determine the existence of human rights violations and reparation, the lack of universality, coherence, systematization and consistency among the existing solutions is evident. Victims lack universal judicial mechanisms, apart from regional solutions (ECtHR, the IACtHR, and the HRCBH). If reparations are due, some states refuse to execute them domestically; consequently, the reparation depends on the goodwill of states.

Moreover, the solutions adopted reveal inconsistencies, to the detriment of the victims' rights. The current situation leads to vulnerability.

The recognition of a right to reparation is related to the individualization of human rights discourse for the protection and promotion of the victims' rights. The definition of this right through different reports presented to the Sub-Commission on the Promotion and Protection of Human Rights and the CHR, by Theo Van Boven and Cherif Bassiouni, respectively, is supplementary to the preoccupation for the codification and progressive development of the law of state responsibility and individual criminal responsibility.[2] Van Boven and Bassiouni analyzed the "right to restitution" as a parallel task to that of the ILC, concerning state responsibility.

A state is responsible for human rights violations within its jurisdiction, and state responsibility emerges from internationally wrongful acts of states.[3] International law recognizes increasingly state obligations toward individuals particularly on human rights issues. The individual is entitled to human rights and counts with *standing* before organs of protection. Cases, petitions or communications against states can be presented if there are breaches of international obligations under human rights law, including tribunals, such as the ECtHR.

Van Boven and Bassiouni recognize the right to a remedy and, in particular, to reparation in the broadest sense, including restitution, compensation, rehabilitation, satisfaction and guarantees of nonrepetition, as an essential requirement of justice, a precondition for reconciliation, and for coming to terms with the past.[4] The Draft Guidelines introduce no new legal obligations, but they consolidate existing norms.[5]

The ILC underlines that the obligation to grant reparation exists also toward persons or entities other than states, for example, "human rights violations and other breaches of international law where the primary beneficiary of the obligation breached is not a State." The *Articles on State Responsibility* do not deal with such rights, "which may accrue directly to [private] persons," but recognizes them.

Van Boven and Bassiouni conceive reparation broadly, but the jurisprudence is more conservative, resorting to classical international law; in particular, the IACtHR cites the famous *Factory Chorzów* case: "It is a principle of international law, and even a general conception of law, that any breach of an engagement involves an obligation to make reparation."[6] According to Van Boven, "There is no doubt that the obligation to provide for compensation as a means to repair a wrongful act or a wrongful situation is a well established principle in international law."[7] Under international law, the violation of an international obligation originates the duty of reparation. The next step is the notion of beneficiary and whether an individual right to reparation exists.

Cherif Bassiouni requires five successive stages in the progressive development of human rights law: (1) enunciation (the emergency of certain common values perceived internationally); (2) declarative (the declaration on an international document or instrument of certain interests or human rights identified as such); (3) prescriptive (a wording of those rights on international instruments — general or specific — or on binding conventions); (4) implementation (search for or development of ways of implementation); and (5) criminalization (development of international penal prescriptions aiming at the protection of such rights against its possible violation).[8] The right to reparation is present in the work of Van Boven and Bassiouni and in general in some case law but also received critiques. There is elaboration corresponding to the second stage (declarative), though some systems recognize the right to reparation in treaty regimes.

Whether and to what extent private persons are entitled to invoke responsibility on their own account depends on each applicable primary rule (e.g., the human rights rule establishing the obligation). Clear and universal primary rules concerning the right to reparation are scarce. For that reason, states should incorporate the work of Van Boven and Bassiouni domestically or through international instruments.[9] Many human rights duties are *erga omnes*,[10] the problem is how to translate them into obligations due to individuals, except if a treaty recognizes them *standing*.[11] Each state decides if it grants access to justice and the right to reparation, and to what extent. Political will and budgetary constraints play a dangerous role.

The former Sub-Commission on Prevention of Discrimination and Protection of Minorities, through Resolution 1989/13, entrusted Theo Van Boven to undertake a study concerning the right to restitution, compensation and rehabilitation for victims of gross violations of human rights and fundamental freedoms, taking into account relevant existing international human rights norms on compensation and decisions and views of human rights organs to explore the possibility of developing basic principles and guidelines.[12] In 1993, Van Boven asserted among the "General Principles" that the violation of any human right originates the right of reparation, particularly gross violations of human rights, among them enforced disappearances. The principles included the duty to make reparation. This obligation refers to every human right, as Nowak asserts.[13] Van Boven articulates the right as the right to a remedy. Bassiouni recognizes three dimensions: access to justice, right to reparation, and access to information.

Van Boven grounded this right on the right to an "effective remedy,"[14] what is asserted in Article 8 of the UDHR, Article 2(3)(a) of the ICCPR, and Article 6 of the DERD.[15] Some instruments include the "right to be compensated in accordance with the law" (Article 10 of ACHR) and the "right to an adequate compensation" (Article 21.2, ACHPR). Article 9.5 of the ICCPR and Article 5.5 of the European Convention include an enforceable right to compensation concerning particular rights. The CAT asserts in Article 14.1 the "enforceable right to fair and adequate compensation, including the means for as full rehabilitation as possible." The DED provides, in Article 19, that the victims and families shall obtain redress and have the right to adequate compensation, including rehabilitation. The compensation is due according to national law (Article 14.6 of the ICCPR; Article 11 of the DAT). The CERD,[16] in Article 6, asserts the right to seek "just and adequate reparation or satisfaction for any damage suffered"; the ILO Convention concerning Indigenous and Tribal Peoples in Independent Countries refers to "fair compensation for damages" (Article 15(2)),[17] to "compensation in money" and "under appropriate guarantees" (Article 16(4)), and to full compensation "for any loss or injury" (Article 16(5)). The CRC indicates that states shall take all appropriate measures to promote "physical and psychological recovery and social reintegration of a child victim" (Article 39).

The Declaration of Basic Principles provides for prompt redress; information about redress; fair restitution to victims, families or dependents, including the return of property or payment for the harm or loss suffered; and reimbursement of expenses incurred services and the restoration of rights. If compensation is not available from the offender, states should provide it, and victims should receive the necessary material, medical, psychological and social assistance and support. Principle 9 provides that governments should review practices, regulations and laws on restitution, in addition to criminal sanctions.

The SMR assert "in order to facilitate the discretionary disposition of juvenile cases, efforts shall be made to provide for community programs, such as temporary supervision and guidance, restitution, and compensation of victims" (Rule 11.4).

Among regional instruments, the ACHR refers to "compensatory damages" (Article 68); consequences should "be remedied" and "fair compensation be paid to the injured party" (Article 63(1)).

The right of reparation is based on international law.[18] The recognition of rights of the victim counts with new examples.[19] The CHR's Resolution 2002/44 (23 April 2002) on "the right to restitution, compensation and rehabilitation for victims of grave violations of human rights and fundamental freedoms," where the CHR recommended to pay attention to the right to a remedy and restitution, compensation and rehabilitation. The CHR recognizes the right to a remedy, but only in "appropriate cases," the right to receive reparation.

The right to reparation is not so clear-cut in the jurisprudence. The IACtHR asserts "the obligation to grant reparation is an international law obligation, though local law is applied as to determine the family regime and applicable rules."[20] The Inter-American Court stresses the duty of the State to grant reparation, instead of the right to reparation of the victim. The HRC has used several formulas: compensation to the victim through payment to his family for any injury suffered,[21] compensation to the husband for the wife's disappearance,[22] appropriate compensation to the family of the person killed,[23] compensation for the wrongs suffered,[24] compensation for physical and mental injury and suffering caused to the victim by the inhuman treatment,[25] and compensation to surviving families,[26] but it has never asserted if a right to restitution exists.

This right has been criticized by Germany when commenting on Van Boven's work, because of the domestic aspects of it, which would belong to the domestic policy of each state.[27] Germany advocated for a real international standard, including a procedure.[28] However, the existent international instruments clearly assert the right to a remedy.

In similar critical tone, Tomuschat has differentiated the rights existent under domestic law from those derived from international law.[29] Most legal systems require a national legal act to confer rights derived from a treaty to individual; consequently, domestic law governs the legal position of the individual. Without universal and general mechanisms giving individual entitlements, Tomuschat asserts that the right to reparation does not derive from available remedies. This point of view is not acceptable.

Bassiouni finds three dimensions, and the first one is the right to a domestic effective and adequate remedy recognized under treaty law (the ICCPR, Article 2.3). Obligations are enforced in domestic law, but human rights law is not conditioned to the adoption of domestic rules because international obligations exist independently from their domestic implementation (Article 27 of the Vienna Convention on the Law of the Treaties, 1969). Duties to respect and ensure are self-executing, concerning all the rights enumerated (*Arg.* Advisory Opinion 7/86, IACtHR).

The second dimension is the right to reparation in a broad sense, derived from the general obligations of all human rights treaties, particularly the duty to ensure or to guarantee, includes the obligation to grant reparation. General international law (custom) recognizes the obligation to give reparation. This counts with a reciprocal right entitlement favoring the individual: the victim's right to reparation. If there are scarce mechanisms of exercise, this does not mean that the right does not exist. The lack of *standing* is linked to the voluntary character of international jurisdictions.[30] Many human rights cannot be protected through judicial mechanisms, but they exist. The third aspect, the right to the truth, is the most problematic for political and social issues that go further than a judicial mechanism.

Van Boven focused on these issues in 1992[31] and elaborated the first Basic Principles and Guidelines on the Right to Restitution of 1993[32] ("the 1993 van Boven Guidelines"), a second version in 1996[33] ("the 1996 van Boven Guidelines"), and a third version in 1997[34] ("the 1997 van Boven Guidelines (revised).") Bassiouni was appointed by the CHR pursuant to Resolution 1998/43 to revise them, according to state comments.[35] He also analyzed the work of Louis Joinet, Special Rapporteur of the Sub-Commission on the question of the impunity of perpetrators of violations of human rights (civil and political).[36] Though Joinet's mandate was separate and distinct, Bassiouni understood that the work was directly related.[37] Joinet concluded that reparation entails individual and general or collective measures.[38] On an individual basis (relatives and dependents), this is the right to an effective remedy. The right to reparation includes *all injuries suffered by the victims.* According to Joinet this is: (a) *restitutio in integrum;* (b) compensation; and (c) rehabilitation. From the collective point of view, Joinet underlines symbolic measures.

Joinet also analyzed the guarantees of nonrecurrence: (a) disbandment of parastatal armed groups; (b) repeal of all emergency laws and courts, recognition of the inviolability and nonderogability of habeas corpus; and (c) removal from office of senior officials implicated in serious violations.

Bassiouni also studied the Declaration of Basic Principles, concerning victims of domestic criminal law and domestic abuse of power,[39] that does not provide for reparation for victims unless they exist domestically (Principles 18 and 19).

Van Boven analyzed gross human rights violations, among them enforced disappearances.[40] Bassiouni referred not to "gross" human rights violations but to human rights violations in general. According to the Maastricht Seminar of 1992, the notion of gross human rights violations included the "practice" of disappearances. Individual cases were not included. Chernichenko studied gross human rights violations and asserted that large-scale violations, as disappearances, are gross human rights violations,[41] Article 1 of the project.[42]

Bassiouni stressed the need to implement the guidelines domestically.[43] The guidelines' status is unclear[44]: Probably they are nonbinding standards, though binding rules would be necessary.

Another problem is the determination of the "victim" status.[45] When the victim is deceased or the injury has consequences for third persons, the need of "third parties" to be "victims" is another issue. Bassiouni asserted in 1999 that there is no consistent and uniform terminology.[46]

The Declaration of Basic Principles and in the work of the Preparatory Commission (PrepComm) for the ICC fourth (penultimate) session contains useful insights. The PrepComm worked on a French proposal.[47] Rule X (Article 15) defined "victim" as any person or group of persons who individually or collectively, directly or indirectly, suffered harm as a result of crimes within the court's jurisdiction. This wording is vague, and the Declaration of Basic Principles' definition is preferred, as it defines "victim" as follows:

> Victims' means persons who, individually or collectively, have suffered harm, including physical or mental injury, emotional suffering, economic loss or substantial impairment of their fundamental rights ... The term "victim" also includes, where appropriate, the immediate family or dependants of the direct victim and persons who have suffered harm in intervening to assist victims in distress or to prevent victimization.[48]

Van Boven, in 1993, included no definition of victim. The guidelines only asserted that the direct victims could claim reparation and, where appropriate, the immediate family, dependents or other persons with a special relationship to the direct victims. Van Boven recognized the need of reparation to groups. In the revised guidelines of 1996, the reference was modified: Reparation could be claimed individually and where appropriate, collectively by direct victims, immediate family, dependents or other persons or groups of persons connected with direct victims. In 1997, the project was slightly modified and "direct victims of violations of human rights and international humanitarian law" and "persons or groups of persons *closely* connected with the direct victims" were added. This concept is stricter than that contained in the Declaration of Basic Principles, because Van Boven includes "direct victims" and later other persons specially related to the victim, though the Declaration of Basic Principles understands that all of them are victims. This interpretation is increasingly accepted in the jurisprudence.

In the Draft IC, Article 22, para. 1, "victim" is the disappeared person and any individual who has suffered direct harm as a result of that person's disappearance. This is a broad definition. Van Boven indicates that to be dependent is independent of a special relationship to the direct victim, and dependents are, in addition, victims. Van Boven counts with a similar view to that of the Declaration on Basic Principles.

Dependent alludes to a person that economically received periodic help from the victim, and the kind of link among them permits to presume that this would continue, if the disappearance had not taken place. Some other persons lack family links and dependence but have been clearly affected by the disappearance, for instance, a fiancée, or persons living in the same household with the victim.

The WG discussed the Draft IC in 2001, asserting that *victim* includes the disappeared person and the next of kin, who suffer moral and psychological damage. The beneficiaries include the victims, heirs, and third parties dependent on the disappeared person and received a regular contribution and would have continued to do so if the disappearance had not occurred. Germany alleged that "dependent who has a direct relationship with her or him"[49] was unclear and should be deleted: If people have been injured themselves when searching the disappeared person, they have their own claim for damages. This ignores the IACtHR's jurisprudence (particularly *Aloeboetoe*).[50] A dependent is not only and not necessary a person injured when searching a person; periodic or constant help by the victim are necessary. Germany asserted that the provision mixes up victims and beneficiaries. Even the ECtHR in *Kurt*,[51] recognized the victim's mother as victim herself, and since *Çakici*[52] a strict standard was developed, followed later [*Timurtaş, Tas*,[53] *Çiçek, Akdeniz*, and *Cyprus v. Turkey*. The family members can also be victims in the Inter-American system, since *Castillo Páez* and *Blake*.

Bassiouni considered a victim a person who, as a result of acts or omissions constituting violations of international human rights or humanitarian law individually or collectively, suffered harm, including physical or mental injury, emotional suffering, economic loss, or impairment of to fundamental legal rights. The project asserts that a victim may also be a dependent or a member of the immediate family or household of the direct victim, as well as a person who, assisting a victim or preventing further violations, suffered physical, mental, or economic harm. A person's status as a victim should not depend on any relationship between the victim and the perpetrator, or whether the perpetrator was identified, apprehended, prosecuted, or convicted.

Bassiouni is clear and a reply to the last concern of Germany,[54] and, at the same time, is coherent with the Declaration of Basic Principles. The Bassiouni project also cares about treatment of victims (compassion and respect for dignity and human rights; appropriate measures to ensure safety and privacy, as well as that of their families). The draft recommends states to ensure that domestic laws provide victims of violence or trauma special consideration and care, particularly avoiding retraumatization in legal and administrative procedures.

The IACtHR has discussed the notion of victim in detail. In *Velasquez Rodriguez*,[55] the victim was only the person disappeared; the *beneficiaries* were the victim's wife, and children; the reparation was divided in equal parts.

In *Aloeboetoe,* all the damages suffered by the victims originated the *right to reparation,* transmitted to their heirs. Only those directly affected by the human rights violation were *victims.* The court differentiated between heirs and third persons affected. The court presumed that the victim's death caused the heirs material and moral damage. The state should prove that the damage did not exist. Those who were not heirs had to prove their right to receive reparation, that is, that they were *dependents* (they received periodic assistance from the victim, need, and a relation between the victim and them justifying the continuity of the assistance).

To determine who are heirs, the general principles of law (Article 38.1.c Statute ICJ) were applied. In most legal systems, they are the children and the spouse; if not them, the parents. The general principles should be interpreted according to national law (the law of the place of commission of the human rights violation), if it is not contrary to the ACHR (e.g., discriminatory).

The IACHR requested that the tribe should be considered victim, because it was responsible toward its members under Saramaca custom. In the traditional maroon society, a person is a member not only of a family but also of a community or tribe. The damage caused to any member damaged the community and deserved reparation. The court rejected the claim because there was no racial problem. This approach deserves critiques. The community lost several of their members, with affective and economic consequences. Van Boven and Bassiouni openly recognized the right to restitution to groups.

Concerning distribution of reparations, the IACtHR in *Aloeboetoe* indicated that a third of the reparation for economic damages was granted to the wives (divided into equal parts if there was more than one) and two-thirds to the children (also in equal parts). Concerning moral damage, half was granted to the children, a quarter to the spouses, and a quarter to the parents. If there was more than one beneficiary, the amount should be divided in equal parts.

In *Caballero Delgado and Santana,*[56] Caballero Delgado's family members were *beneficiaries:* each of the victim's two children would receive a third of the amount corresponding to the victim, and the other third would be received by the concubine, who had also right to the reimbursement of the expenses incurred.

The IACtHR does not use a conservative concept of family, adapting to the circumstances prevailing in each society.

In *Neira Alegría,* the IACtHR repeated previous jurisprudence: The beneficiaries were the victim's wife and children. Some siblings received compensation for searching for the victims.

Few direct victims have survived. The first exception was *Loayza Tamayo.* The court held that the victim's family members were also "injured parties" (Article 63.1) and could present own claims. "Family members" was broadly interpreted, including all persons linked by a close relationship: children, parents and siblings. In *Blake v. Guatemala,* the parents and siblings of the disappeared person claimed to be direct victims. The court recognized their anguish and suffering, and the lack of investigation: They were victims.[57] Moreover, in *Castillo Páez v. Peru,*[58] the Court asserted that "injured party" was the victim disappeared and the next of kin. The beneficiaries or heirs were the victim's father, mother and sister.

In *Durand and Ugarte,*[59] the agreement between beneficiaries and the state established as beneficiaries the victims' parents, sister and brother-in-law. Similarly, in *Barrios Altos,*[60] the IACtHR determined that the beneficiaries should be legal heirs, depending on each case.

In *Bámaca Velásquez,*[61] the IACtHR decided that the injured party consisted of the person disappeared, his wife, father, sister and half-sister. The heirs were accepted according to the general principles of law. The criteria concerning dependence were those of *Aloeboetoe.* The IACtHR understood that the persons suffered moral damage, including a half-sister closely related to the victim. The victim, an elder son in a Maya community, should sustain parents and siblings. The court divided the reparation in equal parts among the wife, victim's father, sister and half-sister. The same criteria were used concerning moral damage. In addition, the victim's wife was a victim herself.

In *Trujillo Oroza*,[62] the victim's family members treated as heirs were the mother, father, and brothers, who were also direct victims. Family members received a symbolic amount for the violation to the right to life of the victim.

In *El Caracazo*, the IACtHR clarified that "victims" refers to direct victims, and "family members," to the persons that were not direct victims, though in strict sense they are also victims because Articles 8 and 25 had also been violated.[63] In disappearances cases, the right to reparation is transmitted to family members.[64] The court applied Article 2.15 the new Rules of Proceeding: Family members are immediate family members (ascendants and descendents, siblings, husband and wife, permanent companions or those determined by the court, according to the case).[65]

The HRC asserted that family members might be victims in *Quinteros*. The HRCBH defined some persons next to the victim as victims themselves (e.g., the disappeared person's wife).[66]

Who are the victims of an enforced disappearance? Bassiouni asserted in 1999 that the standards are not consistent. The definition of the Declaration on Basic Principles is still a good standard, together with the proposal of Bassiouni, who clarifies important aspects. The "disappeared" is clearly the victim, and harm should not be requested. The victim can be an individual and, if appropriate, a collectivity or group, because they could be victimized according to the social and cultural environment. The "racial" element required of the IACtHR is not essential.

Moreover, not only is the disappeared person a victim, but so are other persons who suffer physical or mental injury, emotional suffering, economic loss or substantial impairment in their rights because of a disappearance, which includes the members of the family, who can endure emotional suffering for lack of information, plus the terrible thoughts of what could have happened. This is, according to the IACtHR, a direct violation of Article 5 of the ACHR (inhuman treatment). Moreover, the HRCBH analyzed the disruption of family life as a violation of Article 8 of the European Convention. The economic loss derived from the disappearance is added, plus possible violations of the right to a remedy, for the efforts to obtain information about the fate and whereabouts.

There are further victims: The emotional suffering of a fiancée or a very close friend could amount to the same interpretation of the IACtHR because they mentally represent the torture that could have suffered, mistreatments, and so on.

Concrete persons suffer an economic loss derived from the disappearance, and they are not necessarily family members. *Dependents,* as elaborated by the IACtHR in *Aloeboetoe* and supported by the WG when observing on the Draft IC, reveal particular importance. They received a periodic help from the victim, the disappearance stopped it, and the relation between the dependent and the victim would make one presume that the assistance would have continued (for instance, the help that a person can provide to an old cousin or uncle or to an old friend of the family because of the lack of possibilities to help himself because of sickness or age).

Disappearances may have further victims: persons harmed or harassed because of the disappearance (victim's neighbors and friends), and those who try to impede it, shed light on the case, or investigate the fate and whereabouts of the victim.

In addition to victims, there are possible *beneficiaries,* who, under the applicable law, are entitled to inherit the claim. The IACtHR is actually extensive and deep on this issue by resorting to the general principles of law plus equity. The ECtHR demands the proof of certain elements. The IACtHR has not been consistent, by requesting in some period evidence and in many cases assuming the existence of damages. The appropriate approach is that of the ECtHR, to avoid abuses. The application of these criteria, however, has been too restrictive by the ECtHR. Clearly the petitioner has a strong disadvantage in relation to the state. Some relations, such as parents–children or between spouses, should be presumed to have caused mental harm to the family members, without additional evidence.

The Obligation to Respect and Guarantee International Human Rights and Humanitarian Law

Human rights law creates state obligations, which should implement them in the domestic arena. A state violates international human rights if it fails to respect and ensure the rights protected or if it fails to provide remedies.[67] Measures should be adopted to give effectiveness to the rights enumerated.[68] In the Van Boven Guidelines, the duty to respect and to ensure are included, encompassing the duty to prevent, to investigate, to prosecute, and to afford remedies and reparation to victims, which is consistent with *Velasquez Rodriguez* and Article 1.1 of the ACHR.[69] The Van Boven Guidelines refer not only to reparations but also to remedies, a broader notion.[70]

Van Boven, in 1993, asserted that every state has a duty to make reparation. In the 1996 version, the same duty was asserted "under international law" and concretely concerning "human rights and humanitarian law." In 1997, the word *international* was added to "humanitarian law."

Bassiouni asserts the state obligation to respect, ensure respect, and enforce human rights and humanitarian law norms included, inter alia, in treaties, custom, or incorporated in domestic law. Moreover, Bassiouni asserts that states must ensure that domestic law is consistent with international law. The norm that provides the greatest degree of protection should be applied (principle *pro homine* and the "obligation to adopt measures") also coherently with the IACtHR jurisprudence, in particular since Advisory Opinion 7/86.[71]

Summing up, every violation of human rights is a violation of one or several human rights recognized in treaty law, customary law, or internal law but also of general obligations:

1. Duty to respect human rights. Bassiouni[72] underlines that the *best standard* of protection should be applied.

2. Duty to guarantee or to ensure the full and free enjoyment of these rights. The positive obligation includes:

a. *Duty to prevent human rights violations.* The state must avoid and impede human rights violations, which depends on due diligence in the prevention.

b. *Duty to investigate human rights violations.* The state is obliged to investigate and victims should be allowed to become civil parties as to give effectiveness to their rights, to complement and encourage state activity.

c. *Duty to punish the perpetrators.* Enforced disappearances must be criminally prosecuted, or the corresponding administrative or civil proceedings against perpetrators must be pursued. Joinet refers, in the *Principles on Impunity,* to the right to justice,[73] coherently with the Inter-American system, a right to a fair and effective remedy. Concerning competent tribunals, Joinet asserts that this task belongs to national courts, but if they cannot impart justice or are unable to function, the solutions include ad hoc international tribunals or a standing international court.[74] Finally, if the state does not punish, universal jurisdiction may arise. Joinet encourages "universal jurisdiction" clauses in human rights instruments and legislation to facilitate extradition of offenders.

d. *Duty of reparation.* Bassiouni emphasizes that the state must provide equal and effective access to justice.

In the Draft IC,[75] we find Article 2: to ensure that disappearances are offences under criminal law; Article 3, to prosecute and punishment those who commit or assist the commission of disappearances; Article 4: to establish penalties according to the seriousness of the crime; Article 9: to establish the country's jurisdiction on disappearances. No circumstance should be alleged not to comply with the convention, as political instability, threat of war, state of war, any state of emergency or suspension of individual guarantees. Moreover, state parties undertake to adopt the measures necessary as to fulfill these commitments. The list of obligations does not include prevention, in comparison with the Observations and Recommendations of the International Conference of Governmental and Non-Governmental Experts on "The Missing."[76]

In the first session of the Intersessional open-ended Working Group to elaborate a draft legally binding normative instrument for the protection of all persons from enforced disappearance,[77] the broadest possible jurisdiction by domestic criminal courts was recommended. Clauses are contained in other multilateral instruments (the CAT): the principle of *aut dedere aut judicare*, for instance.

The Right to a Remedy and the Access to Justice

The right to a remedy is a procedural right[78] *(droit à un recours)* referred to access to national and international proceedings, including the investigation of the facts. Global and regional human rights instruments guarantee this right. Provost considers that does not constitute international custom.[79] However, all instruments concerning civil and political rights include it, and so do the works of Van Boven, Joinet and Bassiouni, among others. It is the counterpart of the state obligation to guarantee human rights.

In the 1993 Basic Principles and Guidelines of Van Boven, the right to restitution (not the right to a remedy) was asserted, including the state obligation to maintain prompt and effective disciplinary, administrative, civil and criminal procedures, with universal jurisdiction for human rights violations constituting crimes under international law. The procedures should ensure the right to reparation taking into account the vulnerability of the victims.

The approach was different later. In 1996, the right to a remedy was included (and the right to restitution was deleted), defined as the state obligation to ensure that adequate legal or other appropriate remedies are available to any person claiming that rights have been violated, including access to national and international procedures of protection. In 1997, the amendments were small: the addition of "human" to "rights have been violated," and "any available" before "international procedures," and the insertion of "international" before "humanitarian law."

Similarly, Joinet asserts that the right to justice entails state obligations to investigate, prosecute and punish.

In the Bassiouni Guidelines, the right to a remedy includes three different aspects:

a. Access to justice (or right to a remedy in strict sense);
b. Reparation;
c. Access to the factual information concerning the violations (right to the truth).

Domestically, the right to a remedy implies that the legal system must provide for prompt and effective disciplinary, administrative, civil and criminal procedures to ensure readily accessible and adequate redress and protection from intimidation and retaliation, coherently with the obligation to adopt measures.[80]

The access to justice requires responsive proceedings.[81] Bassiouni asserted that states should

a. Make known, through public and private mechanisms, all available remedies;

b. Take measures to minimize the inconvenience to victims, protect their privacy as appropriate and ensure their safety from intimidation and retaliation, as well as that of families and witnesses, before, during, and after proceedings;

c. Make available all appropriate diplomatic and legal means to ensure that victims can exercise their rights to a remedy and reparation.

From the international perspective, the right includes all available international processes in which the individual has legal standing, without prejudice from domestic remedies.[82]

Joinet,[83] in Principle 19, refers to safeguards against reconciliation or forgiveness to further impunity; effective remedies and reparation are also included. Principle 29 indicates that perpetrators should not benefit from amnesty unless victims were able to avail themselves of an effective remedy and obtained fair and effective decision.

The Universal Instruments

Most international instruments guarantee the procedural right of effective access to a remedy. The UDHR provides that "everyone has the right to an effective remedy by the competent national tribunals for acts violating the fundamental rights granted him by the constitution or laws" (Article 8). The ICCPR contains Article 2.3, calling on states to ensure that any person whose rights or freedoms are violated shall have an effective remedy notwithstanding that the violation was committed by persons acting in an official capacity; to ensure that any person claiming such a remedy shall have the right determined by competent judicial, administrative or legislative authorities, or by any other competent authority provided for by the legal system of the state, and to develop the possibilities of a judicial remedy; and to ensure that the competent authorities enforce such remedies when granted. In the ICCPR, the right to a judicial remedy is not absolutely guaranteed; only the "possibilities" of a judicial remedy must be developed. Van Boven in 1993 asserted that the HRC has repeatedly concluded that the state party is obliged: (a) to investigate the facts; (b) to take action; (c) to bring to justice the responsible; (d) to extend to the victim(s) treatment according to the covenant's guarantees; (e) to provide the victims with medical care; and (f) to pay compensation.

Article 2.3 of the ICCPR is more detailed than Article 13 of the European Convention, but the HRC has refused to declare violations in isolation.[84] In *S. E. v. Argentina*,[85] a woman acted in her own name and on behalf of her three disappeared children whose whereabouts remained unknown since 1976. On 24 December 1986, Argentina passed the Full Stop Act *(Ley de Punto Final)*, establishing a deadline of 60 days for commencing new criminal investigations concerning the dirty war. On 8 June 1987, Law no. 23,521, Act of Due Obedience *(Ley de Obediencia Debida)* was enacted, introducing an irrefutable presumption that members of the security, police and prison services could not punished for such crimes, because they acted under due obedience. The Argentinean Supreme Court held the constitutionality of these acts. The fact-finding commission, CONADEP, opened investigation files on the disappearances but not on the whereabouts of the victims. The author claimed that the laws violated Article 2 of the ICCPR — in particular "to adopt such legislative or other measures as may be necessary to give effect to the rights recognized in the present Covenant" (Article 2, §2), "to ensure that any person whose rights or freedoms as herein recognized are violated shall have an effective remedy" (Article 2, §3(a)), and "to ensure that any person claiming such a remedy shall have his right thereto determined by competent judicial, administrative or legislative authorities ... and to develop the possibilities of judicial remedy" (Article 2, §3(b)) — because the disappearances were not investigated. The HRC repeated that Article 2 cannot be invoked in isolation, only together other articles of the ICCPR. If the human rights violations occurred before the entry into force of the ICCPR, the HRC had no competence. However, the ICCPR reminded that Argentina "is under an obligation, in respect of violations occurring or continuing after the entry into force of the Covenant, thoroughly to investigate alleged violations and to provide remedies where applicable, for victims or their dependants."

In *Villafañe et al. v. Colombia*,[86] the HRC considered that disciplinary and administrative remedies are not adequate and effective remedies in disappearances cases in the sense of Article 2.3.

In *Hugo Rodríguez v. Uruguay*,[87] though not a disappearances case, the HRC interpreted Article 2.3 and asserted that Amnesty Law no. 15,848 and the Uruguayan practice impeded the author's right to an adequate remedy. Uruguay had the obligation to investigate violations committed by a prior regime, especially torture, due to Article 2.3(a) and GCom no. 20 on Article 7.[88]

The HRC concentrates on investigation of human rights violations.

Comparing with the CAT, Article 14 refers to redress and compensation for torture:

> Each State Party shall ensure in its legal system that the victim of an act of torture obtains redress and has an enforceable right to fair and adequate compensation, including the means for as full rehabilitation as possible. In the event of the death of the victim as a result of an act of torture, his dependents shall be entitled to compensation.

The Declaration of Basic Principles contains broad guarantees for pecuniary losses, physical or mental harm, and "substantial impairment of their fundamental rights" through acts or omissions, including abuse of power. Victims have right to redress and to be informed about it. Victims of crime and/or abuse of power should receive access to justice, prompt redress and fair treatment (paragraphs 4–7), restitution (paragraphs 8–11), compensation (paragraphs 12–13), and necessary material, medical, psychological and social assistance (paragraphs 14–17).

The Principles on Prevention assert that effective protection through judicial or other means must be guaranteed to individuals or groups in danger of extralegal, arbitrary or summary executions, including those receiving death threats (§4). These cases should be subject to a thorough, prompt, and impartial investigation (§9), including an adequate autopsy, collection, and analysis of all physical and documentary evidence and statements from witnesses. If the family or victim submits complaints, an independent commission of inquiry or similar procedure should be established (§11).

The Regional Instruments of Protection

Regional instruments require legal and judicial remedies. The ECtHR modeled Article 13 on Article 8 of the UDHR. The standard of the ECtHR is low and does not necessarily a judicial remedy. The provision refers to "national authority" instead of national tribunals. The European Court found violations before systematic violations of human rights,[89] including enforced disappearances, as in *Kurt v. Turkey:*

> where the relatives of a person have an arguable claim that the latter has disappeared at the hands of the authorities, the notion of an effective remedy for the purposes of Article 13 entails, in addition to the payment of compensation where appropriate, a thorough and effective investigation capable of leading to the identification and punishment of those responsible and including effective access for the relatives to the investigatory procedure.... Seen in these terms, the requirements of Article 13 are broader than a Contracting State's obligation under Article 5 to conduct an effective investigation into the disappearance of a person who has been shown to be under their control and for whose welfare they are accordingly responsible.[90]

The applicant argued that her son was taken into custody; this was never seriously investigated; Turkey violated Article 13. In *Çakici v. Turkey*,[91] the court asserted the obligation on states to carry out a thorough and effective investigation to identify those responsible and to punish them, as well as for the effective access to proceedings by the petitioner.[92] In *Timurtaş*, the investigation was qualified as "dilatory, perfunctory and superficial."[93] In *Ihlan v. Turkey*, the court underlined that the need of an "effective" remedy in the practice and in the law.[94]

The ECtHR found easily violations to Article 13 of the European Convention for lack of an impartial, effective, and prompt investigation of serious human rights violations.

In the Inter-American system, Article 18 of the AD, right to a fair trial, asserts that every person may resort to courts to ensure respect for his legal rights. This is a simple, brief procedure to protect a person from acts of authority that violate any fundamental constitutional right. The reference to a court is an important difference, in comparison with the ICCPR and the European Convention.

The ACHR goes further, entitling everyone to effective protection against acts that violate constitutional rights "or laws of the state or by the Convention," even when acts were committed in official functions (Article 25). Paragraph 2 provides for final determination by the competent legal authority, possibilities of judicial remedy and assurances for enforcement of such remedies. The IACHR emphasized that there is a right to a recourse or effective remedy to prosecute and punish officials, and the violation of this right violates the state obligation to respect and guarantee and the right to judicial protection, Article 1(1) and 25 of the ACHR.[95]

The IACtHR asserts that Article 25 of the ACHR is "one of the fundamental pillars not only of the American Convention, but of the very rule of law in a democratic society in the terms of the Convention,"[96] ensuring the access to justice. Article 25 guarantees a simple and rapid recourse so those responsible are prosecuted and reparations are obtained.[97] The IACtHR asserts the duty to investigate the violation, to identify and punish those responsible, and to adopt the internal legal measures necessary to ensure compliance, derived not only from Article 25 but also from Articles 1(1) and 2 of the ACHR.

Article 25 refers to two different issues: if there were adequate and effective remedies, through habeas corpus[98]; second, once alleged a case, the state must investigate, prosecute and punish. The ECtHR and the HRC only analyze the investigation side.

In *Castillo Páez v. Peru*,[99] the IACtHR analyzed the first aspect. As habeas corpus is the adequate and effective remedy, this was obstructed by state agents through the adulteration of the logs of entry of detainees. Habeas corpus contributes to *prevent disappearances* and ensures the right to life. The ineffectiveness of the remedy violated Article 25 with Article 1(1).[100] In *Paniagua Morales,*[101] the IACtHR repeated the habeas corpus should not only exist but be effective.[102]

In *Villagrán Morales v. Guatemala,*[103] the IACtHR asserted that Guatemala violated Article 25 of the ACHR for the lack of investigation.

In *Bámaca Velásquez,*[104] the IACtHR underlined that the state did not recognize the right to judicial protection (Article 25) and repeated that remedies must be effective. The court decided similarly in *Cantoral Benavídez.*[105]

In *Barrios Altos,*[106] the IACtHR addressed amnesties and asserted that they breach the ACHR because they impede the investigation and punishment and breach nonderogable rights. Peru had breached the obligation to adapt internal law to the ACHR. Moreover, the IACtHR asserted that due to the incompatibility of the legislation and the ACHR, these laws lack juridical effect and cannot represent any more an obstacle to investigate the facts supporting this case or to identify and punish the responsible.

The IACtHR has declared violations to Article 25 in cases of enforced disappearances, when the remedies — fundamentally, habeas corpus — did not exist or when they were inefficient or ineffective. A second dimension was emphasized: the obligation to investigate, prosecute and punish.

The IACHR declared violations to the right to judicial protection, Article 25 of the ACHR.[107] The approach includes two dimensions: the remedy/guarantee of habeas corpus and the investigation. Enforced disappearances are a denial of the right to judicial protection. The right devolves to the victim's family, who is entitled to a judicial investigation.[108] The state's obligation to provide effective judicial remedies is not fulfilled simply by the existence of courts or the ability to resort to them. State parties must ensure that the rights are enforced, that is, that a competent court will be willing and able to draw on the capacity of the state to investigate. Habeas corpus had no result, and there was no investigation on the victim's whereabouts.[109]

The Inter-American system combines the right to access to justice with the guarantees of the due process of law, coherently with the report on the right to the fair trial presented to the Sub-Commission. In *Durand and Ugarte,*[110] the IACtHR asserted that Article 8.1 must be *broadly interpreted* in line with Article 1.2 of the DED. Victims and family members must have wide possibilities to be heard.[111] Article 8.1 and Article 25.1 of the ACHR confer on the family members the right that state authorities effectively investigate the disappearance and death, a proceeding is enacted against those criminally responsible, and adequate sanctions are imposed. None of these rights was recognized to the family members of the victims.

In *Blake v. Guatemala*,[112] the IACtHR asserted a breach of Article 8.1: the right to a proceeding within reasonable time, deprivation or denial of justice, as the authorities impeded the investigation. The family members were denied the right to an independent judicial proceeding within a reasonable time, consequently to obtain due reparation, and added that Article 8.1 must be interpreted widely as to pay attention not only to the literal text of the rule as its spirit and has to be appreciated according to Article 29.c of the Convention.[113] Consequently, Article 8.1 confers on family members the right that disappearances are *effectively* investigated by authorities, to have a proceeding against those responsible and to determine the sanctions, as well as to the reparation of damages.

The IACHR adopted a similar approach and combined Article 8 and Article 25. In Report No. 28/92 under "right to a fair trial,"[114] the commission analyzed amnesty legislation in Argentina. The commission understood that the legislation canceled the proceedings. The petitioners were denied their right to recourse and to a thorough and impartial judicial investigation. In many Latin American criminal law systems, the victim and attorney have the right to be the party making the charge in a criminal proceeding. Consequently, the victim has a fundamental civil right to go to courts, to give impulse to the criminal process. Argentina had failed to guarantee Article 25 and violated the convention and the obligation to investigate, Article 1.1.

The commission decided similarly concerning Uruguay, in Report 29/92.[115] A law canceled all criminal trials for past human rights violations and did not constitute any investigatory committee or issued official report. The nature and seriousness of the accusations — for example, enforced disappearances — required an investigation. The victims, family members and injured parties were deprived of the right to a remedy, an impartial and exhaustive investigation, and adequate criminal sanctions. The commission clarified that though the amnesty law did not affect the possibility of compensation, the proof of the illicit act was restricted because the declaration of state officials was impeded by the act, plus the statute of limitations of four years.

In *Pratdesaba v. Guatemala*,[116] the IACHR analyzed the right to due process of law and judicial protection: "Under Articles 8 and 25 of the American Convention every person has the right to recourse to a competent court or tribunal for protection against acts that violate his rights and the State has the obligation to provide the minimum guarantees for the determination of those rights."

The IACHR interpreted Article 25: "It is not sufficient that a State's legal system formally recognizes the remedy in question; instead, it must develop the possibilities of an effective remedy, substantiated in accordance with the rules of due process of law."

When arguing on habeas corpus, the IACHR simply based the conclusions on Article 25 of the ACHR. In *Alarcón Espinoza*, the IACHR asserted that habeas corpus had no success, and after six years the victim's whereabouts were unknown. Article 25 had been violated. The lack of response, effectiveness or result of habeas corpus as violation to Article 25 is frequent.[117] Accepting the differentiation between obligations of means and result, the IACHR sees habeas corpus as an obligation of result: if the victim does not appear and his whereabouts or fate remain unknown, the ACHR is breached.

In *Velasquez Isabela v. Guatemala*,[118] the IACHR, similarly to the IACtHR, recognized the duty to investigate, by asserting that

> under the American Convention on Human Rights, when a protected right or freedom has been infringed, the State is obliged to respond *sua sponte* with certain measures of investigation, actions to sanction and punish the perpetrators, and steps to ensure access to compensation. The victim had a direct right to seek judicial protection and redress. The act of enforced disappearance, where an individual is held incommunicado and the authorities conceal the fact of custody, places the individual concerned outside of the protection of the law. This renders the detainee unable to access the right to file a writ of habeas corpus, the remedy through which judicial protection is normally made available to address an illegal detention.

The remedies must be "truly effective in establishing whether there has been a violation of human rights and in providing redress."

In *Solares Castillo v. Guatemala*,[119] the IACHR declared that disappeared persons suffer per se a violation of the right to judicial protection:

> In cases involving forced disappearance, when individuals are kept incommunicado and the authorities conceal the truth about their arrest, such persons are denied legal protection. That keeps detainees from filing for habeas corpus relief, which is the normal method for securing judicial protection following an illegal arrest. Since the victim is in no fit state to pursue judicial protection, the right to file such remedies necessarily passes on to the victim's relatives or to third parties.[120]

Guatemala should conduct a "serious and effective investigation into the complaint."[121] The commission added that "remedies and judicial mechanisms must not only be formally provided for in law; they must also be effective for establishing whether a human rights violation has occurred and for repairing its consequences."

In *Meneses Sotacuro v. Peru*,[122] the IACHR declared that Peru neither investigated nor initiated judicial proceedings. The IACHR repeated that the state must not evade, under any pretext, its duty to investigate.

In another case,[123] the IACHR clarified that Article 25.1 incorporates the principle that the instruments or procedures for guaranteeing these rights must be effective, and the existence of the case is not enough; an effective recourse must exist with due process.[124]

In cases against El Salvador,[125] the commission analyzed Decree 486, which prevented victims and relatives from obtaining reparation in civil courts. The IACHR recalled that amnesties and their effects may not interfere with the right of the victims and survivors to obtain due compensation for human rights violations as part of the duty to guarantee. The IACHR linked again the right to due compensation to the right to judicial protection enshrined in Article 25 and concluded that El Salvador had violated Article 8(1) with Article 1.1 in torture cases. In the same report, the IACHR interpreted Article 25 of the Convention, asserting the principle of the effectiveness of procedural measures. Through Decree 486, the perpetrators could not be identified, and the right of the relatives was violated, as the decree eliminated all civil liability, preventing survivors and those with legal claims to seek civil compensation.[126] The commission reaffirmed in many cases the right to access to justice.[127]

The ACHPR in Article 7 guarantees every individual the right to have his or her cause heard, including "the right to an appeal to competent national organs against acts violating his fundamental rights as recognized and guaranteed by conventions, laws, regulations and customs in force."

The existence of effective remedies is an essential component of international human rights law. The universal and regional instruments recognize the right to effective remedies, criminal, civil and administrative. Though only the Inter-American system recognizes clearly the right to judicial remedies, the jurisprudence has always underscored that authorities are obliged to investigate. In the Inter-American system, the right to access to justice is linked not only to investigation but also to finding out the fate and whereabouts of the victims. Habeas corpus received special attention. The Inter-American organs of protection link procedural guarantees with substantive guarantees. Consequently, there is not only a right to a judicial remedy, under the rules concerning due process of law, but remedies must be prompt, adequate and effective.

The Instruments Addressing Enforced Disappearances

The DED includes the following provision:

Article 9
The right to a prompt and effective judicial remedy as a means of determining the whereabouts or state of health of persons deprived of their liberty and/or identifying the authority ordering or carry out the deprivation of liberty is required to prevent enforced disappearances under all circumstances, including those referred to in article 7 above.

In such proceedings, competent national authorities shall have access to all places where persons deprived of their liberty are being held and to each part of those places, as well as to any place in which there are grounds to believe that such persons may be found.

Any other competent authority entitled under the law of the State or by any international legal instrument to which the State is a party may also have access to such places.

The remedy—"prompt" and "effective," for the DED—is clearly judicial. This is coherent with the Inter-American system. The provision refers to habeas corpus, especially suitable in enforced disappearances cases, avoiding the ambiguity derived from general provisions protecting the right to personal freedom. The DED clarifies that habeas corpus is useful in enforced disappearances cases. Moreover, Article 13 of the DED ensures the right to complaint to a competent and independent state authority and to a prompt, thorough, and impartial investigation on the complaint. If there are reasonable grounds to believe that a disappearance took place, the state must submit it to that authority for investigation, even without formal complaint. The DED prohibits measures to curtail or impede investigation and requests the state to ensure that the competent authority will have the necessary powers and resources to conduct the investigation effectively, including to compel attendance of witnesses and production of relevant documents and to make immediate on-site visits. The persons involved must be protected against ill treatment, intimidation, or reprisal. The findings must be available to all those concerned, except if this could affect a criminal investigation. Any investigation must continue as long as the victim's fate remains unknown. Article 19 asserts that victims and families shall obtain redress and have the right adequate compensation, including complete rehabilitation as possible. In case of death, the DED dependents are entitled to compensation.

In the Draft IC, Article 22, paragraph 3 covers the right of victims to prompt, fair, and adequate reparation.

Statutes of Limitations

The DED, Article 17, provides for suspension of the statute of limitation if remedies are not available in the sense of the ICCPR. If they exist, they must be substantial and commensurate with the seriousness of the offense. The Draft IC asserts that when enforced disappearances constitute crimes against humanity, international law applies. In the other cases, Article 5 asserts that the statute of limitations would be the substantial and proportional to the seriousness of the offense, starting with the determination of the fate and whereabouts of the victim. In the IACFD, Article 7, the criminal prosecution and the penalty are not subject to statutes of limitations. If there is fundamental norm preventing application of this provision, the period must be equal to that applied to the gravest crime domestically.

When Bassiouni compared the work of Van Boven and Joinet, he asserted that the guidelines contain similar provisions on this point,[128] providing for suspension of all periods until adequate remedies are in place (Van Boven, Principle 9; Joinet, Principle 27; and Principle 24 in the revised version). However, the difference is the nonapplicability of statutes of limitations. Joinet stated that there would be no statute of limitations for the recovery of damages in civil actions brought by victims seeking reparation. Statutes of limitations do not apply to serious crimes under international law, characterized by the nonapplicability of statutes of limitations. However, Van Boven provides the measure for civil actions resulting from a gross violation (Principle 9).

Clearly, this approach differs from of the IACFD, where only criminal actions find statutes of limitations inapplicable. The IACFD addresses the nonapplicability of statutes of limitations in criminal proceedings, related to the previously obligation to prosecute and punish. The *Convention on the Non-Applicability of Statutes of Limitations for War Crimes and Crimes against Humanity* (1968) could be applicable if disappearances constitute crimes against humanity.[129] According to Article 29 of the Rome Statute of the ICC, "the crimes within the jurisdiction of the Court shall not be subject to any statute of limitations."

Consequently, there should be no statutes of limitations when enforced disappearances constitute crimes against humanity. In other cases, the longest period applicable under criminal law should be used. Concerning civil action, this should have the same fate than the criminal action: Statutes of limitation should not apply when enforced disappearances are crimes against humanity, and, in the other cases, statutes of limitation should be the same than for criminal actions. In all cases, the statute of limitations should not run out when the fate and whereabouts of the victim was established with certainty, if there is due process of law and judicial guarantees.

Jurisdiction in Cases of Enforced Disappearances

The guidelines differ in their approach concerning criminal jurisdiction.[130] Van Boven asserts that every state must provide for universal jurisdiction over gross violations that constitute crimes under international law (Principle 5). Joinet only urges that universal jurisdiction should be included in all human rights treaties or instruments dealing with serious crimes (Principle 24, or 21 in the revised version). Moreover, Bassiouni asserts it is not clear if universal jurisdiction exists for all gross violations.

Concerning enforced disappearances, the DED (Article 14) asserts that any person that allegedly committed an enforced disappearance must be brought before the competent civil authorities to be prosecuted and tried (territorial jurisdiction), except in case of extradition. Moreover, the DED asserts that all states should take any lawful and appropriate action available to bring to justice all persons presumed responsible for enforced disappearances who are within their jurisdiction or are under their control. The last wording reveals the notion of universal jurisdiction. The Draft IC, Article 4 asserts that state parties should impose appropriate penalties. Clearly, Article 9 asserts that forced disappearances are offenses in every state party and should take the necessary measures to establish territorial jurisdiction, national jurisdiction (passive and active), and universal jurisdiction. Moreover, the draft asserts no jurisdiction exercised by an international criminal tribunal is excluded, a provision that relates the issue to the ICC Statute that as drafted will only pursue enforced disappearances when they are crimes against humanity.

In the IACFD, Article 4, forced disappearances are offenses in every state party, which are obliged to establish their jurisdiction in enforced disappearances committed within its jurisdiction, if the accused is a national (active personality principle), the victim is a national and that state considers adequate to do so (passive personality principle). Moreover, there is universal jurisdiction if the alleged criminal is in the territory and there is no extradition. The treaty reflects the Argentinean point of view, contradicting the spirit of the instrument: an interpretive clause asserts that the convention does not authorize any state party to undertake in the territory of another state party the exercise of jurisdiction or the performance of functions that are placed within the exclusive purview of the authorities of the other state by domestic law. Enforced disappearances are not in the "exclusive purview of the authorities" of any state: If the state does not prosecute, it should extradite (*aut dedere et judicare*).

In cases of torture, jurisdiction clauses in treaties against torture are fully applicable. Article 12 of the IACAT asserts that every state party shall take the necessary measures to establish its jurisdiction over the crime described in the convention when torture is committed within its jurisdiction. Moreover, the treaty contains the principle of active personality, passive personality when the state estimates it appropriate, and universal jurisdiction. In addition, the provision does not exclude criminal jurisdiction according to domestic law. This treaty would permit avoiding the limitation of IACFD when enforced disappearances could also deserve the application of the IACAT.

In the universal system, Article 5 of the CAT asserts that every state party must adopt the measures necessary to establish its jurisdiction over torture (territorial jurisdiction, active personality; passive personality if the state considers it appropriate; and universal jurisdiction). In similar formula to that of the Inter-American Convention, the CAT does not exclude any criminal jurisdiction exercised in accordance with internal law.

The elaboration of any instrument dealing with enforced disappearances should include a broad spectrum of possibilities. To investigate, prosecute and punish enforced disappearances should be competence of the state where the crime was committed. In addition, active personality should also be recognized. Passive personality is generally left to the discretion of the state. Moreover, universal jurisdiction is essential, in particular, when the states obliged under international law to prosecute and punish (in particular, the territorial state) have revealed the unwillingness to provide for criminal sanctions against perpetrators. Moreover the recognition of the obligation to prosecute in case the extradition is denied constitutes another important tool as to fight against impunity.

Proceedings to Declare the Presumption of Death

The WG has asserted that the content of the right to a remedy depends on the nature of the right violated.[131] Administrative and judicial proceedings for the declaration of the presumption of death are very important in some countries; some civil law issues (e.g., administration of property, possibility of a new marriage, hereditary questions) cannot be solved for the lack of a death certificate because of the nature of the human rights violation. Proceedings to declare the presumption of death are important, because they can replace the function of a death certificate. The legal requirements and procedures leading this presumption are diverse, particularly the minimum time required since the last contact with the individual. As a general principle, no victim should be presumed dead against the will of the family, as the WG understands.[132]

States should grant the necessary facilities to permit family members to continue their lives. Consequently, when death certificates are demanded, special proceedings and documentation to relatives of persons disappeared is part of the implementation of the right to access to justice and right to redress in cases of enforced disappearances.

Access to Justice in Situations of Emergency

In the *Advisory Opinion 8*,[133] the IACtHR pointed out that habeas corpus has an essential role to ensure that a person's life and physical integrity are respected, preventing disappearances or keeping the whereabouts secret, and protecting against torture or other cruel, inhuman, or degrading punishment or treatment. In *Advisory Opinion 9*,[134] the IACtHR stated that "essential" judicial guarantees are not subject to derogation according to Article 27 and they include habeas corpus, amparo, and any other effective remedy before judges or competent tribunals designed to guarantee respect for the rights and freedoms whose suspension is not authorized by the ACHR. The court stated that judicial guarantees should be exercised within the framework and the principles of due process of law expressed in Article 8. Furthermore, the court emphasized that judicial guarantees imply "the active involvement of an independent and impartial judicial body having the power to pass on the lawfulness of measures adopted in a state of emergency." Consequently, the right to adequate remedies facing human rights violations cannot be suspended under any circumstances, though they are not specifically enumerated among the nonderogable rights, but they constitute the clear safeguard for them.

Conclusions

The right to access to justice is essential concerning enforced disappearances. This complex human rights violation puts the victim at the mercy of the captors and accomplices. For that reason, the immediate operation of the judicial and administrative machinery for the sake of the discovery of the fate and whereabouts of the victim is an essential question in all cases.

Instruments addressing enforced disappearances should always include the obligation of state parties to provide prompt, efficient and adequate *judicial* remedies, to present the person disappeared, in good state of health, before a judicial authority. The adequate mechanism is habeas corpus,[135] because this judicial guarantee has the purpose of determining the authority, the place and grounds of the deprivation of the physical freedom and, if they are illicit or arbitrary, the presentation of the person before a judge to order the release. The existence and efficacy of habeas corpus even in state of emergency,[136] does not only permit stopping an enforced disappearance but also preventing it and eventual further damage.

In addition, the right to procedural remedies includes further elements. Because enforced disappearances encompass illicit acts under criminal law, the state has the obligation to initiate the investigation, impartially and objectively, to prosecute those responsible, and to determine adequate sanctions.[137] This obligation cannot be avoided through such arguments as "social peace" or "forgiveness,"[138] for the seriousness of the crimes involved, the need to prevent further cases, and to avoid anomie for the feeling of impunity that follows the lack of punishment. In these criminal proceedings, family members should be authorized to participate to control the proceedings and give them impulse to contribute to their objectivity and avoid becoming a mere formality tending to waste time and pretend that justice is imparted.[139] In case of lack of political will of the state where the crime was committed, universal jurisdiction clauses and engagement among states concerning extraditions are important remedies against impunity.[140] Amnesty legislation and other clauses excluding responsibility should not apply to crimes of enforced disappearances.[141]

Administrative proceedings must control the role of public officers in enforced disappearances and provide, if adequate, the removal of those who should perform a public service, pursuant to pertinent disciplinary rules.[142]

Finally, the right to claim reparation with a wide approach must be enforceable through domestic legislation.[143]

Statutes of limitations should not run out if there are no remedies[144] or they are not impartial, adequate or effective. Second, if enforced disappearances constitute crimes against humanity, statutes of limitation should not apply, both for civil and criminal questions derived from enforced disappearances. Finally, in the other cases, the statutes of limitations should correspond to those applicable to the most serious crimes under domestic law, for both criminal and civil matters.

10

The Right to a Remedy (II): Reparation to Victims of Enforced Disappearances

Reparation means to render justice by removing or redressing wrongful acts and preventing and deterring them. Reparation is performed by the state under domestic law. Only in a subsidiary role is the international community permitted to request reparation and in limited contexts. Reparation today includes restitution, compensation, rehabilitation, satisfaction and guarantees of nonrepetition[1]; Van Boven asserts that the list is not exhaustive.[2]

Reparation in human rights is a recent issue[3]: Every state should redress human rights violations.[4] Moreover, there is an increasing recognition of the right to reparation.[5]

Reparation implies removing the consequences of an enforced disappearance. *Reparation* is a general term, characterizing all types of redress.[6] "Compensation," "restitution," "satisfaction," "guarantees of nonrepetition" and "rehabilitation" cover particular aspects. Van Boven underscored that "restitution" is often not feasible. New forms of reparation are needed. Compensation addresses economically assessable damages. In his view, reparation is not exclusively financial, for the need of restoration of rights and dignity. As MacDonald concluded, compensation does not provide true reparation.[7] Financial means are sometimes not available. Van Boven and Bassiouni advocated for broad reparation.[8] Van Boven affirmed that reparation *relieves the suffering and affords justice* to victims, by removing or redressing, to the extent possible, the consequences of wrongful acts, and preventing and deterring violations.

The DED provides that victims and families must obtain redress and have the right to adequate compensation, including complete rehabilitation, as possible (Article 19). The IACFD does not include a provision on reparation.

In 1998, the WG issued a General Comment to Article 19 of the DED on the obligation to provide *adequate compensation,* deemed "adequate" if "proportionate to the gravity of the human rights violation (e.g. the period of disappearance, the conditions of detention, etc.) and to the suffering of the victim and the family." The WG understood that reparation should be provided for any damage, physical or mental harm, lost opportunities, material damages and loss of earnings, harm to reputation, and costs of legal or expert assistance. In case of death, the victims are entitled to additional compensation. The notion includes rehabilitation (medical and psychological care, rehabilitation for any physical or mental damage, legal and social rehabilitation, guarantees of nonrepetition, restoration of personal liberty, family life, citizenship, employment or property, return to place of residence, and similar forms of restitution, satisfaction and reparation that remove the consequences of disappearance). The WG adopts a broad interpretation of Article 19.

The Draft IC contains in Article 22, paragraph 3, the obligation of state parties to guarantee the right to reparation. Paragraph 4 asserts that the right to reparation includes restitution, compensation, rehabilitation, satisfaction, and the restoration of the honor and reputation of the victims. Rehabilitation must be physical, psychological, professional, and legal. In the 2001 report,[9] the WG expressed asserted that the ex Article 24 should be put in line with the work of Van Boven, Bassiouni and Joinet, in particular, the elements of reparation.

The Declaration of Basic Principles asserts that victims are entitled to prompt redress, fair restitution to victims, families or dependents by offenders or third parties, including the return of property or payment for harm or losses, reimbursement of expenses incurred, and provision of services and restoration of rights. When compensation is not fully available, states should provide it. The approach is broad: The need of material, medical, psychological and social assistance and support for the victims is recognized.

The Statute of the International Criminal Court (ICC) does not deal extensively with compensation,[10] but the "Court shall establish principles relating to reparations" (Article 75.1). Article 79 of the Rome Statute establishes a trust fund for "the benefit of victims of crimes within the jurisdiction of the Court, and of the families of such victims" intermediary between the convicted person, the court and the victims, is to pool together money and other property collected through fines, forfeiture or other sources (e.g., voluntary contributions). The statute defines reparations differently from the Van Boven or Joinet Guidelines: Reparations are restitution, compensation and rehabilitation, Article 75.1, without reference to guarantees of nonrepetition and satisfaction.

In the *Principles on Impunity* of Joinet, Principle 39 refers to the right to reparation: It must cover *all injuries suffered by the victim*,[11] which includes individual measures concerning the right to restitution, compensation and rehabilitation and general reparation measures, such as satisfaction and guarantees of nonrepetition. In the same project,[12] Principle 36 asserts that any human rights violation originates a right to reparation of the victim or beneficiaries, implying the state duty to make reparation and seeking redress from the perpetrator. This includes access to the international procedures, that must be publicized (Principle 38) within and outside the country. In Principle 43, Joinet recommended special measures for disappearances: If the fate of the victim is elucidated, the family should be notified, and if the victim died, the body could be claimed after identification whether or not the perpetrators have been identified, prosecuted or tried.

Bassiouni compared the work of Van Boven and Joinet,[13] and understood that the difference is that Joinet, in the revised version, incorporates the Van Boven Guidelines concerning reparation: he defines by incorporation the Van Boven Guidelines definitions of "restitution," "compensation," "rehabilitation," and "general measures of satisfaction." The revised Joinet Guidelines do not include guarantees of nonrepetition but discuss them as "right to reparation," not as an element. The special measure concerning disappearances of Joinet is not present in the Van Boven Guidelines.[14]

The elements enunciated in the Declaration of Basic Principles are different to the proposals of Van Boven and Joinet.[15] The Declaration does not distinguish between restitution, compensation, and rehabilitation. The restitution section calls for return of property or payment for the harm suffered and reimbursement of expenses incurred (Principle 8). The provision fulfills, according to Bassiouni, the restitution and compensation of the Van Boven and Joinet Guidelines. Moreover, compensation suggests an alternate source of funds (Principles 12 and 13), and the assistance section parallels the rehabilitation section of Joinet and Van Boven (Principles 14 and 17). The Declaration omits collective measures of satisfaction and guarantees of nonrepetition. However, it recognizes the right to reparation.

Van Boven and Joinet do not clearly articulate who is responsible. Collective measures of satisfaction or guarantees of nonrepetition could only fall on the state. Bassiouni asserts that it would be materially impossible that other actors provide for them. Economic compensation counts with not clear solution; the Declaration on Basic Principles asserts that the primary responsible party is the offender. If the offense was committed by a public official on official or quasi-official capacity, responsibility shifts to the state (Principle 11). If the offender is unable to compensate, the state should provide a remedy (Principle 12), when the victim has suffered serious physical or mental injury or claims are brought by dependants of persons killed or disabled.

Chile argued for the state's immediate, direct liability, without prejudice of the right to recover from the offender.

Bassiouni argued for adequate, effective and prompt reparation,[16] proportional to the gravity of the violations and the harm suffered. Proportionality has only appeared in the Inter-American system since *Las Palmeras,*[17] and *Cantos,*[18] where the IACtHR asserted that reparation consists of the measures tending to make disappear the effects of the violations committed; the nature and scope depend on the damage caused. Nowak as judge in separate opinions before the HRCBH shares this approach.[19]

If the party responsible is unable or unwilling to meet the reparation, the state should provide it. States should establish national funds for reparation to victims and seek other funds to supplement these. Domestic and international judgments should be enforced against individuals or entities responsible to avoid the population, through taxes, subsidizing perpetrators.

Currently, disappearances require state link, except in the context of the ICC Statute, when political organizations commit disappearances constituting crimes against humanity. The state, as main passive subject under human rights, should be in charge of restitution. However, nothing should impede the state to claim back the amounts paid to the concrete perpetrators when possible. Redress may include medical, psychiatric, psychological and social rehabilitation or support services, and the state should provide them. The victim should be able to claim to the state directly for reparation, as Chile argued.

Concerning the sources of the international legal obligation to provide redress,[20] Bassiouni underlines that *jus cogens* violations require redress, but there are no binding rules establishing which elements of reparation are due, apart from financial reparation and the principle of *restitution ad integrum.*[21] Mann asserts that international law recognizes the right to restitution in kind.[22] The IACHR refers to *full reparation,* including steps to locate the victim's body and arrangements to respect the family's wishes on an appropriate burial and compensation.[23] The ILC Project on State Responsibility supports, in Article 31, full reparation,[24] reasserted by the states commenting on the project as a customary rule, for example, the United States, France and Germany.[25] However, the IACHR prefers *appropriate reparation.*[26] The IACHR has used the formulas fair and prompt reparation,[27] or simply fair compensation,[28] promptly and adequate,[29] timely and adequate,[30] proper and timely,[31] and so on. The lack of definition of the terms makes contradicting interpretations possible. Reparation is also defined as *integral,* including the right to truth and justice,[32] in particular by the IACtHR[33]; reparation is also qualified as appropriate and just.[34]

The CHR characterizes it as fair and adequate.[35] The Draft IC's formula is prompt, fair and adequate reparation (Article 22, paragraph 3).

The lowering of standards deserves critiques (i.e., from full or integral reparation to lower parameters), when the State Responsibility project (with a more restricted scope and revealing scarce political will of states) accepts full reparation. Human rights organs applying lower standards as "appropriate" or "proper" cannot be understood, except in contexts or massive human rights violations and budgetary constraints.

Concerning the modalities of redress, the source of applicable international law is unclear. Conversely, "general principles" of international law (Article 38 of the ICJ Statute) provide for a first basis for redress and have been applied by the IACtHR. Bassiouni and Van Boven include restitution, compensation, satisfaction and guarantees of nonrepetition, without indicating which measures are appropriate in each case.

Under international law, monetary compensation is the most common form of reparation, though arbitration tribunals assert that reparation must wipe out all the consequences of the illegal act. In the *Lusitania cases,* arbitrator Parker stated that the "remedy must be commensurate with the injury received.... The compensation must be adequate and balance as near as may be the injury suffered."[36] Enforced disappearances are not conducive to an exact rectification. Substitute remedies are required from a victim's perspective. In *Loayza Tamayo* (Reparations),[37] the IACtHR pointed out that the very existence and conditions of the life of a person are altered by human rights violations, by the trust placed in the hands of public authorities, whose duty is to protect and provide security to exercise rights and satisfy legitimate interests. Remedies should reflect the breach of trust and provide psychological and social functions of reintegration and rehabilitation.

Another set of questions is whether there is a *hierarchization of violations and modalities for redress.* Domestic criminal law distinguishes according to the seriousness of crime, attributing different penalties and victims' rights. Bassiouni analyzed whether there should be distinct redress regimes according to the violation,[38] indicating the temptation to use restitution as to sanction the state. This contradicts the classical point of view, which denies an approach to restitution.

Compensation is the most common remedy; *certainty and coherence when calculating damages* avoids under- or overcompensating a victim. Uncertainty and arbitrariness undermine respect for the law; legal certainty is a central concern when looking for order and predictability. Accurate assessment impedes unfair awards, frustrating the purposes of reparation.

Restitution

Restitution is the reestablishment of the situation existing before the violation. *Restitutio in integrum* is impossible or only applicable to some violations.[39] Even if possible, *restitutio in integrum* is not sufficient in enforced disappearances.[40]

Van Boven, Bassiouni and Joinet recognized "restitution." In 1993 Van Boven defined it: "[to] re-establish, to the extent possible, the situation that existed for the victim prior to the violations of human rights. Restitution requires, inter alia, restoration of liberty, citizenship or residence, employment or property." Bassiouni reformulated the notion, indicating that "restitution should, whenever possible, restore the victim to the original situation before the violations of international human rights or humanitarian law occurred. Restitution includes: restoration of liberty, legal rights, social status, family life and citizenship; return to one's place of residence; and restoration of employment and return of property." In Principle 40, Joinet asserted that the purpose is to restore the victim to the former circumstances, entailing the restoration, inter alia, of the exercise of individual freedoms and the rights to citizenship, family life, return to one's country, employment and property ownership. Paragraph 11 of the Declaration of Basic Principles asserts that victims should receive state restitution when public officials violated domestic criminal laws.

If restitution is possible, the state should provide it.[41] The ILC work on State Responsibility, Article 35, asserts that *restitution is the principle, if not materially impossible and not involving a disproportional burden.* However, *restitutio* is strictly interpreted.[42] In the case of *Matanovic,*[43] the HRCBH found it appropriate to secure the victim's release if still alive.

Compensation

Compensation is the element receiving more attention by jurisprudence and doctrine. Every human rights violation entitles the victim to seek compensation, but clear rules for compensation must be developed.[44] Bassiouni asserts that its measure should be clear,[45] The fora to claim damages and the parameters to measure them are unclear,[46] including how to avoid victimization and the dilemma between collective standards or a case-by-case basis approach, and whether there should be similar or different standards for violations committed by state and nonstate actors.

Reparation must be integral. Van Boven in 1993 defined compensation as an element of reparation for any economically assessable damage resulting from human rights violations, such as:

a. Physical or mental harm;

b. Pain, suffering and emotional distress;

c. Lost opportunities, including education;

d. Loss of earnings and earning capacity;

e. Reasonable medical and other expenses of rehabilitation;

f. Harm to property or business, including lost profits;

g. Harm to reputation or dignity; and

h. Reasonable costs and fees of legal or expert assistance to obtain a remedy.

Bassiouni merged the first two paragraphs of the last two versions of Van Boven: "physical or mental harm, including pain, suffering and emotional distress." He also refers to "psychological and social services," absent in the work of Van Boven.

Joinet indicated, in Principle 41, that "compensation must equal the financially assessable value of all damage suffered," particularly (a) physical or mental injury, including pain, suffering and emotional shocks; (b) the loss of opportunities, including education; (c) material damage and loss of income, including loss of earnings; (d) attacks on reputation or dignity; and (e) costs of legal assistance and valuations. Joinet mandates certain level of compensation (equal to the damage), what is absent in the other projects.

The ILC asserts that injury includes any damage, material or moral, caused by the internationally wrongful act of a state (Article 31.2). The notion is stricter than the approach of Joinet, Van Boven and Bassiouni.

The DED, Article 19, mentions the right of victims and their family to "adequate compensation." The General Comment of the WG on Article 19,[47] asserts that the right to compensation belongs to "victims of acts of enforced disappearance and their family," and requires legislative and other measures.[48] The WG indicates that compensation should be "adequate:" proportionate to the gravity of the human rights violation and the victim's and family's suffering. Monetary compensation should repair any damage caused by the disappearance.

Concerning the Declaration on Basic Principles,[49] paragraph 12 asserts that if it is not fully available from the offender or other sources, states should provide it. Injury is required.

Compensation should be paid cash or in kind, which includes health care, employment, housing, education and land. However, this can be expressed in monetary terms.[50] Compensation in kind has not received much attention.[51]

In *Loayza Tamayo — Interpretation of the Judgment on Reparations,*[52] the IACtHR asserted that compensation is not subject to any reduction for tax issues. The ECtHR's approach is different: The amounts are increased to include the tax due.

The rejection of compensation is a problem, analyzed by Juan Méndez[53]: the state has the obligation to offer compensation. *Madres de Plaza de Mayo* officially refused economic reparations, interpreted as the government's attempt to buy their silence and the absence of social and historical recognition.[54] Compensation can be a partial moral recognition of the damage and the victims can at least win something from the State. Danieli asserts compensation is a symbolic act because you can never be really compensated for human rights violations[55]; but compensation confirms the responsibility and wrongfulness, the victim was not guilty, and somebody cares about it. In most legal systems, when damage occurs, money is paid. Danieli advocates for monthly payment, instead of a unique payment. Thinking on Argentina and Chile, he asserts that parents were deprived from their children and the possibility of their help when older. Consequently, compensation for the rest of their lives is more effective than a single lump sum.

The items proposed by Van Boven, Bassiouni and Joinet are not clearly accepted by international tribunals. The IACtHR, in *El Caracazo* (Reparations), asserted that compensation includes actual damages, loss of income, moral damages, costs of proceedings and the patrimonial damage caused to the family group. Physical and mental harm outside moral damages does not receive much attention, as well as loss of opportunities for education, loss of earning capacity and harm to reputation. The reparation of harm to property and business is limited and takes place only in isolated cases, according to the IACtHR.

The IACHR recommended economic compensation,[56] but its broad functions would allow the IACHR to determinate the basis and the types of compensation to afford.[57] The IACHR recommends "reparation," only advocating for a "fair compensation,"[58] as the obligation to "take the necessary steps so that the members of the family ... may be properly indemnified for the violations established herein."[59] The IACHR recommends that reparation should include moral damages.[60] Another recommendation is to pay "compensatory damages to the victim's next of kin."[61] A different formula is to "adopt the measures necessary to ensure that the family members ... receive fair and prompt reparation for the violations here established."[62] In other cases, the IACHR recommended to grant appropriate reparations, including compensation for the suffering caused by the lack of information about the victims' whereabouts.[63]

The most important decision on reparations is the IACtHR's judgment on *Aloeboetoe*. This was not a disappearance case, but the principles asserted are repeated in subsequent cases. All the consequences of an international law violation cannot be repaired, following the arbitral award *Alabama*[64]: Only the immediate effects of the international law violation are repaired and only in the measure protected by law; "indirect" damages are denied. This opposes the idea of integral or full reparation and Joinet that advocates for the reparation of all the consequences. Moreover, the ILC includes causality not limited to the immediate effects of the illicit act. Any consequence of a human rights violation should deserve reparation, notwithstanding the immediate or indirect character. If the victim's family bought a house with a mortgage that could only be paid with the victim's salary, and the family lost that house because the disappeared victim could not pay that amount anymore, although the consequence is indirect, it should deserve reparation, because the house would not have been lost if the state had not caused the enforced disappearance. In this case, the direct consequence is the lack of income of the victim; the indirect consequence is the lack of payment of the mortgage plus the increase of accrued interest. In the view of the IACtHR, the family should lose the house.

The HRC has recommended that states adopt measures, among them compensation to victims or family members, without detailing amounts or criteria.[65] In Case no. 84/1981,[66] the HRC recommended paying *appropriate* compensation to the victim's family. In Case no. 107/1981,[67] the HRC recommended paying compensation for the wrongs suffered. The HRCBH has also granted compensation for human rights violations.[68] In *Medan* (compensation),[69] a proven damage and financial loss were required. The HRCBH granted nonpecuniary damages in cases of authorities' harassment or distress against the victim.[70] In *Palic,*[71] the chamber granted reparation for mental suffering to the victim's wife and nonpecuniary damage concerning the disappeared person. In the first case of *Unkovic,*[72] the chamber granted nonpecuniary compensation for mental suffering. Moreover, in the *Srebrenica Cases,*[73] the judgment included a collective compensation (lump sum) of 2 million convertible marks (KM), payable to the Foundation of the Srebrenica-Potocari Memorial and Cemetery, and, in addition, guaranteed four further annual payments, also to be paid to the foundation, to be used in accordance with the Statute of the foundation.

Physical or Mental Harm, Including Pain, Suffering and Emotional Distress

Joinet defined them in Principle 41: the physical or mental injury caused by the human rights violation, together with moral damages. Van Boven and Bassiouni prefer the term *harm* to *injury.*

Only moral damages are generally compensated, defined as an equitable assessment of compensation for pain and suffering, or *daño moral* in Latin America. The IACtHR also refers to "immaterial damage:" the damageable effects that do not have economic or patrimonial character.[74] It includes suffering and affliction caused to direct victims and the next of kin, damage against important values, as well as nonpecuniary alteration in the conditions of existence. The IACtHR asserts that it has no precise monetary equivalent and can only be compensated in two ways: the payment of an amount or through goods or services with monetary value, determined according to equity. Second, public acts or works are permitted to recover the victims' memory, comfort of survivors and the transmission of official critique to human rights violations, as well as the engagement of nonrepetition. This second aspect is "satisfaction."

In *Velasquez Rodríguez*, the IACtHR decided the reparation of moral damage, on international law grounds and determined on equity.[75] The family alleged the psychological impact suffered and presented expert evidence on the fear, anguish, and depression caused. The court conceded reparation to the wife and children because moral damages had been accredited. In *Godínez Cruz v. Honduras*, the court followed the same approach.[76]

The evidentiary question has changed. In *Aloeboetoe*, the IACtHR asserted that according to the facts, the victim suffered moral damages. *Moral damage is evident for direct victims,* derived from the human nature. Evidence is a very difficult burden for victims and family members. For dependents, the court required evidence, which was not sufficient in the concrete case. The parents were the exception. The court assumed the existence of moral damage. The court presumed their moral damage, in addition to that of the spouse and children.

In *Neira Alegría v. Peru,*[77] the IACtHR repeated the presumption and granted US$20,000 to each family. The same amount was granted in *Caballero Delgado y Santana,*[78] to the relatives of Caballero Delgado. Concerning *Santana,* the amount was US$10,000, to be handed down to the nearest relative. There was no explanation on the different criteria. In *Garrido and Baigorria v. Argentina,*[79] the court granted to Garrido's mother US$75,000 for moral damages. The siblings also claimed moral damages, and the court, though there was not clear evidence, granted US$6,000 to each of them. Baigorria siblings, who had not supplied credible or convincing evidence about the relation with the victim, still obtained similar amounts. Baigorria had two children, and the court set the sum of US$40,000, half for each son.

In *Castillo Páez v. Peru,*[80] the victim's sister proved psychological problems. The court fixed the moral damages at US$30,000, to be divided between the parents and sister in equal parts. The court awarded direct compensation for moral damages to the parents: US$50,000 to each, and US$30,000 to the sister. In *Loayza Tamayo v. Peru,*[81] the victim survived serious human rights violations: deprivation of personal freedom in subhuman conditions; separation from children, parents and siblings; inhumane, humiliating and degrading treatment during detention, isolation, and so on, which also affected children and family members. The court granted US$50,000 to the victim and presumed the impact on children, each entitled to US$10,000. The court presumed moral damages of the parents, who received the same amount as the children. The victim's siblings also received compensation for moral damages: each of them US$3,000. One of the sisters had suffered threatens and persecution, but the amount granted was the same as her siblings. The court did not explain the difference with Castillo Páez.

In *Blake v. Guatemala,*[82] the family referred to "emotional injury" for the disappearance, the victim's death, and the cover-up by authorities. The court granted US$30,000 to each family member. The parents obtained almost double the amount as Blake's father, without explanation by the court.

In *Bámaca Velásquez,*[83] the IACtHR resorted to equity and presumptions to determine compensation for moral damage.[84] Concerning the victim's sisters, the IACtHR presumed the moral damage. In the Mayan culture, the loss of the emotional and economic support of the eldest brother caused extreme suffering, because they could not bury the victim. Alberta Velásquez, half-sister of Bámaca, due to her relation and affection between them also obtained reparation. The direct victim obtained US$100,000; his wife, US$80,000; his father, US$25,000; each sister, US$20,000; and his half-sister, US$5,000.

In *Trujillo Oroza,*[85] the IACtHR asserted that the victim's mother looked for her son for 30 years; his stepfather took care of the victim since the age of 3 years, and he supported the victim's mother all that time. The victim's siblings were deeply affected. The IACtHR repeated the presumption of the moral damage,[86] which was extended to family members in close contact with him. The court granted the victim US$100,000; his mother, US$80,000; the adoptive father, US$25,000; and each brother, US$20,000.

In *Paniagua Morales,* the IACtHR asserted the guiding role of the jurisprudence.[87] The siblings emigrated to Canada and the United States, and the family disintegrated.[88] The sister-in-law received reparation because she lived with her husband and the victim and recognized the victim's body. The tribunal decided US$54,000 for moral damages,[89] US$20,000 for the victim's daughter, US$15,000 to the mother, US$5,000 to the father, US$5,000 to the wife, US$5,000 to the brother, US$1,000 to other family members. There were several victims, and the amounts were always different, without clarification of the reasons.

In *Villagrán Morales,* the IACtHR attended to the exposure of the young victims, clandestinely detained, severely beaten and subjected to physical and psychological torture before being killed. Three of them were minors, particularly vulnerable, who deserved special protection. The victims' mothers and the grandmother of one suffered two types of moral damages: First, they were affected by the disappearance, torture and death; in addition, they suffered human rights violations. The victims' siblings were also affected and were victims.[90] The direct victims received between US$23,000 and US$30,000; the mothers and grandmothers, US$26,000; and the siblings, US$3,000.

In *El Caracazo,* the court fixed a sum for damage caused to victims and family members: US$20,000 to the mother, father, spouse or permanent companion, daughter or son and US$5,000 to each sibling. The court liberalized the criteria for determining moral damages concerning siblings, because they obtained compensation independently of their relation to the victim. In the same case, the court repaired the immaterial damage to the relatives for lack of access to judicial guarantees: US$5,000 to the father, mother, spouse or permanent companion, son or daughter and US$2,000 to each sibling. The court used unique criteria for different cases. They did not need to prove the lack of a remedy. The surviving victims obtained US$5,000 for violation of the judicial guarantees.

In *Las Palmeras,*[91] the IACtHR returned to the previous approach: concerning Article 8–25 of the ACHR, those who claim reparation must prove the damage. The IACtHR declared that to be a family member was not enough, and moral damage should be accredited, except for very close relatives or persons such as the husband, wife or permanent companion. Moreover, the court attended to condition of those entitled to reparation.[92] As a victim was denied justice and was wife and mother of victims, she deserved reparation. If victims suffered concrete difficult problems, the amount to pay increased. Finally, one of the victim's nieces obtained the same reparation as the siblings, because she lived with the family for six years. This should be the criterion to follow in subsequent cases.

The ECtHR, in *Kurt v. Turkey,* declared a violation of Article 5 and awarded GBP15,000 for moral damages, to be paid to the applicant (the victim's mother) and distributed among her son's heirs. The applicant was not assisted in her search for the truth; the court granted her GBP10,000 for moral damages.

In *Çakici v. Turkey,*[93] the court granted GBP25,000 for nonpecuniary damage to be held by the applicant for his brother's heirs. The court had not found a breach of Article 3 concerning the applicant; however, he obtained GBP2,500, which was granted for his sufferings.

In *Taş v. Turkey,* the ECtHR decided a case of arbitrary detention or torture before disappearance. The ECtHR granted GBP20,000 to the applicant, held by him for his son's heirs. For the breach of Article 3 and 13 against the applicant, the ECtHR granted GBP10,000.

In *Timurtaş v. Turkey,* the court clarified that reparation should be granted if there was arbitrary detention or torture before disappearance or death, sums to be held by the family for the person's heirs. The court granted the same amount as in *Taş* concerning the victim and the applicant, which was repeated in *Çiçek v. Turkey*. In *Ertak*,[94] the court awarded the same amount concerning the victim but only GBP2,500 to the applicant on equity.

In *Mahmut Kaya v. Turkey*,[95] the court recognized that the victim suffered serious ill treatment after six days' detention. GBP15,000 was paid to the victim's heirs. The applicant obtained GBP2,500.

In *Ihlan v. Turkey*, the court found severe, life-threatening injury amounting to torture and lack of an effective remedy. The court awarded GBP25,000, as in *Çakici*. However, the applicant did not obtain a favorable award, following *Salman v. Turkey:* The authorities were responsible for the death of the applicant's husband, tortured in police custody before he died; the authorities failed to investigate the case effectively; and the applicant was intimidated. The applicant obtained, as victim, GBP10,000.

In *Bilgin v. Turkey*, the court awarded FRF200,000 for nonpecuniary damage for the applicant for his brother's heirs. On equity, the ECtHR granted the applicant FRF25,000.

The ECtHR is more coherent than the IACtHR, as the compensation was justified in each case.

The HRCBH based the decisions on nonpecuniary damages on equity.[96] In *Palic*,[97] the tribunal granted KM15,000 to Mrs. Palic for the disappearance of Mr. Palic because of her mental suffering; concerning her husband, for compensation for nonpecuniary damage, KM50,000 was awarded, to be held by her for her husband or his heirs. In another case, the applicant sought nonpecuniary compensation for "mental suffering, pain and sorrow" resulting from the uncertainty.[98] However, the chamber granted compensation only as nonpecuniary damage.[99] The HRCBH awarded nonpecuniary damages.[100]

In the *Srebrenica Cases*,[101] a collective compensation (lump sum) of KM2 million was included to be paid to the Foundation of the Srebrenica-Potocari Memorial and Cemetery, and in addition, four further annual payments to be paid to the foundation.

Moral damages are not the only ones analyzed, but so were further elements following Bassiouni and Van Boven.

Concerning physical harm, only one case deserved reparation. In *Bámaca Velásquez*, the victim's wife requested indemnification in equity for damages caused to her health derived from the disappearance and the ineffectiveness of the internal proceedings. The health damages were proved, and the IACtHR awarded US$25,000. In many cases, mental and physical harm were subsumed in moral or immaterial damages.

A more coherent approach is needed, except when there are differences in the facts. The ECtHR is more coherent.

Family members are direct victims, deserving the reparation of moral damages not only as heirs but also as direct victims.

Loss of Opportunities, Including Education

The notion is different than that of loss of earnings. A human rights violation could impede the victim to accede to certain benefit, not linked to a concrete source of income but to a probable possibility, objectively forecasted, frustrated by the human rights violation. This includes the loss of educational opportunities and is present in the works of Van Boven, Bassiouni and Joinet. In Chile, the reparation included benefits to relatives of disappeared persons up to 35 years of age: educational scholarship for registration and tuition fees, plus a monthly subsidy for daily expenses. This recognizes that education is frustrated if parents are not alive (or disappeared).

In *Velásquez Rodríguez,* the IACtHR granted the victim's children the possibility of education until 25 years of age. In *Barrios Altos,* the agreement included educational services: scholarships, education materials in elementary school, to try to obtain gifts of official books for elementary school and high school; clothing, and so on. In *Cantoral Benavides,*[102] the IACtHR included a scholarship for graduate studies and living expenses during the studies.

Concerning loss of chance, in *Castillo Páez,* the court asserted the possibility of whether there was a possible improvement in the victim's future income. In the case, the court rejected the reparation because there was no evidence. Family members argued that the victim would have increased his income once he had graduated. The court rejected the petition because the victim was not a good student.

In *Loayza Tamayo,* for the first time, the IACtHR granted reparation for the "life project" or "life plan,"[103] a notion different from that of special damages and loss of earnings: This refers only to the loss of future economic earnings that can be quantified by using indicators. The life plan concerns the full self-realization of the person, according to particular circumstances, potentialities, and ambitions, permitting the person with reasonable and specific goals to attain them. The concept is based on individual options.

In *Bámaca Velásquez,*[104] the petitioners requested the reparation of the project of life of the victim's wife for her goals with her husband, independently from the notion of moral, material damage and the punishment of those responsible, and considered that it should be compensated on equity. The court asserted that the disappearance would have radically altered the course of her life, and the damage to the "life plan" existed, an expectation both reasonable and attainable: the loss or severe diminution, irreparably or very difficult to repair, of a persons prospects of self-development, in the context of *restitutio in integrum.*

The "loss of opportunity" is not essential in the decisions of compensation. Only the loss of educational opportunities has been accepted. In addition, the Inter-American Court recognized the notion of life plan. The claim of "loss of chance" has not deserved the same support. However, the court has not refused to deal with the concept per se.

In the Inter-American system, the IACHR has requested the reparation of the right to life or the value of life, different from the project of life. In *Castillo Páez v. Peru,*[105] the IACHR defined it as the worth that can be attached to "every individual's life that transcends his earning potential, since every individual is an essential and unique part of his family, his community, his nation and humanity," that was calculated at US$100,000. The court interpreted it broadly as referring to the right of a nation, a community and a family not to be denied the life of one of its members (cf. Article 32(1) ACHR). However, recalling previous jurisprudence, in particular *Aloeboetoe,* the court asserted that there was not collective compensation (though collective compensation had not been requested), except in very specific communities that could prove the damage caused to them. Concretely, the loss of life per se did not originate compensation.

In *Bámaca Velásquez,* the petitioners argued for the right to life as an autonomous value, because in case of death, this cannot be compensated as moral or material damage. This would benefit the victim's family and transcend any materialistic calculus with determination on equity. The IACHR added the impossibility of "self-realization" and "life options" of the victim, claiming at least US$25,000. However, the court rejected the claim. The same happened in *Trujillo Oroza*[106]; US$100,000 was requested.

The organs of protection should be more sensitive to fair needs of the victims, in particular relating to the loss of opportunities, including education.

Material Damages and Loss of Earnings, Including Loss of Earning Potential: Damages Caused to the Business or Property

Material or actual damages include all forms of direct and indirect out-of-pocket expenses caused by the human rights violation, for which reparation is normally recognized, including by Van Boven, Bassiouni, and Joinet.

In the IACtHR jurisprudence, the court requested first concrete evidence of material damages, of the expenses, but later made flexible the criteria by granting compensation on equity (that is, without clear evidence).[107]

In *Velasquez Rodriguez*[108] and *Godínez Cruz,*[109] the court rejected actual damages for lack of evidence. In *Caballero Delgado and Santana* (Reparations), the court reimbursed the Santander Teachers' Union and the Andean Commission of Jurists the expenses incurred; in the Merits Judgment, expenses were only recognized to the relatives' representations to the Colombian authorities. The court indicated that the victim's relatives "should have incurred in expenses" and fixed an amount. The change of approach is evident, because the lack of evidence did not impede reparation.

In *Blake,* the victim's relatives requested US$300,000 for actual damages, but the court ordered for "reasonable expenses incurred" only US$16,000. The Inter-American tribunal normally refers to "reasonable expenses incurred."

In *Loayza Tamayo,* the victim requested the reimbursement of expenses incurred while she was illegally in prison; the IACtHR only compensated medical (US$1,000) and travel expenses incurred by the next of kin (US$500).

In *Castillo Páez,* the victims claimed expenses incurred because of the sister's exile in the Netherlands and Sweden. The court, in equity, granted US$25,000 and did not pay attention to actual expenses. The same criteria were used in *Bámaca Velásquez,* as the petitioner demanded reparation of expenses of his wife to obtain information. The IACtHR asserted that though the pertinent receipts were not fully submitted, the victim's wife had made them. In equity, the IACtHR granted US$20,000.[110] In other cases, the court followed similar patterns. In *Paniagua Morales,* the IACtHR asserted the lack of evidence but a general patrimonial damage to the family should be compensated, on equity. The amounts were different in each case.

In *Suárez Rosero,* the victims requested the reimbursement of the cost of a driver and domestic help for the victim's wife, with health problems, and her physical and psychological treatment. The court granted all these items (from US$1,500 to about US$4,000). With similar approach, in *Cantoral Benavides,* the court reimbursed medical expenses (US$1,000), transport (US$500), and medical and psychological treatment to the victim's mother (US$1,500).

In *Trujillo Oroza,*[111] the victim and family members requested the reparation of damages for 28 years of search in Bolivia and abroad and the costs of medical treatment incurred by the victim's mother, impunity, and the uncertainty on the victim's whereabouts. The court accepted all the petitions, some based on actual receipts and some on equity.

In *El Caracazo,*[112] the court granted in equity US$600 to each family, for funerary services, and US$1,000 for the expenses incurred searching for the victims. For the first time the court granted to every petitioner the same amount. The court conferred to three surviving victims US$7,000–15,000 because of medical expenses, also on equity.

The ECtHR has not granted compensation for actual damages. In *Ertak,* the ECtHR understood that there were no losses. In *Çakici v. Turkey,*[113] the applicant requested the reimbursement of money taken from the victim on apprehension. The court considered that there was no evidence.

The ECtHR does not understand that the search per se means expenses.

The solution of the IACtHR is fair. The evidentiary criteria should be high concerning important expenses; only reasonable expenses should be reimbursed.

Under this heading, the *loss of earnings* should be analyzed, including earning capacity, loss of income related to a human rights violation. In the *Principles on Impunity,* Joinet includes it as "loss of earning capacity,"[114] if the victim survives and suffers a reduction in the normal physical or mental capacities to perform a job or lucrative activity.

In *Velásquez Rodríguez,* the IACtHR enumerated the factors necessary to evaluate the loss of earnings: the victim's age, past jobs, salary level, social security system information and tax declarations, academic and professional background, property, family situation, spouse's rights according to family law, existence of a concubine, names and ages of children, educational and health needs of them (e.g., if they have any disability), name and age of the victim's parents, information about economic situation and existence of dependence, names and situation of other heirs, including every dependent; life insurance, current national mortality tables for men and women in the country, civil rights of heirs and dependents according to labor and civil law, persons with right to alimony, legal criteria to determine a pension, beneficiaries of pensions for death or permanent incapacity, and legislation and jurisprudence for indemnization in case of death, accidental or not.

The court asserted that the most favorable treatment possible for the family under domestic law should be applied and denied the application of the rules of accidental death to a disappearance.[115] Consequently, guidelines such as life insurance were not applied. In addition, the court differentiated the situation of victims disabled from other dependents who had an actual or future possibility of working. In *Godínez Cruz* the court decided similarly.

In both cases, the court rejected actuarial calculus, but the compensation was inferior to that resulting from such a calculus. The only plausible explanation is to avoid a burden to the state economy.

In *El Amparo,*[116] the IACtHR employed different criteria as basis of calculus to determine the loss of earnings. The basic salary should be an amount noninferior to the basic family consumption basket, which was superior to the basic salary of a farm worker, the victim's activity. This parameter was never used again.

In *Neira Alegría,*[117] the court asserted the point of view that is followed today: Reparation was based on the annual income of the victims, according to their ages and the years remaining until reaching the normal life expectancy in Peru. The calculus should determine what amount, invested at normal interest rates, would produce the amount of the monthly income the victim would have received during his probable lifetime in that country, at the end of which time it would be extinguished. Interest should have accrued until payment and should be added to that sum. The commission had assumed an annual increase of 2 percent in the minimum living wage, which the court rejected for lack of evidence. Finally, the court criticized the commission's reasoning, which did not deduct personal expenses, estimated at one quarter of the income, deducted from the total amount

There was no information about the monthly minimum wage, the court, on equity grounds, and considering the economic situation of Latin America, fixed it at US$125. Since this case, when the salary of the victim was not proved, the court used as basis of calculus the minimum salary of the activity. Examples are *Caballero Delgado and Santana*,[118] *Villagrán Morales*[119] (where most victims were children; the petitioners alleged the minimum salary for nonagricultural activities) and *Cantoral Benavides*.[120]

In *Blake v. Guatemala*,[121] the victim was a young U.S. journalist. The injured party requested more than US$1,000,000. The court rejected the claim because the reparation should be limited to the violation of Articles 5 and 8(1)/Article 1(1) of the ACHR, and not because of the disappearance, which took place before Guatemala accepted the court's jurisdiction. A question was open: What would the court have decided if Guatemala had been party at that time? For the first time, the court related the reparation to the concrete violations, though before it limited the calculus to the presumed or actual victim's income with the elements asserted in *Neira Alegría*. This link of violation–reparation would not be followed later.

In *Loayza Tamayo*,[122] the court studied a case where the victim was alive. There was no deduction for personal expenses and the salary could be proved, and that amount was used as basis of calculus, not the legal minimum.

In *Castillo Páez v. Peru*,[123] the court considered that an "equitable point of departure" was the minimum monthly wage in Peru, minus 25 percent for personal expenses, plus the current interest rate. An average salary in the area the victim was working, if the salary cannot be proved, could be a fairer solution. The minimum salary is arbitrary and unsatisfactory. Another possibility is the solution of *El Amparo:* the family consumption basket of basic goods, if minimum salaries are inferior to them. However, this "equitable point of departure" (the minimum salary) has been the predominant approach, see *Suarez Rosero v. Ecuador*,[124] and *Paniagua Morales*.[125] Moreover, in *Garrido Baigorria v. Argentina*, the court considered that there was no credible evidence on the economic activities of the victims or economic support to mother or siblings; consequently, there were no material damages. The court considered that the victims lived on criminal activities.

In *Bámaca Velásquez,*[126] the IACtHR rejected the reparation for the time the victim was guerrilla commander (from March 1992 to March 1997). Afterward the IACtHR asserted the occupation or income of Bámaca were not proved. In equity, the IACtHR granted US$100,000 as loss of income.[127] The IACtHR also granted loss of income to the wife, because to look for her husband impeded her work (on equity, US$80,000). The minimum salary was not applied, opting again for equity. This happened again in *Trujillo Oroza:* The IACtHR decided that Bolivia should indemnify the amounts that the victim could not receive from his graduation on, totaling US$130,000, on equity, to be paid to his mother as heir.

In *El Caracazo,* the court followed the same guidelines: loss of income derived from salaries, determined on minimum salary in the country at the time of the human rights violations, with current value, previous discount of 25 percent of the minimum salary, to cover personal expenses. Moreover, no discount applied to surviving victims, except to one of them that was not impeded to work. The amounts ranged from US$35,000 to US$37,000.

The ECtHR granted loss of earnings in several opportunities. In *Çakici,* the petitioners claimed them according to the victim's estimated monthly income. The court requested a clear causal connection between the damage and the human rights violation. The loss of financial support to the widow and children was due to the disappearance. The applicant had submitted a detailed presentation, an actuarial basis of calculation of the capital sum to reflect the loss of income due to the death. The court awarded a sum to be held by the applicant on behalf of his brother's surviving spouse and children. The criteria were applied in *Ihlan v. Turkey* and *Salman v. Turkey.*

In *Bilgin v. Turkey,* and *Mahmut Kaya v. Turkey,*[128] the court rejected awarding reparation because of lack of information about the help the victim provided to the family.

However, equity has been an important ground in *Çiçek v. Turkey,* where the amounts granted were asserted "on an equitable basis" to the victim's children.

The ECtHR was more coherent concerning loss of earnings. The applicants before the ECtHR have been more precise concerning the victim's income than the petitioners before the Inter-American System, where the shadow economy in Latin America plus the lack of information led the court to use the minimum salary as basis of calculus. The solution is unfair: The basket of goods of an average family or an average salary would be more appropriate. The IACtHR should adopt a consistent approach.

Another related issue is the *interest rate*. In Article 38, Interest, the ILC work on State Responsibility asserts that interest on any principal sum due is payable when necessary to ensure full reparation. The interest rate and mode of calculation must be set as to achieve that result. Interest runs from the date when the principal sum should have been paid until the date the obligation is fulfilled.

The IACtHR used the current rate of interest of the obliged state. The ECtHR applied the statutory rate of interest applicable not in Turkey, but in the United Kingdom or in some cases in France when the amount was calculated in FRF. In *Kurt v. Turkey* the statutory rate in the United Kingdom at the date of the judgment was 8 percent per annum. In *Ertak v. Turkey*,[129] was 7.5 percent. The same solution was adopted in *Salman v. Turkey, Ihlan v. Turkey, Taş v. Turkey, Kaya v. Turkey*,[130] *Timurtaş v. Turkey*, and *Çakici v. Turkey*.[131] In *Bilgin v. Turkey*, the rate applicable in France was 4.26 percent per annum.

Interest rate is always recognized in decisions on reparation, and the only dissenting point is which rate of interest should be used. Clearly the method chosen in the Inter-American system favors the victims, as interest rates are higher in developing countries than in developed countries. Moreover, the victims and their next of kin live in developing countries, and the compensation is many times the only means of subsistence for future years.

Another issue is the damages caused to the business or property of the victim or his or her next of kin. This was emphasized by Van Boven. A human rights violation not only causes actual damage and loss of earnings but also damages to the company or business the victim ran or administered.

In *Castillo Páez*, the petitioners requested the reparation of the nuclear family's patrimonial damages: US$200,000. The IACtHR considered

> especially inasmuch as it is impossible to establish the causal nexus between the fact and the consequences alleged to have followed from it ... a general patrimonial injury was done to the family group by the disappearance of one of its members, for reasons imputable to the State. The disappearance caused economic and other types of problems for the family that must be redressed based on principles of equity.

The reparation granted was US$25,000.

In *Cesti Hurtado*,[132] not discussing a disappearance, the IACtHR analyzed a similar issue: Cesti Hurtado requested US$6,000,000 for the lack of activity in the company caused for human rights violations, plus other expenses incurred in relation to them as the cost of a security system and personnel. The family and company were suffered threats, robbery, spy systems, and so on. Cesti also requested US$4,000,000 to reestablish the prestige of the company, US$43,907.21 for the interruption of insurance, US$1,070,000 for the embargo decreed, and US$67,316.48 because tax payments were defaulted for the embargo. The IACtHR considered that the reparation should be granted according to domestic law.[133] The IACtHR ordered the state to grant indemnization for material damages, taking into account the material damage.

There is some prejudice by the organs of protection as to deal with property issues, actual economic damages should receive concrete reparation.

Harm to Reputation and Dignity

Van Boven, Bassiouni and Joinet recommended the reparation. In *Bámaca Velasquez,* the petitioners claimed compensation for the campaign of hostility and threats against the victim's wife, damaging her image and credibility. The court asserted that the state should perform a public act of recognition of its responsibility of the facts and publish in the official newspaper and in other newspapers of national circulation the judgment and the facts: Satisfaction, not compensation, was ordered, as Van Boven, Bassiouni and Joinet advocated.

Costs Required for Legal or Expert Assistance, Medicines and Medical Services, and Psychological and Social Services

This notion is found in the proposals of Van Boven, Bassiouni and Joinet. In the jurisprudence of the IACtHR, only since *Garrido and Baigorria* is this repaired, concerning legal assistance. The previous approach appears in *Aloeboetoe:* Judicial fees were denied because the court understood that OAS members, through the annual budget, cover the organs of the Inter-American system. The system did not allow direct participation of the petitioners and victim's attorney, but only the case presentation before the court by the IACHR. This changed later, but only for reparation. Clearly, in *Neira Alegría v. Peru,*[134] the court asserted that the Commission incurred expenses for the internal work structure through the assessment of costs.

In *Garrido and Baigorria v. Argentina,* the victims' families petitioned the court attorney fees for 15 percent of the reparation, plus other litigation expenses: US$40,000. The court asserted that reasonable costs of domestic proceedings before the IACHR and IACtHR on an equitable basis should be reimbursed, considering the "sufficient connection" existing between costs and the results achieved. The factors were the performance of the attorney, the evidence introduced, knowledge of international jurisprudence and, in general, everything that would demonstrate the quality and relevance of the work, as well as the role in the proceedings. Consequently, the court fixed US$45,500, US$20,000 of it as fees for both attorneys. In *Loayza Tamayo,*[135]

Bámaca Velásquez,[136] *Suárez Rosero,*[137] *Cesti Hurtado,*[138] *Villagrán Morales,*[139] and *Trujillo Oroza v. Bolivia,*[140] the court ordered the payment of attorney fees and costs. In *Castillo Páez,*[141] *Blake v. Guatemala,*[142] and *Cantoral Benavides,*[143] only costs were paid.

Expert assistance (medical and psychological services) are included under "actual damages" (*Trujillo Oroza*).

In the European system, the court always grants this item, even adding any added-value tax, including the costs incurred, for instance, to attend hearings in Strasbourg. This happened in *Kurt v. Turkey* (where, in addition, the court asserted that the applicant was free to designate her legal representative, even with seat in the United Kingdom), *Çakici v. Turkey,*[144] *Ertak v. Turkey,*[145] *Ihlan v. Turkey, Timurtaş v. Turkey, Salman v. Turkey,* and *Çiçek v. Turkey.* In all the cases, the court deducted the amount advanced as legal aid by the Council of Europe. However, in *Bilgin v. Turkey, Kaya v. Turkey,*[146] and *Taş v. Turkey* the ECtHR concluded that there was no evidence supporting the claims. On equity, the court awarded an amount.

This item also deserved reparation before the HRCBH.[147]

Rehabilitation

Rehabilitation concerns services addressed at the restoration of the dignity and reputation of the victim.[148] Principle 42 of the *Principles on Impunity* include under "Measures of Rehabilitation" the costs of medical, psychological or psychiatric care, as well as social, legal and other services. Van Boven included medical and psychological care, legal and social services.[149] The difference with Joinet is that this author includes psychiatric care and other services. Some have advocated for rehabilitation, in particular, psychological,[150] for the individual, family, community and society. It does not mean to restore the status quo ante. The Declaration of Basic Principles supports the access to necessary material, medical, psychological and social assistance and support.

The General Comment of the WG on Article 19 of the DED asserts that redress includes "the means for as complete a rehabilitation as possible." This refers to medical and psychological care and rehabilitation for physical or mental damage, as well as legal and social rehabilitation; guarantees of non-repetition; restoration of personal liberty, family life, citizenship, employment or property; return to one's place of residence and similar forms of restitution; satisfaction; and reparation.

Article 22, paragraph 4, of the Draft IC recognizes rehabilitation in reparation. Germany asserted that moral rehabilitation is already caused by the criminal conviction of the offender and recommended the deletion of this passage.[151]

The position is hardly acceptable: Many disappearances have remained unpunished. Consequently, "rehabilitation" should not depend on such an issue. Second, rehabilitation refers to other kind of measures, in particular, professional assistance (medical, psychological, legal, etc.) to victims and family members. Germany confuses rehabilitation with satisfaction.

Rehabilitation is a necessary consequence of disappearances. The criminal prosecution of the author is important, but the traumatizing effects are not repaired with that measure.

In *Blake,* the petitioners requested the IACtHR the payment of the expenses for the future treatment of the victim's brother, who suffered acute depression. The court granted him in equity an amount. In *Loayza Tamayo,* the court granted an amount to face future costs of the rehabilitation for victim and children; the same happened in *Cantoral Benavides,* but concerning the victim's brother. In *Durand and Ugarte,*[152] the parties agreed in other forms of reparation, including health services (expenses for health services of victims' family members, including medicine costs). Psychological services and interpersonal development were agreed. In *Barrios Altos,* the agreement included health services (health expenses, free hospital services, diagnosis, medicines, specialized attention, internment, operations, births and dentistry).

In *Trujillo Oroza,* as rehabilitation, the petitioners requested rehabilitation (psychological and physical treatment) for the mother and siblings, which was accepted by the court.

In *Ihlan v. Turkey,* future medical expenses were requested to the ECtHR. However, the court did not award them, considering the claim largely speculative. The HRC, in Case no. 181/1984 recommended that Colombia to provide medical care to the victims.

The jurisprudence has not adequately dealt with rehabilitation. Only the IACtHR has conceded this form of reparation, once accredited the need and requested by the interested party. Only health issues were relevant, not further aspects. Even when petitioners do not claim rehabilitation, the court should request the state to cover medical and psychological services that the victims may need to overcome suffering after the disappearance. The other macro aspects of rehabilitation can only be addressed by policy makers and reviewed not through individual cases but, for instance, through state reporting, in particular, before the HRC and IACHR.

Punitive Damages? Jurisprudence

In international law, punitive damages are normally rejected, though they are granted before common law courts concerning serious human rights issues, among them, enforced disappearances.

In *Filartiga v. Peña Irala,* a U.S. court decided a case of torture followed by death of the victim in Paraguay.[153] Though punitive damages were admittedly not recoverable under the Paraguayan Civil Code (applicable to the case) and the U.S. court asserted that it would apply Paraguayan law to the case under analysis, the tribunal asserted that the prohibition of torture could only be vindicated by imposing punitive damages. The court found "some [international] precedent for the award of punitive damages in tort" against states in the *I'm Alone (Canada v. United States)*[154] "While punitive or exemplary damages, as such, have rarely been awarded by arbitrators; they have at times apparently been assessed in diplomatic settlements." The court noted that $2 million as punitive damages were awarded in *Letelier v. Chile.*[155] The court imposed the damages under domestic law, mentioning that the "tortuous actions" were "in violation of international law."

Lillich analyzed further cases before US courts before serious human rights violations.[156] The amounts granted are considerable, in comparison with cases already analyzed: *Siderman v. Republic of Argentina* ($2,707,515.63); *Trajano v. Marcos* ($4,407,966.99)[157]; *Letelier v. Republic of Chile* ($5,062,854.97); *Forti v. Suarez-Mason* ($8,000,000)[158]; *Martinez-Baca v. Suarez-Mason* ($21,170,699)[159]; and *Rapaport v. Suarez-Mason* ($60,004,852).[160] In *Forti v. Suarez-Mason,* plaintiffs demanded damages for official torture, prolonged arbitrary detention, summary execution, causing a disappearance, and cruel, inhuman and degrading treatment. The awards were not specifically linked to international, U.S. or Argentinean law. In *Trajano v. Marcos,* the torture and death was "a tort in violation of the laws of nations," using various provisions of the Philippine Civil Code. In *Martinez-Baca v. Suarez-Mason,* another disappearance in Argentina, the district court, after stating that the "plaintiff's claims arise under international law and California law," based damages on international law. International law incorporated in common law provided a way to calculate damages. Punitive damages were permitted to punish and deter such acts and promote human rights. The ground was international law, statutory and common law of the United States, and common law of California.

Lillich understood that when the U.S. courts found gross violations, they ordered compensatory damages and, in addition, in some cases such as *Filartiga, Forti, Rapaport,* and *Martinez-Baca,* punitive damages.

In India, exemplary damages have been granted in enforced disappearances.[161] In *Sebastian M. Hongray v. Union of India,* a court decided the case of two missing persons who were illegally kept under army custody. The court issued a writ of habeas corpus. As the missing persons were not presented, the court, in contempt jurisdiction, ordered exemplary costs to be paid to the widows.

The human rights–monitoring bodies reject punitive damages. In *Velasquez Rodriguez and in Godínez Cruz*,[162] the IACtHR interpreted "fair compensation," Article 63(1) of the ACHR, "to refer to a part of the reparation and to the 'injured party,' is compensatory and not punitive. Although some domestic courts, particularly the Anglo-American, award damages in amounts meant to deter or to serve as an example, this principle is not applicable in international law at this time."

The IACtHR expressed the opposition to punitive damages in subsequent cases.[163] In *Garrido Baigorria v. Argentina,* the court rejected the indemnization "that would go beyond the realm of compensation for damages caused, and into the punitive realm." The relatives demanded "exemplary damages." The court asserted that

> such functions are not in the nature of this Court and are not within its power. The Inter-American Court is not a criminal court and, in this particular matter, its competence is to determine the reparations that States that have violated the Convention must make.... Their quality and their amount depend on the damage done both at the material and at the moral levels. Reparations are not meant to enrich or impoverish the victim or his heirs.

Americas Watch expressed years ago a favorable opinion concerning punitive damages for particularly cruel and wanton acts (in international law, for crimes against humanity), as a condemnation against them.[164] In the Inter-American system the most important barrier is Article 63 of the ACHR. However, *de lege ferenda,* punitive damages can deter future human rights violations. In particular, human rights violations are sometimes committed by states that accept domestically punitive damages and have resources to grant such reparations. Punitive damages could be a useful tool against systematic human rights violations. This is not advocacy for the enrichment of the victims. The sums could permit the creation of trust funds to deal with lack of payment to victims of enforced disappearances by other states that are reticent or unable to satisfy legitimate claims. In some civil law jurisdictions *astreintes* exist: The court can fix a fine to the party that does not abide by an obligation to do, not to do, or to pay, which increases daily if the obligated party does not adjust the conduct to what is required by law or judicial order. This is not compensatory, but addressed to punish the lack of compliance.

Satisfaction and Guarantees of Nonrepetition

Satisfaction contributes to the promotion and protection of human rights and prevention of violations,[165] by adding an additional dimension to the compensatory approach. Article 37 of the ILC work, titled Satisfaction, asserts that the state responsible for an internationally wrongful act is under the obligation to give satisfaction for the injury caused by that act, insofar as it cannot be made good by restitution or compensation. Satisfaction can be the acknowledgment of the breach, an expression of regret, formal apology or another appropriate modality. However, satisfaction has limits: It should be proportional to the injury and cannot humiliate the state obliged.

Guarantees of nonrepetition imply that the state should take all necessary measures to prevent human rights violations.[166] This is included in Article 30 of the ILC work: Cessation and Non-Repetition, as the state responsible is under the obligation (a) to cease the act, if it is continuing; (b) to offer appropriate assurances and guarantees of nonrepetition, if circumstances so require.

Van Boven included in 1993 satisfaction and guarantees of nonrepetition by encompassing:

a. Cessation of continuing violations;
b. Verification of the facts and full and public disclosure of the truth;
c. A declaratory judgment in favor of the victim;
d. Apology, including public acknowledgment of the facts and acceptance of responsibility;
e. Bringing to justice those responsible;
f. Commemorations and paying tribute to victims;
g. Inclusion of an accurate record of human rights violations in educational curricula and materials;
h. Preventing recurrence of violations by
  i. Ensuring effective civilian control of military and security forces;
  ii. Restricting the jurisdiction of military tribunals;
  iii. Strengthening the independence of the judiciary;
  iv. Protecting the legal profession and human rights workers;
  v. Providing human rights training to all sectors of society, in particular to military and security forces and to law enforcement officials.

Bassiouni indicates that "satisfaction and guarantees of non-repetition" should include, where applicable, any or all of the following, with important modifications, in comparison with Van Boven: Paragraph (b) includes, concerning disclosure of the truth, the limitation "to the extent that such disclosure does not cause further unnecessary harm or threaten the safety of the victim, witnesses, or others."[167] Paragraph (c) is added: "The search for the bodies of those killed or disappeared and assistance in the identification and reburial of the bodies in accordance with the cultural practices of the families and communities." The new paragraph (d) (paragraph (c) in the work of

Van Boven) adds social rights to legal rights. Paragraph (h) (paragraph (g) in Van Boven's version) is redrafted by asserting "inclusion of an accurate account of the violations that occurred in international human rights and humanitarian law training and in educational material at all levels." Among guarantees of nonrepetition, the protection does not only include legal and human rights defenders (paragraph iv), but also "media and other related professions." Bassiouni adds two interesting paragraphs: paragraph (vi) concerns "promoting the observance of codes of conduct and ethical norms, in particular international standards, by public servants, including law enforcement, correctional, media, medical, psychological, social service and military personnel, as well as the staff of economic enterprises"; and paragraph (vii) "creating mechanisms for monitoring conflict resolution and preventive intervention."

Pursuant to Principle 44 of the Joinet *Principles on Impunity,* satisfaction includes symbolic measures as moral and collective reparation to satisfy the duty to remember, which include

a. Public recognition by the state;
b. Official declarations rehabilitating victims;
c. Commemorative ceremonies, naming of public thoroughfares, monuments, and so on;
d. Periodic tribute to victims;
e. Acknowledgment in history textbooks and human rights training account of serious violations.

Joinet includes Guarantees of Non-Repetition (Principle 45): appropriate measures to ensure that victims cannot be confronted with new violations. Among them, the rapporteur prefers

a. Measures to disband parastatal armed groups;
b. Measures repealing emergency provisions conducive to violations;
c. Administrative or other measures vis-à-vis state officials implicated in serious human rights violations (Principles 46–48).

Principle 49 encourages an inventory of positions of responsibility with decision-making power and the obligation of loyalty to process in progress, primarily in the army, police and judiciary. Assessing each individual situation, considering

a. The human rights record, particularly during repression;
b. Noncorruption;
c. Professional competence;
d. Skill in promoting peace and/or democratization, particularly concerning the observance of constitutional guarantees and human rights.

Cessation of Continuing Violations

A violation of international law must be stopped, as doctrine, reports of codification and resolutions of UN organs assert.[168] Cessation implies the respect for the primary rule.[169] Cessation is part of due reparation.[170] In enforced disappearances, the idea relates to the "appearance" of the victim in good state of health. However, this is impossible in most cases. The human rights violation continues until the clarification of the fate and whereabouts of the victim and, if possible, the indication of the place where the victim is buried to hand the body to the family members for burial according to customs and beliefs. Enforced disappearance is a *continuing violation of international human rights,*[171] as the IACtHR often asserts.[172] The violation persists until the fate or whereabouts are disclosed.

The IACtHR interpreted that the cessation is an immediate consequence of the violation.[173] In *Bámaca Velásquez,* the IACHR requested that Guatemala should adopt measures to recover Bámaca's body and allow the family access to procedures to locate and rebury the body according to ethnic traditions and culture. The commission urged the court to return the body and order the government to reveal evidence of the crime and end the impunity. The court required the cease by investigating the disappearance. The court ordered not only that Guatemala should investigate but also provide reparation by returning Bámaca's body to his family within six months after the judgment.

The ECtHR has used "continuing violation" in *Loizidou v. Turkey.*[174] In *Cyprus v. Turkey,* the court considered that Turkey had committed continuing violations of the European Convention. In the remedies, no reference was made to the cease. The ECtHR has neither ordered the cessation under Article 41 of the European Convention nor understood that this is a clear consequence of the duty to respect.

Stopping continuing human rights violations is not seriously included in jurisprudence but in the work of organs with extrajudiciary mandate. The WG appeals to all governments to release immediately all persons held in secret detention and hopes that future clarification is based on the ground that disappeared persons are released or found alive.[175] Moreover, State Reports of the IACHR also recommend cessation.[176] The recommendations of the Report on the Situation of Human Rights in Chile (1974) include "that, in order to safeguard the rights referred to in Article XXV of the American Declaration, a rapid survey should be made of the status of all persons who are still deprived of their liberty without any charges being brought against them, in order to release all those who do not constitute a serious and certain danger for the maintenance of public peace."[177] The idea is present in the work and recommendations of NGOs.[178]

The scarce decisions concerning cessation are inked to the limitations in the rules determining the competence and jurisdiction of the organs of protection. The minimum decision of an organ of protection should be to reassert the international obligation: The state should stop the human rights violations that are still taking place. The proposal of Van Boven and Bassiouni should receive more attention.

Verification of the Facts and Full Disclosure of the Truth

The verification of the facts and full disclosure of the truth are advocated by Joinet and Bassiouni. Principle I of the *Principles on Impunity* is titled "The Inalienable Right to the Truth," and asserts that "every people has the inalienable right to know the truth about past events and about the circumstances and reasons which led, through the consistent pattern of gross violations of human rights, to the perpetration of aberrant crimes. Full and effective exercise of the right to the truth is essential to avoid any recurrence of such acts in the future."

The right to know is present in Principles 3 and 4 of the same project, as a substantive right,[179] before being analyzed (see chapter 7). The proposal recognizes the truth as a consequence of human rights violations, irrespective of legal proceedings, the right of victims, families and dear ones to know the circumstances in which human rights violations took place and the victim's fate. States should adopt appropriate action.

This question is present in the jurisprudence of the organs of protection. The HRC, in case no. 30/1978, asserted that the government should reconsider the position and take effective steps to establish what happened to the victim since October 1975. In case no. 84/1981, the HRC recommended establishing the facts. In case no. 107/1981, the committee understood the mother of the disappeared daughter had the right to know what had happened to her; the government should take immediate and effective steps to establish what happened to the disappeared person since 18 June 1976 and secure the release. Moreover, the HRC requested to be kept informed about the investigations pursued.

The same concern is expressed by the IACHR, for example, in *Guarcas Cipriano,*[180] where the IACHR indicated that the families should know the truth about what happened and to use that information to seek reparation.

In *Garrido and Baigorria,* the IACHR requested the court, as reparation, that "the Argentine State publicize the report of the ad hoc Commission and the findings as widely as possible." Because the judgment required Argentina to investigate the case and punish those responsible, the court preferred to leave the question out of the judgment. However, in *Cantoral Benavides,* the court asserted that the state should publish in the official newspaper and another of national circulation the resolution of the final judgment. In *Castillo Páez,* family members requested the publication of the judgment in the official newspaper and a press communiqué transcribing the proven facts and the operative part of the judgment.

In *Durand and Ugarte,* the parties agreed on the publication of the court's decision. The same happened in *Barrios Altos,* where the agreement contained the publication of the judgment in the official newspaper and promotion of its content in further media, within 30 days of the signature of the agreement.

In *El Caracazo,* some deaths were not been attributed to the state, but the court asserted the right of family members to know the whereabouts, for violations to Articles 8 and 25 of the ACHR.

In *Las Palmeras,*[181] the IACtHR asserted that criminal prosecutions should be pursued until the truth was found. The state should publish the judgment so the Colombian society could know the truth.

In the *Srebrenica Cases,* the HRCBH decided that the Republika Srpska had "to release all information presently within its possession, control, and knowledge with respect to the fate and whereabouts of the missing loved ones of the applicants" (§211); "full, meaningful, thorough, and detailed investigation into the events" (§213); and publish the entire decision in full in Serbian in the *Official Gazette* of the Republika Srpska within two months (§214).

The right to the truth is asserted in doctrinal works but not widely in the jurisprudence as satisfaction. The HRC and the IACHR recognize it as to guarantee full reparation. Moreover, the society must know what really happened and who were the victims and perpetrators, to avoid the repetition of similar events, to allow real pacification and reconciliation, and to impede misperceptions about the responsible parties.

Consequently, the disclosure of the truth is a necessary reparatory measure that any state should endeavor to achieve.

Search of the Bodies and Burial of the Victims

Another essential measure is the search of the bodies by the state because the family members to be able to bury the victims according to own customs or beliefs. Without bodies and funerals, the relatives are unable to visualize the death of their loved ones and accept it as real.[182] This is highlighted by Joinet in the *Principles on Impunity,* Principle 43: Enforced disappearances require special measures. This author recommended if the fate is elucidated, the victim's family must be notified. The need of a proactive policy is encouraged, instead of reactive solutions: well- structured, highly organized, adequately funded and properly equipped local, regional and international centers capable of handling the recovery and identification of the victims' bodies.[183]

If the victim died, family members should be able to claim the body after identification, whether or not the perpetrators were identified, prosecuted or tried.

There were formal barriers impeding exhumations. In Argentina, they require judicial order and express request of the relatives. In Chile, if there is information, a complaint must be lodged with the competent courts, the remains exhumed, and the necessary forensic measures taken to establish the victim's identity. In Peru, a judicial order is necessary.[184]

The IACHR included in its reports the recommendation of "making the arrangements necessary as to locate the remains and to facilitate the wishes of his family as to an appropriate final resting place."[185] In the IACtHR jurisprudence, in *Bámaca Velásquez*, the petitioners requested the victim's body to repair the "obstructive actions" of state agents and to find the whereabouts of the victim. In addition, they solicited that the victim's wife could take part of these events. The court considered that Guatemala was obliged to make the necessary investigations to find the corpse, hand it to family members, and bury him in the place of their choice at the expense of the state.[186] Finally, as additional measure of satisfaction, the court asserted that Guatemala should follow a national plan of exhumations. In *Durand and Ugarte*, the parties agreed to find and to identify the victims' bodies to hand them in to family members. In *Villagrán Morales*,[187] the family of one victim requested to bury him; the IACtHR recalled the family right to find out the whereabouts of the victim. This was a fair expectation that the state should satisfy with the available means. In addition, Guatemala should transport the body to a place chosen by the family without additional cost. This was also present in *Trujillo Oroza*, where the IACHR requested the investigation of the whereabouts of the disappeared person and devolution of the body. The victim had been disappeared for 30 years.

In *El Caracazo*,[188] the court asserted that the recovery of the bodies is reparation per se, because it leads to the dignity of the victims, to recognize honor for their memory and to allow the burial. The court underscored the obligation to find, exhume, and identify the bodies through reliable techniques and instruments. The costs and the inhumation in a place chosen by the family should be borne by the state. One of the victims was born in Dominican Republic, where the burial should take place, at Venezuela's expense.

In *Las Palmeras*,[189] the victim's corpse was not found. Colombia should perform all necessary steps to identify him within a reasonable time and to find and perform the exhumation the remains, as well as to hand the body to the relatives for adequate burial, at the expense of the state. In another case, the victim was still in the morgue, and the court ordered that the body should be handed down to the family.[190]

Official Declarations or Judicial Decisions

Official declarations and judicial decisions are forms of satisfaction: They constitute an official "truth," contributing to the recognition of victims. Monitoring organs declare that the state has committed violation of human rights,[191] with expressions such as "to condemn energetically the official practice of enforced disappearances, including the concrete case," included in the final decision and recommendations in concrete cases.[192]

This form of satisfaction is important, though is not alternative to other forms of reparation if there are further damages.[193] The publication of a report containing the declaration of the violations, as well as recommendations, is also satisfaction. This is common in the Inter-American system, as the IACHR is authorized to publish resolutions adopted in the IACHR's Annual Report to the GA of the OAS.[194] In *Castillo Páez,* the IACtHR emphasized the role of the judgment publication as satisfaction.

In *Cantoral Benavides,* the family members requested the publication of the final judgment and the judgment on reparations in the official newspaper and several mass media. The court rejected the request, arguing that the judgment of the IACtHR is per se a form of reparation.[195]

The presentation of a case before an international proceeding and the publication of are a form of satisfaction. However, this is not the only measure, in particular when the image of the victims has been damaged before the public opinion.

In *Bámaca Velásquez,* the petitioners requested the vindication of victim's image through the publication of a message written by the victim's wife, through the media, at the cost of the state. The same concern was present in *Loayza Tamayo,* where the petitioners requested the guarantee of restoration of the victim's and the next of kin's honor before the public and the international community, and in *Castillo Páez,* where the petition requested that the victim's good name should be restored; or in *Cantoral Benavides,* where the petitioners requested that the state should publish communiqués asserting that the victim was innocent. In none of the cases did the IACtHR accept the petition, replying that the judgment was a measure of satisfaction.

This point of view is unacceptable: The restoration of the victim's good name is linked to the declaration of the truth. When the IACtHR declares that the state has violated human rights, it does not mean a declaration on the victim's honor. Every person is entitled to all human rights, independently of the crimes committed. The situation of many victims is that they were publicly accused of criminal activities, as if to "justify" the use of state violence, what requires special measures of reparation, different from the declaration of human rights violations by the state.

The IACtHR flexibilized its position in *Las Palmeras*[196]: As satisfaction, the state should publish in the public newspaper and in a press bulletin of the national police and the armed forces of Colombia the judgment and the reparation resolution.

Apology, Including Public Acknowledgment

Apology, as proposed by Bassiouni and Van Boven, is a very delicate issue. States can recognize a human rights violation, but apologies to the victim and families are uncommon. In *Loayza Tamayo v. Peru*,[197] the victim and family members requested the state apology to the victim and next of kin, which should be published in important newspapers. The same happened in *Castillo Páez* and *Suárez Rosero*.[198] In all cases, the court refused and asserted that the judgment was enough. Only in *Cantoral Benavides*[199] did the court order public apologies in Peru through the recognition of responsibility.

Furthermore, in *Trujillo Oroza*, the family members requested symbolic acts, including the recognition of international responsibility and public apology through the media. However, the IACHR did not support this request: The withdrawal of the preliminary exceptions, the recognition of the facts and the acceptance of the international responsibility were sufficient. However, recognition is not the same as apologies, as the last concept implies something else: not only are the facts recognized but also the wrongfulness.

Apologies are included in agreements on reparation. In *Durand and Ugarte*, the parties agreed in the publication of the agreement a public expression of request of pardon to the victims for the serious damages caused and the ratification of the will of nonrepetition. In *Barrios Altos*, the parties to the agreement accorded to publish apologies and request forgiveness to victims for the damages.

The IACtHR's reticence to order the state to apologize has concrete reasons included in the ILC Draft Articles: Satisfaction cannot be humiliating for the state. To impose apology through a judicial decision would go further than what is acceptable under international law. However, apology is the first step toward reconciliation and cannot be obtained through a judicial order. It must be part of a process of change in a society. Nonjudicial conflict resolution proceedings are more appropriate for apologies, except, of course, when the state decides *motu proprio* to apologize. Notwithstanding this thought, only when the wrongfulness is recognized, expressly or implicitly through state measures (e.g., removal from office with due process of law), real reconciliation exists and prevention of new violations is guaranteed.

Judicial and Administrative Sanctions against the Perpetrators

The investigation, prosecution and punishment are a clear form of satisfaction,[200] and an obligation derived from human rights treaty law before serious human rights violations.[201] The trial of perpetrators is linked to fairness in social relations and accountability. The suffering of victims makes it unacceptable that perpetrators escape punishment. Where no action or insufficient action is taken domestically, the obligation falls on the international community.

The duty to prosecute is not new, as arbitral jurisprudence is rich where the subject matter is this state's duty.[202] Amnesties were questioned before arbitral tribunals as violations of the duty to prosecute serious crimes. Lillich cites significant cases.[203] In *Cotesworth and Powell*,[204] the British-Colombia Mixed Commission in 1875 asserted that "one national is not responsible to another for the acts of its individual citizens, except when it approves or ratifies it," which could be inferred, concretely, from the pardon or amnesty to the offender. The commission asserted that "by pardoning a criminal, a nation assumes the responsibility for his past acts." In *Mallén*, the award asserted that a state cannot relieve itself of this obligation under international law, because of a draft amnesty law and a ministerial circular.[205] In *Montijo*,[206] arbitrator Bunch asserted that "the grantor of an amnesty assumes as his own the liabilities previously incurred by the objects of his pardon towards persons and things over which the grantor has no control."

There is an obligation to define enforced disappearances as crimes under domestic law, contained in the DED, as interpreted by the WG, the Draft IC, and a clear treaty law obligation for the states parties to the IACFD. These instruments include clauses expanding jurisdiction far from the territorial principle. Moreover, enforced disappearances can be crimes against humanity that must be tried by the state with territorial or active personality jurisdiction, or they can fall within the jurisdiction of the ICC if the pertinent state is party to the 1998 Treaty of Rome.

The obligation to investigate and punish illicit acts derives from international human rights, in particular, general obligations of human rights treaties.[207] The leading case is *Velásquez Rodríguez*. The court interpreted Article 1(1) with Article 7 to mean that

> States must prevent, investigate, and punish any violation of the rights recognized by the Convention and ... if possible to restore the right violated and provide compensation as warranted for damages resulting from the violation.... The State has a legal duty to take reasonable steps to prevent human rights violations and to use the means at its disposal to carry out a serious investigation of violations committed within its jurisdiction, to identify those responsible, to impose the appropriate punishment and to ensure the victim adequate compensation.

The obligation does not only entail "to effectively ensure ... human rights" but also that investigations are conducted "in a serious manner and not as a mere formality preordained to be ineffective.... If the State apparatus acts in such a way that the violation goes unpunished ... the State has failed to comply with its duty to ensure the full and free exercise of those rights to the persons within its jurisdiction." This is a due diligence requirement, binding "independently of changes of government over a period of time and continuously from the time of the act that creates responsibility to the time when the act is declared illegal." The obligations are applicable to new governments not in power at the time of the violation. The court suggests that an isolated violation is enough.

This was confirmed by subsequent cases decided by the IACtHR and the IACHR related to the right to a remedy (Article 25 of the ACHR) and due process of law (Article 8), read together with the obligation to ensure respect (Article 1). Consequently, blank amnesties are forbidden.

Van Boven, Bassiouni and Joinet reinforce the obligation to prosecute perpetrators. Chernichenko emphasized this question by asserting that though states are responsible for gross violations of human rights, perpetrators incur in criminal and civil responsibility.

Bassiouni underscored that the 1993 Van Boven version involves impunity concerning criminal prosecutions to prevent impunity. However, there were no provisions on noncriminal methods of accountability, such as truth commissions. The 1996 version eliminated those references and included the phrase: "particular attention must be paid ... to the duty to prosecute and punish perpetrators of crimes under international law"; concerning satisfaction and guarantees of nonrepetition, the phrase "bring to justice the persons responsible for the violations" was replaced by "judicial or administrative sanctions against the persons responsible for the violations." Bassiouni understood that the change gives the impression that the "judicial or administrative sanctions" are optional or discretional.

The 1996 version enunciates the "duty to prosecute and punish," but in the Bassiouni opinion, it lessens the emphasis on criminal sanctions. Finally, concerning respect to those obliged to make reparation and ensure respect; the 1993 version states that "where these principles refer to States, they also apply, as appropriate, to other entities exercising effective power." This was absent in 1996.

After *Velasquez Rodriguez,* the IACtHR asserted as satisfaction the investigation, prosecution and punishment of authors of disappearances. In *Caballero Delgado v. Santana,* Colombia was obliged to investigate and punish crimes committed against the victims. In *Bámaca Velásquez,*[208] the petitioners requested a real criminal proceeding to finish with impunity and to establish the facts seriously, quickly, impartially and effectively. The court replied affirmatively. In *Cantoral Benavides* the family members requested the investigation and punishment of the material authors, instigators and accomplices. The court reasserted the duty to investigate and sanction.[209] Concerning *Cesti Hurtado*,[210] the IACtHR asserted that the state should investigate exhaustively, seriously and impartially to individualize the authors.

Moreover, the question has been included in extrajudicial agreements monitored by the IACtHR, as in *Durand and Ugarte,* where the parties agreed to investigate and punish all those responsible and to advance the investigation before domestic tribunals.

In *Trujillo Oroza,* the IACHR recommended the investigation and effective punishment of authors and accomplices. Moreover, the IACtHR asserted that the state must avoid and combat impunity, defined as the lack of investigation, persecution, capture, trial and condemnation of those responsible. Once again, in *El Caracazo,* the court underlined the breach of the duty to investigate, as 13 years later no investigation had taken place.[211]

In *Las Palmeras,*[212] extrajudicial executions were discussed; the petitioners requested a decision asserting that Colombia should investigate and punish the perpetrators. The court recalled that the ACHR guarantees the access to justice to every person to protect rights and that the state is obliged to prevent and investigate human rights violations, as well as to identify and sanction perpetrators and accomplices. Consequently, every human rights violation encompasses the duty to investigate effectively to individualize those responsible and, if that corresponds, to sanction them. Thus the court asserted the state's obligation to effectively finish criminal proceedings, to identify those responsible and to punish them, what is a treaty law obligation that must be performed ex officio effectively, independently of the activity of private parties.

In the HRC, there are recommendations concerning the duty to investigate, prosecute and punish. In case no. 30/1978,[213] the HRC asserted that the government should bring to justice any person responsible for the death, disappearance and ill treatment of the victim. The same recommendation was issued in cases No. 84/1981, 107/1981, 161/1983,[214] and 181/1984.

The IACHR recommended the state urge the competent authorities to investigate the case[215] or perform the "most exhaustive investigation possible" within a maximum period (generally, 60 days.)[216] The orientation is similar to that of the IACtHR.[217] Moreover, the IACHR recommended determining the authorship of the facts and the whereabouts and location of the victim and, according to the domestic laws, punishing those directly and indirectly responsible.[218] In other opportunities the investigation was qualified as full and impartial[219]; full, swift and impartial[220]; impartial and effective[221]; serious, impartial and effective[222]; exhaustive, rapid and impartial[223]; exhaustive[224]; "complete, impartial and effective"[225]; "exhaustive, impartial and effective"[226]; or "thorough, rapid and impartial."[227] If bringing to justice the perpetrators is impossible, the state must continue the investigations and try to find the truth.[228]

The CHR has urged governments "that have long had many unresolved cases of disappearances, to continue their efforts to shed light on the fate of the individuals concerned and to set appropriate settlement machinery in train with the families of those individuals,"[229] together with a fair and adequate reparation. This is also addressed under the item "impunity."[230] The WG has emphasized this problem, though it has never addressed responsibility for specific disappearances, concentrating on the fate and whereabouts of the missing person, for its humanitarian, nonaccusatory approach to disappearances. The WG has also insisted on the moral aspects of impunity and the need to satisfy one's sense of justice and public respect for the rule of law.

Consequently, in all frameworks, except in the ECtHR, the organs of protection have requested the state to take measures concerning investigation, prosecution and punishment of perpetrators.[231] The ECtHR repeatedly asserted the violation of the right to an effective remedy concerning the obligation to investigate. However, the ECtHR does not include references to the necessity of investigation. Monetary compensation cannot substitute for the lack of investigation. State responsibility is not relieved only through compensation. If perpetrators are free, they are in office, the duty to prevent human rights violations are also breached, as well as the duty to investigate and prosecute.

Commemorations and Tributes to the Victims

Danieli proposed the adoption of measures of commemoration and education in enforced disappearances,[232] as rituals heal the rupture that victimization created between society and survivors.[233] Danieli asserts something that requires great dignity and a feeling of honor for those who suffered, died; it also has preventive purposes. The same orientation is present in the work of Van Boven, Bassiouni and Joinet.

In *Castillo Páez v. Peru*, the family unsuccessfully requested that the public garden where the victim disappeared should bear his name and a memorial sign. In *Trujillo Oroza*, the family members requested the construction of a public monument in the memory of the victim, establishing 2 February as the National Day of the Detained-Disappeared, and arranging of public events and ceremonies in education centers to commemorate the date.

In *Barrios Altos*, the parties agreed on building a monument to remember the case in a place agreed on with the City Hall of Lima within 60 days.

In Chile, acts in public spaces as sport stadiums used as detention and torture centers are considered a "ritual of purification."

Moreover, in Sri Lanka,[234] the Interim Report of the Commission of Inquiry recommended

> the creation of a "Wall of Reconciliation wherein are inscribed the names of all who have disappeared or died in this tragic period of our country's history." Your Commissioners consider this recommendation to represent a very important aspect of national reconciliation. This Memorial Wall which will contain names denoting all sections of the Sri Lankan people will be a symbol of our essential unity to future generations, a place to which everyone in this country could come and pay respect to those lost to us.

In the *Srebrenica Cases*,[235] the High Representative issued a decision on the location of a cemetery and a monument for the victims (OG RS no. 39/00 of 16 November 2000).

These measures have only taken place when the state decided it, and not through judicial order. Memorials and commemorations not only provide satisfaction to family members, but work as preventive measures as well.

Inclusion of the Violations in Training and Educational Materials

The inclusion of the human rights violations in training and educational materials deserves a serious approach in countries that suffered enforced disappearances, to prevent serious human rights violations. This requires time.

Sometimes education took place thanks to the assistance and recommendation of human rights organs,[236] in particular, public information and education campaigns, including seminars, trainings, lectures, and talks for priority sectors, dissemination activities through media for the police, public officials, government employees and students.[237]

In Sri Lanka nonformal human rights education began as legal education in the aftermath of massive human rights violations in the 1980s and early 1990s. Recipients ranged from human rights activists or professionals to community leaders, government officials, public servants, and elected village leaders. In addition, the teaching of human rights was integrated into history and social studies subjects in years 6–11 of education. Textbooks were revised to enlarge human rights content.[238]

However, education requires time, and human rights culture must impregnate all sectors of society, in particular police and security forces, whose role in enforced disappearances is essential.

Preventing the Recurrence of the Violations

Though many issues are related to prevention of human rights violations (e.g., education, the verification of the truth, commemoration and tributes to victims, etc.), special measures are addressed at the prevention of enforced disappearances. The obligation to guarantee or to ensure, including prevention of human rights violations, is a due diligence obligation: to maintain and organize the state apparatus and system to prevent human rights violations. One example is Article 19 of the DED, including the obligation to adopt legislative and other measures to enable victims to claim compensation, to permit access of national authorities to places of detention, habeas corpus, maintenance of centralized registers of persons detention, and so on.[239] The WG reminded governments of these obligations not via the clarification of individual cases but through more general action. For instance, concerning Sri Lanka, the WG recommended a mechanism to clarify the fate and whereabouts of missing persons.[240] Several preventive measures were adopted,[241] including visits to detention units and police stations by human rights officers,[242] official communication of detentions performed by military officers,[243] ruling that women and children should only be placed in a women's detention unit, a unique register for detentions,[244] and human rights courses for personnel of the security forces and police.

On prevention, the ECOSOC Resolution 1997/33 devoted to "Elements of Responsible Crime Prevention: Standards and Norms" included the concept of crime prevention, through nonpunitive measures, as a legitimate response of the society to criminal instances.

In *Castillo Páez v. Peru,* family members requested a commitment that similar events would never take place. Concerning apologies,[245] the court rejected the petition. In other cases, the engagement was included in the reparations agreement, for instance, in *Durand and Ugarte* and *Barrios Altos.*

The jurisprudence of the HRC included, as in case no. 107/1981, the assertion that the State should ensure that similar violations would not occur in the future. The HRC, in case no. 84/1981, recommended ensuring strict observance of all procedural guarantees prescribed to ensure that similar violations will not occur in the future. The preventive aspect of remedies is constantly underlined by the HRC in its frequent calls on state parties "to take steps to ensure that similar violations do not occur in the future." Equally, the HRC considers that state parties should take immediate steps to ensure strict observance of the provisions of the ICCPR. In *Sanjuán Arévalo,* the HRC asserted interest in information on any relevant measures introduced by the state party concerning the committee's views.

Concerning prevention, in *Bámaca Velásquez,* family members requested that the state should adapt the juridical system to abide by human rights. In *Caballero Delgado and Santana,*[246] the IACHR requested the inclusion in the legal system the habeas corpus and the criminalization of enforced disappearance and that judicial proceedings should remain within the jurisdiction of ordinary courts and not be transferred to military courts. In *Garrido and Baigorria*,[247] the victim's family members sought the criminalization of forced disappearance under the criminal code as federal offense. The court did not analyze this issue, because the state declared that the government had already introduced in the National Congress a preliminary bill defining the crime, according to the IACFD.

In *Barrios Altos*, the agreement contained, as satisfaction, respect of the interpretation of the IACtHR, which declared the ineffectiveness of the amnesty legislation, to begin the incorporation of extrajudicial execution as crime within 30 days of the signature of the agreement, and to begin the proceeding to sign and promote the ratification of the International Convention on Inapplicability of Statutes of Limitation to Crimes against Humanity within 30 days of the signature. In the concrete case, state parties are obliged to adopt all measures necessary not to subtract any person of judicial protection and exercise a simple and effective remedy.

The IACHR recommended that the state accede to the IACFD to prevent further cases.[248] In other cases,[249] the IACHR recommended to "derogate or leave without effect any domestic measure, legislative or other, that would tend to prevent the investigation, prosecution and punishment of those responsible for the arrest and disappearance of [the victim]," or to suspend domestic measures, legislative or of any other sort, to hinder the investigation, indictment, and punishment of those responsible.[250] Similar recommendations were issued concerning Chile.[251] Similarly, the WG recommended the amendment of legislation permitting the practice of disappearances,[252] for example, in Sri Lanka, the legislation to fight against terrorism and emergency regulations had this effect, in particular, concerning due process of law and treatment of prisoners.

Concretely, the IACtHR ordered states to derogate legislation in reparation judgments, as in *Cantoral Benavides*,[253] referring to emergency rules. The same happened in *Villagrán Morales*.[254]

Moreover, measures to prevent disappearances include the dismissal from public office of persons participating in human rights violations, through pertinent administrative or disciplinary processes, with due process of law.

The definition of enforced disappearance as a crime under internal law, with the characteristics indicated in the DED and the IACFD is the main concrete measure to adopt. However, this measure should be framed in a broader context to prevent enforced disappearances: due process of law, habeas corpus, and the essential elements of the rule of law.

Competence of the Monitoring Bodies to Grant Reparation

Pursuant to the *Principles on Impunity,* the right to reparation includes access to the applicable international procedures. Clearly, reparation before international organs is subsidiary to domestic jurisdiction. Apart from international responsibility,[255] state responsibility may be declared by international monitoring organs, particularly judicial bodies (the IACtHR, the ECtHR, the HRCBH, and the African Court), with competence to grant "reparation" defined in the instruments of creation. Other monitoring bodies, nonjudicial or quasi-judicial, have a more limited competence: They only can declare the violation of the rights and make recommendations.

Both the ECtHR and the IACtHR have interpreted their mandate classically. Only recently and for the influence of Cançado Trindade in the court, the IACtHR developed further principles and departed from *Factory of Chorzów*, case "adopted" since *Aloeboetoe*. The HRCBH benefited from the broader mandate of Annex VI of the Dayton Agreements.

In the European system, the individual victim has direct access to the court, which hears violations to the European Convention and its protocols. The judgments are compulsory for states, and the Committee of Ministers is in charge of the follow-up of the decisions of the court. The European Convention asserts in Article 41 the notion of "Just satisfaction": "If the Court finds that there has been a violation of the Convention or the protocols thereto, and if the internal law of the High Contracting Party concerned allows only partial reparation to be made, the Court shall, if necessary, afford just satisfaction to the injured party." Clearly, the provision does not refer to restitution, or to a right to restitution. The solution adopted in 1950 in Rome is more restrictive than the original proposal, which had referred to the possibility of the court to annul, suspend, amend, incriminate, and so on.[256] In the conditions established, the European Court would only grant reparation when it found a violation together with the absence of measures in the internal domain (and the court has denied having power to determine the particular measures that should be taken in the domestic system).[257] The court considers that only in the own state system a court decision is to be executed in good faith.[258] The court power on reparation is subsidiary and cannot be exercised except when domestic law does not allow it or is imperfect as to delete the consequences of the violation.[259] Reparation is, in the European system, a matter of discretion, until a certain point arbitrary and clearly subsidiary. However, as Nowak asserted, the court grants just satisfaction when facing gross violations of human rights, in particular, nonpecuniary damages. In addition, costs and expenses incurred and rate of interest have been recognized. To afford "just satisfaction," the requirements are generally: (1) a violation of the convention; (2) the impossibility of completely eliminating the consequences of the violation; (3) damage; (4) cause–effect relation between violation and damage.[260]

In the Inter-American system, the IACHR may receive petitions from individuals and NGOs recognized in one of the member states of the OAS as to denounce violations to the AD and, if the state is party, to the ACHR. If the state is party to the IACFD, it can apply this instrument.

If the IACHR finds human rights violations, a report with recommendations is issued. If the state is party to the ACHR and accepted the jurisdiction of the IACtHR,[261] and has not paid attention to the recommendations, the IACHR must transmit the case to the IACtHR, except if there is a majority decision against this possibility, according to the new Rules of Procedure. The grounds are the position of the petitioner, the nature and seriousness of the violation, the need to develop or clarify case law, the future effect of the decision in the legal systems of member states, and the quality of the evidence available (Article 44, Rules of Procedure 2002, IACHR).

If the IACHR presents the case to the court, the individual has no direct access (the commission presents the case, not the petitioner), except in the reparation stage, according to the Rules of Proceeding of the court. The court is an autonomous judicial organ[262] and issues binding judgments, pursuant to the ACHR, that must be executed in internal law according to the pertinent procedures of execution of judgments. The IACtHR considers that the obligation to abide by a judgment derives from state responsibility, backed by international jurisprudence, and the principle *pacta sunt servanda.*[263]

Article 63.1 of the ACHR crystallizes state responsibility for human rights violations. The provision contains a customary rule. When an illicit act is committed, there is a duty of reparation and to stop other consequences of the violation[264]: The court shall rule that "the injured party be ensured the enjoyment of his right or freedom that was violated." Clearly, the convention orders the court to include in the judgment measures as to restore the status quo ante. In addition, the court, "if appropriate," shall rule "that the consequences of the measure or situation that constituted the breach of such right or freedom be remedied and that fair compensation be paid to the injured party." Paragraph 2 refers to provisional measures.

Since *Velasquez Rodriguez,* the IACtHR clarified the principle of international law indicating that every violation of an international obligation resulting in harm creates a duty to make adequate reparation. The court ruled that reparation "consists in full restitution (*restitutio in integrum*), which includes the restoration of the prior situation, the reparation of the consequences of the violation, and indemnification for patrimonial and non-patrimonial damages, including emotional harm." According to the court, Article 63 (1) is not limited by the defects, imperfections or deficiencies of national law, but functions independently. This is a clear reply to any intended analogy concerning Article 41 of the European Convention, absolutely subordinated to domestic law.

Regarding the scope of reparation, the court addressed investigation, punishment, public condemnation and in fact the merits judgment reparation. On the other hand, punitive damages are not included in "fair compensation."

The court includes within its competence to decide that a proceeding should be reviewed, or, in *Barrios Altos,* that a law contrary to the Convention lacks legal effect.

Though the IACtHR has interpreted its own competence restrictively,[265] it has later preferred a broad interpretation, not limited to the ACHR but also providing for other adequate measures of reparation, to declare internal rules without effect. Apart from that, the court can adopt preventive measures.[266]

The African Court's jurisdiction, pursuant to the Protocol to the African Charter on Human and People's Rights on the Establishment of an African Court on Human and People's Rights (1998) extends to all disputes and cases concerning the interpretation and application of the ACHPR, the protocol, and "any other relevant Human Rights instrument ratified by the States concerned" (Article 3). This impedes the fragmentation of international human rights law, by judging the acts of a state through the complex framework of obligations voluntarily assumed. Article 30 asserts that the state parties must comply with the judgment within the time stipulated by the court and to guarantee the execution. The protocol does not contain special rules on consequences of human rights violation.

The HRCBH is bound by Article 11 of Annex 6 to the Dayton Agreements (1995), which asserts that after conclusion of the proceedings, the chamber issues a decision, asserting whether there was a breach by the party concerning the obligations under the agreement, and if so, what steps shall be taken to remedy such breach, including orders to cease and desist, monetary relief (including pecuniary and nonpecuniary injuries), and provisional measures. This is currently the most complete provision for jurisdiction of a human rights tribunal concerning measures of reparation. In *Hermas v. the Federation of Bosnia and Herzegovina,*[267] the chamber clarified Article 11: When the chamber found a breach of the agreement, it may order the respondent party to take steps that will remove, alleviate or prevent damage to the applicant, as well as compensation. Moreover, compensation may be awarded concerning pecuniary or nonpecuniary (moral) damage and may include costs and expenses incurred to prevent the breach or to obtain redress. Moreover, the chamber may order the responding party to cease or to desist, that is, to discontinue, or refrain from taking, specific action. In a subsequent case, it clarified that it cannot award reparation because the damages took place before the entry into force of Annex 6, that is, 14 December 1995,[268] or to obtain redress therefore.

In *Matanovic*,[269] the HRCBH found it appropriate to order the respondent to take all necessary steps to ascertain the whereabouts or fate of the applicants and to secure the victims release, if still alive, which reveals the broader mandate of the chamber (to grant orders to cease.) Moreover, the chamber ordered the respondent to report to the chamber on the steps taken and the results of investigations carried out, leaving open the possibility of ordering further steps to be taken by the respondent party as appropriate in the future and monetary relief.

Nowak has asserted that the chamber decides normally on restitution of costs and expenses, plus nonmonetary damages. Though some decisions are criticized for the low compensation granted, the tribunal follows the jurisprudence of the ECtHR: The petition determines the amount to be awarded. If no amount was requested, the ECtHR does not grant "just satisfaction."[270] The chamber does not increase the sums, though they could appear insufficient or ridiculous. In *Ostojic*, Nowak questioned the amounts provided, asserting that the chamber should develop its own jurisprudence on reparations, based on the work of Van Boven before the subcommission. The chamber interprets the reparation clause wrongly, as the judge understood that Article 11 contains a wider provision than Article 41 of the European Convention, interpreted in the famous *Vagrancy Cases* against Belgium.[271]

Consequently, Nowak asserted that "Article XI (1) of Annex 6 resembles more the concept of an emerging right of victims of human rights violations to reparation under contemporary human rights law." He highlighted the work of Van Boven asserting that reparation must be proportionate to the gravity of the violations and the resulting damage and must include restitution, compensation, rehabilitation, satisfaction and guarantees of nonrepetition. Consequently, the chamber should develop its jurisprudence under Article 11(1) of Annex 6 along the emerging right to reparation rather than by following strictly the case law of the European Court. When dealing with monetary relief, that is only one of the elements of reparation, the chamber should take into account not only the applicants claims but other types of reparation and the principle of proportionality to the gravity of the violations and the resulting damage. Article 11(1) does not bind the chamber to follow the applicant's claim. Consequently, the chamber is authorized to afford an element of reparation different from that explicitly claimed or an amount higher than the amount claimed by the applicants. In Nowak's opinion, the chamber should either have refrained from awarding compensation and order other types of reparation, or it should have awarded a more substantial amount to all applicants proportionate to the gravity of the violations and the pecuniary as well as nonpecuniary damages suffered.

In *Kevesevic*, Nowak expressed again a partly dissenting opinion concerning the remedies that the chamber is authorized to grant, questioning the practice of reserving for further consideration monetary compensation, by inviting the applicants to put forward detailed claims and to issue "Decisions on the Claim for Compensation," with similar approach by the ECtHR, repeating that the ECtHR has weak competence to decide on compensatory claims, in contrast with Article 11(1), which would allow a broad interpretation. The author emphasized that the chamber is not bound by the claim, and that the judicial organ should assess the seriousness of the human rights violations and the amount of suffering caused, granting if possible full restitution, a fair amount in the form of a lump sum. The change of jurisprudence is remarkable in subsequent cases, in particular, in the *Cases of Srebrenica,*[272] the chamber ordered several important measures under its wide powers: The Republika Srpska "as a matter of urgency" was ordered to release all information presently within its possession, control, and knowledge concerning the fate and whereabouts of the missing persons, including if they are still alive and in that case, where they are detained, and if corresponding, the location of the mortal remains. Moreover, the chamber ordered the immediate release of persons in illicit detention. Another urgent measure was to disclose to the ICRC, the ICMP, and the State and Federal Commissions and the ICTY, as well as to the OHR, the OSCE Mission to Bosnia and Herzegovina, and the Office of the Council of Europe in Bosnia and Herzegovina all information concerning gravesites, individual or mass, primary or secondary, of the victims of Srebrenica. The text of the decisions adopted in the case should be published in full. Finally, a lump sum of KM 2 million was to be paid to the Foundation of the Srebrenica-Potocari Memorial and Cemetery, and in addition, four further annual payments were guaranteed.

The HRC is the organ created by the ICCPR that may receive communications from victims if the state is party to the ICCPR and to the first OP. If communications are admissible, at closed meetings, in the light of all written information available, the HRC issues views to the state party and to the individual (Article 5). If there is a violation of the ICCPR, it recommends to the state party appropriate steps to remedy the violation. Though the HRC can only issue recommendations, a follow-up mechanism exists,[273] in the charge of a special rapporteur, who must regularly report to the plenary about the activities.

The CAT may receive individual complaints concerning the violation of the provisions of the treaty. With information provided by the individual and the state concerned, the committee considers the communication and formulates its views. The proceedings conclude with the transmission of the final views to the author and the state, which is also invited by the committee to inform of the action taken according to the committee's views. The committee includes in the annual report a summary of the communications examined, the explanations and statements of state parties concerned, and its own views.

In *Bleier*,[274] the HRC urged the government to reconsider its position and to take effective steps (1) to establish what happened to Eduardo Bleier since October 1975, to bring to justice any responsible for the death, disappearance or ill treatment, and to pay compensation to him or family for any injury suffered; and (2) to ensure that similar violations will not occur. In *Quinteros v. Uruguay*,[275] the HRC decided that the mother had the right to know what happened to her daughter and that the government should take immediate and effective steps (1) to establish what happened to the disappeared person since 18 June 1976 and secure her release; (2) to bring to justice any persons found to be responsible for the disappearance and ill treatment; (3) to pay compensation for the wrongs suffered; and (4) to ensure that similar violations will not occur in the future. In case no. 161/1983 (*Joaquin David Herrera Rubio v. Colombia*) the HRC asserted that the state party is under an obligation, according to the ICCPR, to take effective measures to remedy the violations and to investigate the violations, to take action as appropriate and to take steps to ensure that similar violations will not occur in the future. In *Sanjuán Arévalo*,[276] the HRC stated information on any relevant measure taken by the state party will be welcomed, in particular inviting the state party to inform on further developments in the investigation. In some cases, the HRC recommended compensation to the victim (the disappeared person) for any injury suffered (no. 30/1978), compensation for the wrongs suffered (no. 107/1981), or compensation to the surviving families (nos. 146/1983 and 148, 154/1983).

The preventive aspect of the remedies is underlined by the HRC calling on state parties "to take steps to ensure that similar violations do not occur in the future." Equally, the committee repeatedly expressed the view that state parties are obliged to take immediate steps to ensure strict observance of the ICCPR. In *Sanjuán Arévalo*, the HRC welcomed information on any relevant measures introduced by the state party concerning the HRC's views and, particularly, invited the state party to inform them about further developments in the investigation.

The human rights judicial system does not reach many countries, in particular in Asia. New regional mechanisms and the strengthening of the current universal system in a clear-cut form (e.g., strengthening concerning civil and political rights) appears as a necessary measure to provide for a better international system to deal with disappearances and prevent them.

There are several intents of changing the content and the extent of reparation, though the traditional compensatory approach prevails. Rehabilitation is gaining space, with clear limitations. Further attention to the work of

Van Boven and Bassiouni would contribute to enrich the jurisprudence with appropriate solutions for the protection of victims.

Conclusions

Different questions related to the protection of victims have been discussed. A broad definition of *victim* was supported, as including not only the person disappeared but also the family members and other persons affected, such as, for instance, dependents.

Moreover, the duty to protect victims is included in the dimensions of the respect of the general obligations, concerning civil and political rights, the obligation to respect, ensure or guarantee the enjoyment of human rights. The duty to ensure or guarantee includes several dimensions: the obligation to prevent through adequate state structures, the obligation to investigate, to prosecute and punish perpetrators and to grant reparation.

Bassiouni indicates that the right encompasses three different dimensions. The first one consists on the right to access to justice, fundamentally, to access to competent and impartial judicial organs as to decide promptly, independently and adequately questions related to the human rights violation. The second dimension is the right to reparation. Under general international law every state is obliged to provide reparation under international law before an illicit act, the individualization of the international law discourse through human rights law has the recognition of the right to the victim to reparation as counterpart. However, in the practice the right is recognized only to a limit, dependent on the goodwill of states, except when international mechanisms permit the state to receive a judgment asserting that reparation is due (e.g., the ECtHR, the IACtHR, the HRCBH). Concerning the content of reparation, international human rights depart from classical international law, where compensation is the most important element. Elements include also restitution, satisfaction, rehabilitation and guarantees of nonrepetition. Consequently, the attention to the proposal of Van Boven/Bassiouni as well as the *Principles on Impunity* of Joinet, could enrich the jurisprudence of the human rights organs and provide actual reparation.

These elements are all interrelated, and the classification was followed just to present a fairly clear framework. Judicial remedies are the only channels to obtain and exercise the right to reparation. The right to access to information was in practice only exercised through judicial remedies, though other channels should be put in action. For example, the encouragement and promotion of investigations addressed to deal with the truth, the establishment of museums, could be measures useful as to achieve this goal, as in the *Srebrenica Cases*. The right to reparation is linked to the access to justice.

11

The Right to a Remedy (III): Access to Factual Information Concerning the Violations

Bassiouni recognized that "states should develop means of informing the general public and in particular victims of violations of international human rights and humanitarian law of the rights and remedies contained within these principles and guidelines and of all available legal, medical, psychological, social, administrative and all other services to which victims may have a right of access." This is the weaker paragraph in the proposal, as though the title refers to information concerning violations (the truth), the content argues for information about remedies.

As Joinet indicated,[1] there is not only a right of an individual to know what happened, right to the truth, but also a collective right to prevent future human rights violations. This is the "duty to remember," to avoid historical revisionism or negations. Political and technical factors have been alleged as obstacles for the truth.[2]

The access to factual information must be guaranteed by the state through procedural measures, as component of the right to a remedy.[3] The victims and society should be informed on remedies and the outcome of proceedings dealing with human rights violations.[4] The Argentinean case permits us to understand the problems derived from the lack of judicial remedies as to exercise this right.[5] Though the truth should be investigated *ex officio*, in many cases this has not happened. For families, judicial mechanisms provide not only a reliable mechanism for establishing legal violations but also an official and public statement recognizing that a violation occurred and that victims were harmed. In addition to individual accountability, judicial mechanisms permit applicants to hold the system accountable, either directly or indirectly. Most important, they give a signal that impunity is inadmissible and affirm the state's commitment to judicial redress and human rights.[6] Investigations by federal courts, for example, in La Plata, into past "disappearances" continued in proceedings known as *Juicio por la Verdad* (the Truth Trial), directed to uphold the right to the truth of the relatives.[7]

In *Aguiar de Lapacó*,[8] Lapacó requested a federal court of appeals in 1995 to issue a written communication to the headquarters of the Army Chief of Staff of the Argentinean Ministry of Defense to obtain all existing information on the fate of persons who disappeared by the army and the security and intelligence branches under the operating orders of the First Army Corps from 1976 to 1983, because of the right to the truth from an individual and collective perspective. The court decided to allow the petition, asserting that "it was appropriate for it to exercise its jurisdictional power," and that although the amnesty legislation and pardons had benefited members of the armed forces, they did not imply the culmination of all kind of proceedings. The Secretary-General of the army responded to the court's petition stating that the armed forces had no information. Consequently, Mrs. Lapacó suggested that official communications could be sent to other organizations. The court asserted that this was beyond its jurisdictional powers, exhausted when the amnesty laws were passed, and the tribunal sent the file to the Secretariat for Human Rights (Ministry of the Interior). Consequently, the petitioner filed an extraordinary remedy with the Supreme Court, and the Attorney General supported their arguments. However, the Supreme Court rejected the extraordinary remedy on the grounds that investigative proceedings determine the existence of a punishable act and identify its perpetrators; given the amnesty legislation, that was not possible.[9] *Aguiar de Lapacó* presented a petition before the IACHR, which led to a friendly settlement, where Argentina accepted and guaranteed the right to the truth, "which involves the exhaustion of all means to obtain information on the whereabouts of the disappeared persons. It is an obligation of means, not of results, which is valid as long as the results are not achieved, not subject to prescription." The right was recognized concerning the petitioner's daughter. Moreover, Argentina asserted that the federal courts had exclusive jurisdiction, assuming the engagement to adopt the necessary laws to ensure that the criminal federal system throughout the country would try these cases to determine the truth regarding the fate of persons disappeared before 10 December 1983. In the same agreement, Argentina arranged for the Office of the Attorney General to assign an ad hoc group of prosecutors to act as third parties in cases involving inquiries into the truth and the fate of disappeared persons. This agreement was approved by the IACHR, which kept monitoring functions over it.

In the practice, the lack of a judicial remedy for the victim (in a broad sense) is a very important problem. When the political authorities decide or agree to conceal the truth, only an effective remedy addressed as the truth permits victims and family to exercise their rights. Only remedies empowering the victims to present claims can solve the problem, at least from the individual point of view. Habeas corpus was a useful remedy for years, in the absence of other solutions, because it was the adequate and effective remedy in disappearances (apart from the criminal cases where some persons were concretely investigated). The Habeas Corpus Act 23.098 (1984) asserts that it can be presented when an act or omission of public authority is denounced, and it implies the limitation or current threat of physical freedom without written order of public authority, or in case of illegitimate aggravation of the form and conditions of a licit deprivation of physical freedom (Article 3). The law authorizes the victim or any person in his or her favor to present it (Article 5). This is very important, as it recognizes *broad standing* to introduce the action (it is not necessary to allege the violation of a subjective right). The judgment of the magistrate (habeas corpus) issues orders to the requested authority to achieve the immediate presentation of the person detained with a report including the grounds, form and conditions of detention, and if there is written order of competent authority, the reasons and place of detention. If the authority holding the person detained is not known, the judge issues orders to the highest authorities of the government branch as indicated in the denouncement. If a person is in custody, detention or confinement, and she or he would be transported out of the territory or the victim would suffer irreparable damage, habeas corpus can be issued *ex officio,* ordering the competent authority to bring the person before the judicial organ.

Habeas corpus was used to find out the fate and whereabouts of persons disappeared. The insufficiency of the existing legislation facing the reality of unsolved cases of enforced disappearances plus the progressive development of human rights law, made some human rights lawyers use habeas corpus creatively.

A particular question was raised when the Argentinean Constitution was amended in 1994. Article 43 contains a series of judicial guarantees devoted to protect urgent cases, when human and civil rights are violated or threatened. The first paragraph refers to *amparo,* the action addressed at the protection of all human rights constitutionally protected, treaties or laws, except physical freedom. More important, the third paragraph of Article 43 included *habeas data,* an action addressed at knowing the data referring to a person and their finality, included in public registers or databases or those private ones intended to provide reports. In case of falseness or discrimination, the action can be presented to demand the suppression, rectification, confidentiality or update. Finally, Article 43, paragraph 4 recognized constitutionally the habeas corpus, and it included, in one of the grounds for its presentation, the case of forced disappearance of persons.

Habeas data was not immediately specified through legislation, and new judicial presentations took place. This judicial guarantee was used to protect the right to the truth, and even the Supreme Court agreed. Consequently, the judiciary asserted that the lack of legislation was not an obstacle for the exercise, that should be provisionally encompassed by judicial organs.[10] Moreover, the Supreme Court extended *habeas data* (originally restricted to protect the right to privacy), to other persons when the person with standing was impeded to do it, facing presumptive death, and the petitioner was a member of the direct family.[11] In *Urteaga,* the Supreme Court asserted that the disappeared person's brother had the right to obtain the information existing in public registers or databases permitting him to clarify the death of the person disappeared and, if it was the case, to know the destiny of his corpse, that is, to have access to the "data" protected by *habeas data.* However, some judges have understood it in a stricter sense (protecting only the right to privacy) and considered that the petitioner had standing and cause of action, but according to *amparo,* was of generic character. Moreover, the judges asserted that the brother had the right to clarify the circumstances of the death, and if appropriate the fate of the corpse. The right of the petitioner to obtain information from state organs was guaranteed, to determine if there was information in registers on the death of the person disappeared and/or the place of burial. In another opinion, the habeas data was understood to protect the right to privacy in family life, arbitrarily restricted because the right to mourn or to bury the relatives had been violated.[12] Moreover, another judge expressed that to grant action was the only way to abide by the principles of the IACFD.[13]

Finally, the law on Habeas Data was passed (Act 25.326). The purpose, according to Article 1, is the integral protection of personal data, including the guarantee of the right to information. The act recognizes the right to access, that is, to request and obtain the personal data included in public databases or in private databases to give reports. The responsible user has 10 days to respond. If that is not satisfied, the action of protection of personal data can be presented. In case the data concern a person that died, the legal heirs can present the action. Clearly, Article 23 asserts that the law applies to the data kept by the armed forces, security forces, police and intelligence organisms, and those on personal antecedents that proportion those data to administrative or judicial authorities pursuant to the law.

Article 33 refers concretely to the judicial remedy. Concerning standing, Article 34 clearly recognizes the person affected, legal representatives, and heirs in direct line or collateral until the second degree, personally or through representative. The ombudsman can participate in these proceedings. Federal tribunals are competent when the action is presented against public databases of national organisms or interjurisdictional or international organs. The proceeding is the same existing for *amparo,* pursuant to Article 37.

The Argentinean case reveals the problem of the lack of judicial remedies to exercise the right to the truth. Any solution should pay attention to the need to define under internal law adequate, effective and prompt judicial remedies to permit the victims to find out the truth, in particular, the fate and whereabouts of the victims. However, no solution can be limited to the judicial arena. Though discussing the problem of "the missing," in the context of the ICRC, humanitarian, political and extrajudicial mechanisms have been recommended in the domestic arena, permanent commissions to which the requests of information on the victims could be addressed.[14]

The last element of the right to a remedy, as presented by Bassiouni the access to the factual information is perhaps the most difficult issue, especially when the state, for alleged pacification grounds, has preferred to forget the truth. Mechanisms to give access to it and to encourage state organs to perform their obligation of investigation should be set up.

12

Conclusions: The Need for a Comprehensive and Coherent Framework of Prevention and Protection in Cases of Enforced Disappearances

In the previous chapters, different aspects of human rights concerning enforced disappearances are analyzed. Through the comparison between case law and the existing rules addressing enforced disappearances, lack of coherence among the systems of protection and eventually *lacunae* within those systems were revealed. Few binding rules are applicable in the framework of enforced disappearances. The codification and progressive development of international human rights should someday permit to speak about universal "rules" and perhaps a system in this field (see chapter 1). The current situation does not provide a high level of protection, and the lack of clear rules places the victims at the mercy of monitoring organs and the political will of states, which motivates the absence of coherent solutions and makes obstacles of the realization of justice. Concerning enforced disappearances, the international system does not work as a system of collective guarantee but as inconsistent regimes that function as if the other mechanisms would not exist (see chapter 1).

In particular, the DED still provides the most comprehensive framework in the universal arena. However, because this is a declaration, it lacks binding character per se, which requires further treaty law rules concerning enforced disappearances. In particular, the definition of enforced disappearances in a binding instrument is a pending matter. Though there is a definition in the IACFD, this represents a lost opportunity, because the definition is more restrictive than the current practice.

The importance of the DED consists in expressing *opinio juris, besoin de droit*. Through in this resolution, unanimously adopted by the General Assembly of the United Nations, the international community expressed the rejection for enforced disappearances, when declaring that every case is a grave, serious and flagrant violation of human rights. Moreover, the WG has repeatedly addressed the states' understanding that some obligations derive from this instrument, fundamentally, the obligation to prosecute and punish perpetrators. The WG asserted that states should actively adapt domestic legislation to human rights law to prevent enforced disappearances. The WG underscored the need to define the crime of enforced disappearances. In addition, Article 18 of the DED asserts that amnesty laws are not permitted concerning disappearances (see also chapter 9). These assertions would be impossible if no obligation would derive from the DED.

Though the prohibition of disappearances is clear under international law, the definitions are not coherent. The DED still provides for a very good definition, though the enumeration of the acts depriving the physical freedom deserves critiques, which is corrected by the IACFD (see chapter 1) and Draft IC through a general introductory phrase. Moreover, the assertion that the victim must be placed outside the protection of the law is also eliminated in the Draft IC. That is a consequence and not an element of a case of enforced disappearances. The definition of the IACFD is defective, as it links disappearance to lack of domestic remedies, which does not respond to previous practice or the DED. Disappearances take place even when judicial mechanisms function adequately.

The biggest deficit of existing definitions is to omit the action of nonstate actors. Only the ICC Statute links disappearances to nonstate actors: Only political organizations are included, a concept that appears to be too broad. The future jurisprudence of the ICC can solve borderline cases as action of economic groups with political purposes. The ICC Statute only refers to enforced disappearances as crimes against humanity.

Nothing impedes states from characterizing enforced disappearances in a broader way than the existing international instruments, particularly if the state lost the monopoly of the use of force, to avoid impunity.

Enforced disappearance is a deprivation of the physical freedom of a person, in whatever form or way, and, under current international law, committed by state officers or that receive state support or acquiescence, with subsequent lack of information about the fate and whereabouts of the victim, denial of the detention or information about the victim. The first constitutive act is the arbitrary or illegal deprivation of physical freedom, but some cases have taken place against persons in prison after trial and prosecution. The notions arguing for the need of a reasonable amount of time are critical, as the IACtHR expressed. Enforced disappearances include situations in which the victim's body victim appeared 20 hours after kidnapping. The suffering cannot depend on fixed amounts of time but on a case-by-case analysis.

One particular problem is the characterization of enforced disappearances as continuing violations. Though this is present in the existing instruments, it has been hardly applied by the organs of protection. Preparing a binding instrument concerning enforced disappearances, this issue should be reinforced, as the illicit act subsists until the fate and whereabouts of the victim are not clarified. As a result, the clear consequence is that the statute of limitations does not start running until clarification. If a state accepts the jurisdiction of an international body, and this takes place after the disappearance, the character of continuing violation makes the pertinent body competent.

Concerning statutes of limitation, there are divergences among the DED, the IACFD, the Draft IC and the ICC. The best solution is a differentiated regime in which enforced disappearances constitute crimes against humanity, and the rest of cases do not. Moreover, the civil action should follow the same fate as the criminal action. Crimes against humanity should not be subject to statutes of limitation, so as to be coherent with the ICC Statute. In the other cases, the statute of limitation should be the longest existing under domestic law.

Clearly, enforced disappearances can take place in isolated cases. However, where enforced disappearances have been systematic or have amounted to a practice, the declaration of the existence of a practice contributes to the facilitation of the evidentiary task by the injured party. In *Velasquez Rodriguez,* the IACtHR considered that once accredited the practice and that the victim would fall within the target group, the burden of the proof shifts to the state, which has to prove, for instance, that the person escaped or is legally detained. This approach was always rejected by the ECtHR in cases against Turkey, arguing the lack of necessity. The injured party is at disadvantage in comparison with the state, because of lack of access to evidence essential to the solution of the case.

Another inconsistency is the characterization of enforced disappearances as crimes against humanity. In the Inter-American system, the terminology is not used strictly, but almost as synonym of gross or serious violations of human rights. However, this point of view is unacceptable. The terminology should keep relation with the Statute of the ICC: Enforced disappearances that are massive and systematic and addressed against civilian population are crimes under humanity. One consequence is the nonapplicability of statutes of limitations of the crime, as indicated.

This lack of clear treaty rules addressing the disappearances has led different organs of protection and petitioners to use the traditional frameworks in the field of civil and political rights (e.g., the multiple-rights approach; see chapter 2) to frame the phenomenon in the existing rules. Moreover, practically all rights allegedly violated in enforced disappearances are nonderogable rights. In addition, only the IACHR has been proactive when declaring human rights violations, that is, substituting the wrongly alleged violations for a more coherent framework, which is important when granting reparation, according to the work of Bassiouni and Van Boven and the WG (see chapter 10): Reparation should be proportional to the human rights violations committed. However, not even within the same system of protection was the same set of rights allegedly violated (see chapter 2).

In the Inter-American system, the multiple-rights approach is present in all decisions, which is not clear in the other systems. The organs have often declared the violation of several rights protected but not argued clearly in favor of the multiplicity of violations. In that sense, the lack of quotations concerning the DED is emphasized.

The situation of the direct victim and other persons next to him or her should be differentiated. Concerning the direct victim, following all organs of protection, every case is a violation of *the right to physical freedom*. If the victim was detained without judicial order, or on arbitrary or illegal grounds, there is a violation to this right (see chapter 4). However, unfortunately there have been disappearances where the detention was also originally legal or nonarbitrary, but the case derived from an enforced disappearance. In any case, as the disappeared person is maintained in incommunicado detention, without possibility of questioning the legality of the situation and without presentation before a judge, there is always a violation of the right to physical freedom. The European Court has presented the most elaborated jurisprudence on this point, asserting since *Kurt* that there is a complete negation of the right and the most grave violation to Article 5 of the European Convention.

To prevent and protect victims, habeas corpus is the most adequate remedy to address enforced disappearances, in particular when the guarantee recognizes broad standing (in particular, if any person can present habeas corpus for the victim). In this sense, the organs of protection, particularly in the Inter-American system, have emphasized that this guarantee is breached concerning victims and that habeas corpus cannot be suspended in states of emergency because of this essential role. In cases of state of emergency, the authorities have recognized the possibility of detaining persons without judicial order, but this power is not unlimited and does not mean that the person is left at the mercy of state authorities. Consequently, habeas corpus permits family members and persons next to the victim to know where the person is detained, under which authority and on which grounds. Additionally, the existence of accurate registers of detention (available to all persons interested) and periodic visits to centers of detention guarantee of the right to communication of the person detained and appear to be essential measures of prevention. Independent monitoring should be underscored.

Every case of enforced disappearances violates or threatens seriously the right to life (see chapter 3). In many cases, the victim has suffered extrajudicial execution. When the body did not appear, the time elapsed was the key element to figure out that the victim had died. Incommunicado detention places the victim at serious risk. However, the ECtHR has been demanding at the time of declaring violations to Article 2 of the European Convention, paying attention to circumstantial evidence based on concrete elements that would lead to the conclusion beyond reasonable doubt that the victim has been extrajudicially executed, in particular that the victim suffered mistreatment. Moreover, the ECtHR declared procedural violations to Article 2, indicating the lack of investigation. This opinion does not constitute an appropriate approach because it does not provide for coherent responses: Some procedural violations are considered under Article 13; in the case of the right to life, the court analyzes them under Article 2.

The right to life requires from states not only the duty of respect but also an active approach of prevention.

Moreover, every disappearance includes, as a minimum, inhuman or degrading treatment. Clearly, a person in incommunicado detention suffers a terrible state of anguish, caused by the isolation, lack of contact with the family and the external world in general, and the fear for the final fate (see chapter 5). This requirement is not justified: Every victim of a disappearance is evidently in a situation of distress of arbitrary and painful character. In addition, in some cases, when it could be accredited, more serious violations to the right to physical and mental integrity have been declared and, in the most extreme form, torture. Additional evidence is necessary to achieve the conclusion.

Moreover, enforced disappearances constitute violations of the right to juridical personality, as the victim is placed outside the protection of the law and impeded from the exercise of all rights (see chapter 6). Originally the provisions recognizing this right referred to entitlement to rights, not to the impediment to exercise. However, enforced disappearances were not in the agenda of drafting bodies in the 1950s and 1960s. Consequently, the dynamic interpretation of human rights instruments would provide an additional and necessary element as, effectively, the victim is deprived from the possibility of exercising the rights to which he or she is entitled.

However, the human rights violations depend on the characteristics of each case, as other questions may arise, for example, rights of the children, freedom of movement, and so on (see chapters 2 and 4).

Concerning victim's relatives and persons near them, they can also be direct victims. In this context, there are two approaches. Some monitoring organs emphasize the possibility of inhuman or degrading treatment, because of the sufferings and anguish that those close to the victim endure, as of the uncertainty on the fate and whereabouts of the victim and the kind of treatment undergone. This is the model applied, for example, by the IACtHR in *Blake* (see chapter 5). In this point the ECtHR has also expressed a dissenting view, requiring the presence of "special factors" and clarifying that it does not establish a right in favor of the family members. Though those who allege to have suffered such a treatment should present evidence, the standard required by the European Court is too high and hardly justified. Those who have proved a very close link to the victim should be exempted from the presentation of further evidence, as obviously the disappearance caused them distress that deserves recognition in the human rights arena. Moreover, the insight provided by the jurisprudence of the HRCBH in *Palic* and repeated in the *Srebrenica Cases* is relevant, where the violation of the right to family life was alleged in enforced disappearances, as the person disappeared is taken out of his normal familiar context and isolated, impeding any communication with those close to them, applying Article 8 of the European Convention.

In addition, family members can be victims of the violation of the right to know the truth (see chapter 7), because the fate and whereabouts of the victim are hidden. This right derives from the DED, in particular, Articles 9 and 13, and has been recognized by the IACHR, the HRCBH, the CHR and the WG. There is also dissent among the systems of protection. The IACtHR does not understand the truth as an autonomous right but as a derivation from the obligation to investigate. Moreover, the ECtHR has not referred to the right to the truth but to the obligation to investigate, depending on the case, derived from Article 2 or Article 13 of the European Convention, once accredited a human rights violation.

They can also be victims of the violation of the right to a judicial remedy, when the investigations do not take place, there is no prosecution and punishment, and the habeas corpus does not provide result.

At this point, the definition of victim must be highlighted. The Declaration of Basic Principles and Bassiouni provided broad definitions to protect victims (see chapter 9). *Victim* does not only refer to the person disappeared: Family members are also victims per se, because they suffer anguish for the absence of the person loved, plus uncertainty on the fate and whereabouts, and lack of possibility of performing an adequate burial, and so on. Moreover, those close to the victim (in particular, spouse or permanent companion, children, siblings and parents) should not be requested to provide additional evidence other than the proof of their family link to be victims themselves, in particular concerning inhumane treatment. In addition, some persons do not count with such a close link, but they could be treated similarly if they accredit the existence of a close relation that would have derived in special suffering: other family members, a fiancée, very close friends. A disappearance can affect persons economically dependent on the victim, and they may not belong to any of these categories. The standards elaborated by the IACtHR in *Aloeboetoe* still apply: Periodic help, the necessity, and the link with the victim make the court presume that the help would have continued.

The problems that children can suffer is also addressed (see chapter 8). Children have been victims of enforced disappearances and further illicit acts linked to the enforced disappearances: abduction of children, especially in Latin America. In some cases, the children were illegally adopted by family linked to the perpetrators of the disappearance. In another cases, the adoptive parents ignored the origin of the children. The principle that asserts that the best interest of the children should be considered must always be applied. Dramatically, there are contradictions with the legitimate claims of family members of the disappeared person. If the identity is in doubt, any judicial measure should pay attention to the protection of the allegedly abducted child. In particular, the organs and claimants should avoid presenting the question to the media before a final solution is adopted, because the person affected can suffer irreparable damages. Moreover, the case should be put under the consideration of the same young person, especially when the age and personality permit to do it. This delicate process should be accompanied with psychological expert assistance to the minor, as well as to the claimant family members, and adoptive parents if they had no knowledge of the origins of the children. The expert assistance should have an important role to play to advise the judge if it is appropriate to go ahead with the investigation or if the parties involved are not ready to do it. Moreover, compulsory blood or DNA tests should not take place, to protect the personality of the minor. This should be differentiated from the advice and support to the minor; further victimization of the minor should be avoided. If parents participated in some criminal act concerning the abduction and suppression of identity, they should be prosecuted and punished and not protected simply because the minor is at stake. This is a different issue. In the cases where it is accredited that the adoptive parents participated in the commission of criminal acts, most authors and reports propose that the adoption should be declared void *ab initio,* and the judge should decide who should have the custody of the minor. If the parents had no knowledge or participation in the case, the judge could confirm the custody, if that is in the best interest. In all cases, if the actual family of the children does not obtain the custody, they should obtain periodic visits to keep contact with the minor and to restore broken links.

Van Boven and Bassiouni have recognized the right to a remedy (see chapter 9), with emphasis on restitution, compensation, satisfaction and guarantees of nonrepetition. Joinet on impunity also addressed the consequences of disappearances. The right of victims to a remedy in general, and in particular the right to restitution, compensation, satisfaction and guarantees of nonrepetition, is recognized. Though under international law, every state that violates international law is obliged to grant full reparation, pursuant to the jurisprudence and the work of the ILC, this issue has not been so clear concerning the right of the individual victim. The research and systematization of Bassiouni, Van Boven and Joinet counts with the importance of recognizing this individual right, which takes place in the context of recent jurisprudence of the organs of protection, such as the HRCBH and the IACtHR. Though the future of these projects is still uncertain, and the best solution would be to convert them into binding rules, the political will of states is limited when dealing with victims.

Bassiouni and Van Boven have highlighted the obligations to respect, guarantee and to adopt measures to adapt the domestic system to international human rights law. The proposal is in line with the jurisprudence of the Inter-American system, particularly after *Velasquez Rodriguez*. Several measures are included in the DED, the Draft IC, and several instruments of the UN system dealing with treatment of prisoners, for instance, the recording of the persons detained, the periodic supervision of centers of detention, the prohibition of clandestine prisons, the definition in criminal law of enforced disappearances with an appropriate penalty, the existence of proceedings to claim irregularities in centers of detention, and so on. These measures help prevent enforced disappearances. Moreover, in general, the rule of law and respect for human rights as part of the everyday culture are the most efficient way to prevent enforced disappearances. To achieve this goal, the human rights education of public officers and the establishment of adequate mechanisms of removal facing irregularities are important deterrent factors.

The classification of Bassiouni is followed, identifying three aspects in the right to the remedy that are interrelated: (a) the right to access to justice, (b) the right to restitution, (c) the right to access to information concerning violations.

The right to access to justice means access to a judicial remedy, even to find out where is the victim detained. The elaboration and the functioning of judicial procedures as habeas corpus, with wide standing to allow any person interested to investigate the fate and whereabouts of the victim. Habeas corpus is only highlighted in the Inter-American system. In contrast, all the organs of protection understand that there is a state obligation to investigate *ex officio*. The investigation of serious offenses is a state obligation, independent of any possibility to participate in domestic proceedings. This investigation must comply with requirements of impartiality, celerity and independence. For achieving this goal, clauses permitting the possibility of the injured party to participate in criminal proceedings is an interesting factor of control. If this participation is not allowed, there is a risk that investigations are carried out just as a formality, waiting for the statute of limitation to run out or caducity rules to apply. The establishment of enforced disappearances as a crime, with an additional type concerning crimes against humanity, should pay attention to the problem of statutes of limitation. First, statutes of limitation should not run out when there are no remedies, or they fail to function, they are dilatory or the victim is impeded concretely to exercise them. Second, statutes of limitation should not apply when enforced disappearances are considered crimes against humanity. Third, in the other cases, statutes of limitation should be substantial to the seriousness of the human rights offense committed.

Apart from the obligation to investigate, the obligation to guarantee includes the obligation to prosecute and punish. To that end, those who are still working in official functions should be removed to guarantee the impartiality of the proceedings and to prevent further violations. As asserted previously, the injured party should be allowed to intervene in criminal proceedings to control the activity of the state and to perform and propose evidentiary measures. Finally, the obligation to guarantee includes the obligation to grant reparation, analyzed shortly.

Among general obligations derived from general international law, every state must adapt the national system to obligations assumed under international law. This includes, particularly in the Inter-American system for states parties to the IACFD, the definition of enforced disappearances as a crime under national law.

The obligation to grant reparation exists under classical international law but not so clearly in the field of human rights. However, the individualization of the human rights discourse, as Nowak has underscored, includes the right to restitution, compensation, satisfaction and guarantees of nonrepetition as one of its main features. This right to restitution is understood in a broad sense, limited to not only the monetary aspects of reparation but to different sides. Restitution in cases of enforced disappearances is practically impossible (see chapter 10), except if the victim is still alive and liberation is possible. However, even in this case, this would not be sufficient, and other measures should complement the victim's release.

Compensation is the most traditional form of reparation, responding to the extensive jurisprudence on reparations for injuries to aliens. In the field of international human rights, the parameters, the basis of calculus and the applicable law are questions without clear solution. The most detailed system is present in the IACtHR, as Van Boven and Bassiouni provide simply for proportionality. The IACtHR uses these criteria only in *Blake*. Joinet addressed this question with the broadest approach, by asserting that all the consequences of the human rights violation should be faced. The IACtHR asserts in *Aloeboetoe* that only immediate consequences deserve reparation. Joinet emphasized that full reparation should be guaranteed.

Among the items deserving compensation, only moral damages are generally granted, and the amounts were calculated on equity. Tribunals should be coherent so as not to give the impression that some enforced disappearances or victims are more important than others. The justification in each case is a rule to follow. In *Las Palmeras,* the IACtHR used these criteria for the first time.

The other elements generally included under compensation have received diverse attention. Concerning actual damages, that is, the concrete expenses incurred because of the enforced disappearance, the IACtHR has been the organ with a better approach, by asserting that only reasonable expenses should be reimbursed. Small amounts are granted on equity grounds, understanding that to present receipts of every small expense is difficult.

Concerning loss of income, the IACtHR counts with the most extensive jurisprudence. Different factors are taken into account: the basis employed by the court deserves to be criticized for resorting to the minimum salary as the first element, when family members could not prove the victim's salary. This leads to unfair situations. Moreover, many Latin Americans work in the shadow economy. Consequently, they cannot prove their income. Alternative solutions include that present in *El Amparo:* the cost of the basic basket of goods, or the average of salaries of the activity that the victim was allegedly performing. If this last amount is inferior to the basket, the basket should be used. The court tries to avoid granting important sums to victims. The issue that the victim's family has to subsist for years with the sums adjudicated is forgotten. Concerning the ECtHR, it grants reparation for loss of earnings if there is sufficient connection with the human rights violation.

Concerning loss of opportunities, the IACtHR paid particular attention to school opportunities for children of victims and left opened the possibility that once accredited, loss of chance would deserve reparation.

In the Inter-American jurisprudence, there are two new concepts: the project of life and the right to life. The project of life alludes to the plan of the person concerning the future; sums are calculated according to equity.

The right to life alludes to the value of the life per se and tries to assign a reparation for cases of arbitrary deprivation of life.

As for legal costs, they are adjudicated and recognized. Other expert costs have only been recognized once alleged, for instance, medical treatment in particular in the IACtHR. The sums adjudicated have been increased by the application of an interest rate. On this last point, the opinion of the ECtHR was criticized because it does not apply the interest rate of the place of payment but the interest rate of the United Kingdom or France. This does not allow the adequate reparation, because the victims and their families have to pursue their lives and incur in expenses not in those countries but where the violations of human rights took place.

Rehabilitation was not commonly guaranteed. Only the IACtHR granted future medical and psychological treatment when the injured party has alleged it. Rehabilitation policies should be implemented ex officio by the state to address trauma suffered by victims and families.

Concerning satisfaction, the measure that has received more acceptance clearly and obviously is the declaration of the tribunals of the human rights violations. Other measures, such as publication of the judgments and the truth and recognition of the facts, play an important role but only because the state agreed to them. This is the problem concerning satisfaction: Judicial organs order states to do things that they would not agree to do voluntarily, and consequently, they do not perform the judicial order. Some tribunals deny satisfaction and the judicial declaration of the violations, understanding that they place the state in a very uncomfortable situation.

Perhaps the measure of satisfaction that received more attention by the human rights violations is investigation.

A very important measure of satisfaction is handing down the corpses to families, if possible. For achieving that goal, the state should investigate ex officio the fate and whereabouts of the victims, an obligation of continuing character until the content is not satisfied. Moreover, centralized and permanent organs to respond to consultations and needs of the families are essential measures.

To find out the truth is a state obligation and should be pursued ex officio. This presents several aspects: the right of the individual family members and persons near to them to know what happened to the victim, why it happened, and who is responsible. Finding the fate and whereabouts of the victim is essential. However, the truth has a collective aspect, because the society should have conscience of the past and dramatic circumstances that members of its society endured to avoid future repetition.

The state has often impeded finding the truth, sometimes alleging the need of reconciliation and social peace. This interpretation is unacceptable, because the truth permits one to differentiate between the good and the bad, the victim and the perpetrator. If the truth is not openly revealed, the society runs the risk of anomia, as rules appear to exist only for some persons, whereas others, with the pretext of reconciliation, can freely operate in the society. The lack of respect for rules and lack of enforcement with equality, where everybody must respect the same laws and any perpetrator should suffer the same consequences. If impunity pervades the social matrix, if those who committed the most perverse atrocities remain free and those who commit small crimes go to prison, the scale of values is perverted and only more violence can follow.

For these reasons, if the state decides to deny the truth, the victims should be empowered to find it out. To that end, mechanisms addressed at the disclosure of archives, databases, and through judicial or administrative proceedings, are the only remedy to guarantee victims the possibility of approaching the truth. Moreover, when disappearances reach international forums, the organs of protection should emphasize that the investigation should continue.

Consequently, the framework of analysis and protection of victims of enforced disappearances lacks coherence and is incomplete. The only universal mechanisms are in charge of the WG applying the DED. Though some states have cooperated with the WG, formally or substantively, many have ignored its recommendations for lack of enforcement mechanism. The WG constitutes a link between families and governments and to act in urgent cases to prevent further damages.

The absence of an internationally binding instrument is felt in different areas. However, a new treaty cannot solve all problems, in particular the lack of application of the DED by the existent organs of protection, in particular, the recognition that enforced disappearances are continuing violations of human rights and the restrictions to statutes of limitations. Consequently, the first recommendation is to pay more attention to this instrument, whose rules still provide for a good framework of protection.

In the Inter-American system, the most extensive analysis of enforced disappearances has taken place. However, there are serious inconsistencies in the jurisprudence, which should be solved to avoid that victims under the same circumstances receive a different treatment, particularly the declaration of different violations of human rights in similar factual contexts. A system of human rights protection should not have "special" victims and victims of second or third class (or states with fewer cases against them in the IACtHR, in comparison with others state members of the same system). However, the recent reform to the Rules of Procedure of the commission has considerably limited the discretion at the time of submitting cases to the court. The IACtHR has been the organ that settled the most important precedents on enforced disappearances, particularly in *Velasquez Rodriguez.* The jurisprudence has evolved, but the court is more conservative than the commission when deciding the rights violated. In particular, the court denies the violation of the right to juridical personality and the right to the truth; the point of view of the commission deserves support because it is more protective concerning the victim and more complete when addressing the different faces of a disappearance.

The IACtHR is the organ with more elaborate jurisprudence concerning reparations. However, the court addresses reparations from a classical point of view, applying international law as evolved in arbitral jurisprudence on state responsibility. The violation of the project of life is a new concept, but the framework is still similar to *Aloeboetoe,* the most important decision concerning reparations in the Americas. The organs of the Inter-American system should pay more attention to the work of Bassiouni, Van Boven and Joinet concerning the elements of reparation and provide a more proactive approach at when granting reparation.

The HRCBH has initially followed the ECtHR, which is even more conservative than the IACtHR, by strictly interpreting the clause empowering the judicial tribunal to grant "just satisfaction" subsidiarily when the state does not repair the human rights violations in the domestic arena. Both tribunals attach the decisions on reparations to the petitioners' claims. This is criticized by Nowak as judge of the HRCBH, as the clause recognizing competence of the HRCBH to grant reparations is wider than in the other systems of protection, permitting a broader notion of reparation that should follow the guidelines of Bassiouni and Van Boven, instead of the jurisprudence of the European Court. Recent jurisprudence reveals changes to be welcomed, in particular, in the *Srebrenica Cases.*

Consequently, only with a more coherent framework can victims be protected. On this issue, both states and international monitoring organs share the burden of assuming brave solutions, further engagement, and a perspective where the center is placed in the victim.

To conclude, the current practice permits the formulation of the following recommendations.

• A universal and binding framework to deal with enforced disappearances should be developed, with standards equal or higher to those recognized by the DED. Enforced disappearances require a system of "collective guarantee."

• Any definition of enforced disappearances should be supported on the concept contained in the DED and the working definition of the WG.

• The possibility of commission of enforced disappearances by actors not linked to the state should be included in any document to be adopted, following the significative step represented by the ICC Statute. The state is not exempt from responsibility, if it fails to prevent, investigate, prosecute and punish disappearances.

• Enforced disappearances should be recognized as crimes against humanity, in a coherent approach with the ICC Statute.

• The notion of victim should be broad enough as to include not only those disappeared but close family members and, if appropriate, other family members and permanent relations, as well as dependents.

• The recognition of the right of any persons not to be subjected to enforced disappearances should be recognized. Moreover, the right to be protected against enforced disappearances should deserve special attention.

• Even with a definition of enforced disappearances as a right, disappearances should be recognized at a minimum as a violation of the right to physical freedom, humane treatment, and a violation or a serious threat to the right to life, to the right to judicial personality and to judicial guarantees.

• The other victims are also victims of human rights violations, in particular inhumane treatment, disruption of the family life, right to judicial guarantees and right to the truth.

• Enforced disappearances should be recognized as crimes under domestic law. Differentiated regimes should apply to crimes against humanity.

• Enforced disappearances are continuing violations of human rights and continuing illicit acts while the fate and whereabouts of the victim are not clarified.

• Statutes of limitations should not apply when disappearances constitute crimes against humanity. They should be substantial in the other cases.

• Amnesty legislation and pardons should not be applicable to enforced disappearances.

• The guarantee of habeas corpus should be guaranteed under domestic law in all times and circumstances, as the basic instrument to address disappearances. Broad standing should be recognized to present action in favor of the person disappeared by third persons.

• States should investigate without any excuse cases of enforced disappearances, until they find out the fate and whereabouts of the victims and investigate, prosecute and punish perpetrators.

• States should provide full reparation to victims of enforced disappearances, except when the amount of victims or lack of state resources make it impossible.

• Any instrument concerning enforced disappearances should include the right to a remedy as access to justice, restitution, compensation, rehabilitation, satisfaction and guarantees of nonrepetition, as well as the right to the truth.

• The results of investigations should be public, accessible to all, and included in education programs and history books.

• States should include in the criminal legislation the principles of active and passive personality to prosecute perpetrators of enforced disappearances. Moreover, states should include universal jurisdiction, in particular concerning crimes against humanity.

• States should grant the right to the injured party to participate in criminal proceedings to coadjuate the state obligation to investigate, to propose evidentiary measures and to control the engagement of state authorities in the development of the case.

• States should develop diverse preventive mechanisms, in particular, concerning logs of detainees, conditions of detention, places of detention, education of the security and police officers, and a clear system of sanctions and administrative proceedings to denounce irregularities in the security and police forces. In case a binding instrument is adopted, this obligation, as well as the obligation to criminalize enforced disappearance, should have a deadline, established in the same instrument.

• If state remedies fail and the cases reach the international organs of protection, a perspective that pays attention to the victim should be used.

Notes

Chapter 1

1. Krausnick, H., and Broszat, M., *Anatomy of the SS State,* 216 (London: Paladin, 1970), cited by Blanc Altemir, Antonio, *La violación de los derechos humanos fundamentales como crimen internacional,* 335 (Barcelona: Bosch, 1990), (hereafter, Blanc Altemir, *La violación*). E/CN.4/ 2003/WG.22/CRP.2, *Commission de Droits de l'Homme, Groupe de travail intersessions à composition non limitée, chargé d'élaborer un projet d'instrument normatif juridiquement contraignant pour la protection de toutes les personnes contre les disparitions forcées Première session, Project de Rapport, Organisation des travaux,* §4–5, 13 January 2003; E/CN.4/2003/71, *Report of the intersessional open-ended working group to elaborate a draft legally binding normative instrument for the protection of all persons from enforced disappearance,* 12 February 2003; Also E/CN.4/WG.22/ WP.2, October 2004. The Working Group met again 01/31–02/11/05 in Geneva (E/2004/260).

2. IACtHR, *Velasquez Rodriguez* (Merits), series C, no. 4, 29 July 1988, §149 (hereafter *Velasquez Rodriguez*); IACtHR, *Godínez Cruz* (Merits), series C , no. 5, 20 January 1989, §157 (hereafter, *Godínez Cruz*).

3. UN GA, Resolution 3450 (XXX) on persons disappeared in Cyprus (1973); UN GA, Resolution 33/173 on disappeared persons (29 December 1978).

4. The CHR created the WG through Resolution 20 (XXXVI) of 29 February 1980; Andreu Guzmán, Federico, "Le Groupe de travail sur les disparitions forcées des Nations Unies," *IRRC,* vol. 84, no. 848 (December 2002), 803–818.

5. E/CN.4/1994/26, *Question of enforced or involuntary disappearances. Report of the Working Group on Enforced or Involuntary Disappearances* (22 December 1993), §89 et ss.; E/CN.4/1995/ 36, *Question of enforced or involuntary disappearances* (21 December 1994), §57 et ss.; E/CN.4/ 1996/38, *Question of enforced or involuntary disappearances* (15 January 1996), §61 et ss.; E/CN.4/1997/34, *Question of enforced or involuntary disappearances* (13 December 1996), §36 et ss.; E/CN.4/1998/43, *Question of enforced or involuntary disappearances* (12 January 1998), §76 et ss.; E/CN.4/1999/62, *Question of enforced or involuntary disappearances* (28 December 1998), §23 et ss.; E/CN.4/2000/64, *Question of enforced or involuntary disappearances* (21 December 1999), §24 et ss.; E/CN.4/2001/68, *Question of enforced or involuntary disappearances* (18 December 2000), § 33 et ss.; E/CN.4/2002/79, *Question of enforced or involuntary disappearances* (18 January 2002), § 27 et ss.; E/CN.4/2003/70, *Question of enforced or involuntary disappearances* (21 January 2003); E/CN.4/2002/71, *Report submitted by Mr. Manfred Nowak, independent expert charged with examining the existing international criminal and human rights framework for the protection of persons from enforced or involuntary disappearances, pursuant to paragraph 11 of Commission resolution 2001* (hereafter, Report of Manfred Nowak), §46 (8 January 2002), 4.

6. E/CN.4/2002/71, ibid., §70, 30.

7. A/RES/47/133, *Declaration on the Protection of all Persons from Enforced Disappearance* (18 December 1992) (hereafter, DED).

8. Abellán Honrubia, V., "Aspectos Jurídico Internacionales de la Desaparición Forzada de Personas como práctica política del Estado." in *Estudios Jurídicos en Honor del Profesor Octavio Pérez-Vitoria,* I, 16 (Barcelona: Bosch, 1983).

9. Pasqualacci, Jo M., "The Inter-American Human Rights System: Establishing Precedents and Procedure In Human Rights Law," *U. Miami Inter-Am. L. Rev.,* vol. 26, 323 (Winter 1994–1995).

10. A/RES/56/83, *Responsibility of States for internationally wrongful acts—Annex,* Articles 4–11 (28 January 2002).

11. Blanc Altemir, *La violación,* 340.

12. DED.

13. Brownlie asserted that in the practice of the International Court of Justice (ICJ) there are two approaches. In many cases the ICJ assumes

the existence of *opinio juris* on evidence of a general practice, or consensus in the literature, or in previous determinations of the court, or in other international instruments: Brownlie, Ian, *Principles of Public International Law,* 5th ed., 7 (Oxford: Oxford University Press, 1998) (hereafter, Brownlie, *Principles*). However, the same author underscores that, in other cases, the court has adopted a more rigorous approach, calling for more positive evidence of the recognition of the validity of the rules in question in the practice of the state. The approach depends on the nature of the issues and the discretion of the court.

14. Dailler, Patrick, and Allain Pellet, *Droit International Public,* 6th ed., §212, 328 (Paris: L.G.D.J., 1999) (hereafter Dailler, *Droit*), referring to *coutume sauvage,* in opposition to *coutume sage.* The first one obliges to pay attention to the context and circumstances surrounding the adoption of the new rules.

15. American Law Institute, *Restatement (Third) of the Foreign Relations Law of the United States,* §701–702 Reporters' Note 2 (Philadelphia: West Publishing, 1987) (hereafter, *Restatement*), cited by Henkin, Louis, Gerald Neuman, Diane F. Orentlicher, and David Leebron, *Human Rights,* 319 (New York: Foundation Press, 1999) (hereafter, Henkin, *Human Rights*).

16. See the reports cited in note 5.

17. E/CN.4/2001/68, §123 et ss.

18. OEA/Ser.L/V/II.102, Doc. 9 rev. 1, *Third Report on the Situation of Human Rights in Colombia,* §33 (26 February 1999) (hereafter *Third Report Colombia*).

19. Lillich, Richard B. and John M. Paxman, "State Responsibility for Injuries to Aliens Occasioned by Terrorist Activities," *Amer. Univ. L. Rev,* 25–2 (1977), 246.

20. OAS/Ser.P AG/doc.3114/94 rev.1, *The Inter-American Convention on Forced Disappearance of Persons* (9 June 1994) (hereinafter IACFD).

21. ECtHR, *Mahmut Kaya v. Turkey,* application no. 22535/93 (28 March 2000) (hereafter *Mahmut Kaya*). Two persons were kidnapped and their bodies appeared five days later; the case was considered an enforced disappearance.

22. OEA/Ser.L/V/II.74, Doc. 10 Rev. 1, IACHR, *Annual Report 1987–1988* (16 September 1988).

23. *Third Report Colombia,* §33.

24. OEA/Ser.L/V/II.98, Doc. 6, Report no. 11/98, *Samuel de la Cruz Gómez,* Case 10.606 (Guatemala), *Annual Report 1997* (17 February 1998), §19 (hereafter *Samuel Gómez*).

25. OEA/Ser.L/V/II.98, Report no. 41/97, *Estiles Ruiz Dávila,* Case 10.491 (Peru) (17 February 1998) (hereafter, *Ruiz Davila*).

26. *Mahmut Kaya.*

27. OEA/Ser.L/V/II.98, Doc. 6, Report no. 43/97, *Héctor Pérez Salazar,* Case 10.562 (Peru),

Annual Report 1997, §14 (17 February 1998) (hereafter, *Pérez Salazar*); Report no. 42/97, *Angel Escobar Jurado,* Case 10.521, §12 (hereafter *Escobar Jurado*); OEA/Ser.L/V/II.102, Doc. 6 rev., Report no. 19/99, *Pastor Juscamaita Laura,* Case 10.542 (Peru) (hereafter, *Laura*), 16 April 16 1999. At §13, the IACHR asserted that "the essential consideration is that individuals are deprived of their liberty by agents of the State, or with the appearance of legality, followed by the refusal or inability of the State to explain what has happened to the victim or to provide information on his whereabouts." At §18, it underscored that "experience has shown the Commission that the principal cause of forced disappearances lies in the abuse of the powers granted to the armed forces of the State during a state of emergency. Under a state of emergency, arbitrary arrests become more frequent, individuals are arrested without charges and are held without trial or court order, they are deprived of their access to judicial remedies and their arrest is not recorded: all of this in flagrant violation of the rule of law."

28. The ECtHR has not used a multiple-rights approach; see next chapter.

29. ECtHR, *Kurt v. Turkey* (15/1997/799/1002) (25 May 1998), §68 (hereafter *Kurt*).

30. *Convention for the Protection of Human Rights and Fundamental Freedoms,* ETS no. 005, Rome (4 November 1950).

31. E/CN.4/WG.22/WP.2, Working Paper, Geneva, 4–8 October 2004. Compare with E/CN.4/Sub.2/1998/19, *Report of the sessional working group on the administration of justice,* Annex (19 August 1998) (hereafter *Draft IC*).

32. E/CN.4/2003/WG.22/CRP.3, *Intersessional open-ended Working Group to elaborate a draft legally binding normative instrument for the protection of all persons from enforced disappearance* (13 January 2003), §1–2 (hereafter, *Intersessional WG*).

33. Report of Manfred Nowak, §71.

34. A/CONF.183/2/Add.1, *United Nations Diplomatic Conference of Plenipotentiaries on the Establishment of an International Criminal Court, Report of the Preparatory Committee on the Establishment of an International Criminal Court, Addendum* (14 April 1998) (hereafter ICC Statute).

35. PCNICC/2000/1/Add.2, *Elements of Crimes,* 16–17 (2 November 2000); ICC-ASP/1/3, *Assembly of States Parties to the Rome Statute of the International Criminal Court,* 122–123 (3–10 September 2002) (hereafter, *Elements of Crimes*).

36. See, e.g., the definition proposed by Abellán Honrubia.

37. *Intersessional WG,* §15.

38. *Restatement:* "A State violates international law if, as a matter of State policy, it practices, encourages or condones: (a) genocide; (b) slavery

or slave trade; (c) the murder or causing the disappearance of individuals; (d) torture or other cruel, inhuman or degrading treatment or punishment; (e) prolonged arbitrary detention; (f) systematic racial discrimination; (g) a consistent pattern of gross violations of internationally recognized human rights"; Lillich, Richard B., "The United States Constitution and International Human Rights Law," *Harv. Hum. Rts. J.* 53–3; and *Siderman de Blake v. Republic of Argentina,* 965 F.2d 699 (9th Cir. 1992).

39. Brownlie, *Principles,* 5.

40. *See, however, Forti v. Suarez Mason,* 672 F. Supp. 1531 (1987), where the U.S. District Court for the Northern District of California, understanding that the plaintiffs did not cite any case finding that a disappearance constitutes a violation of the law of nations, rejected the analysis of the tort "causing disappearance." The court analyzed that as to apply §1350 of the Alien Tort Act, should be first satisfied that the legal standard to apply was one with universal acceptance and definition. The Court understood that there was no international consensus of a customary international norm. The decision was issued before *Velásquez Rodríguez.*

41. A/CONF.157/23, para. 91, section E, Part II (1993) (hereafter *Conference of Vienna*).

42. UN GA Resolution 217 A (III), *Universal Declaration of Human Rights* (10 December 1948) (hereafter UDHR).

43. A/RES/55/103, *Question of enforced or involuntary disappearances* (2 March 2001), §2; A/RES/57/215, Question of enforced or involuntary disappearances (28 February 2003).

44. Resolution 2002/41, *Question of enforced or involuntary disappearances,* §5 (23 April 2002).

45. E/CN.4/2001/68, §124–125.

47. Report of Manfred Nowak.

47. A/34/583/Add.1 (21 November 1979), §165 and 177.

48. E/CN.4/2001/69/Add.1, *Question of enforced or involuntary disappearances Switzerland,* 6 (14 March 2001).

49. *Third Report Colombia,* §26.

50. E/CN.4/2001/68.

51. A/RES/56/83, *Responsibility of States for internationally wrongful acts,* 28 January 2002, Annex (hereafter *State Responsibility Resolution*); see , State Responsibility, Titles and texts of the draft articles on Responsibility of States for internationally wrongful acts adopted by the Drafting Committee on second reading, Responsibility of States for Internationally Wrongful Acts, 26 July 2001, Article 14, para. 2 and Art. 15.

52. Brownlie, Ian, *State Responsibility,* I, §192 et ss. (Oxford: Oxford University Press, 1983) (hereafter Brownlie, *Responsibility*); Pauwelyn, Joost, "The Concept of a Continuing Violation of an International Obligation: Selected Prob-

lems," *BYIL* 66, 415 (1995); and Wyler, Eric "Quelques Reflexions sur la Realisation dans le Temps du Fait Internationalement Illicite." *RGDIP,* 45, 887 (1991).

53. *Draft IC,* Art. 16.

54. IACtHR, *Blake* (Merits), Series C, no. 36, 24 January 1998 (hereafter, *Blake*).

55. HRCBH, Case No. CH/96/1, *Josip, Bozana and Tomislav Matanovic against the Republika Srpska* (11 July 1997) (hereafter *Matanovic*).

56. *Dayton Peace Agreement for Bosnia and Herzegovina*/General Framework Agreement, and Annexes 4, 6 and 10, 21.11.1995; 14.12.1995, *HRLJ* 18, 309 (1997) (hereafter Dayton Agreement).

57. ECtHR, *De Becker v. Belgium* (27 March 1962).

58. *Velasquez Rodriguez; Godínez Cruz,* id.

59. OEA/Ser.L/V/II.102, Doc. 6 rev., Report no. 56/98, Cases: 10.824 (*Eudalio Lorenzo Manrique*) 11.044 (*Pedro Herminio Yauri Bustamante*) 11.124 (*Eulogio Viera Estrada*) 11.125 (*Héctor Esteban Medina Bonet*) 11.175 (*Justiniano Najarro Rua*), Peru, §127 (16 April 1999) (hereafter, *Eudalio Manrique*).

60. *Mahmut Kaya.*

61. ECtHR, *Timurtaş v. Turkey,* Application no. 23531/94, §115 (13 June 2000) (hereafter, *Timurtaş*).

62. ECtHR, *Taş v. Turkey,* Application no. 24396/94, § 152, 169 (14 November 2000) (hereafter, *Taş*).

63. ECtHR, *Ylhan v. Turkey,* Application no. 22277/93 (27 June 2000) (hereafter *Ilhan*).

64. ECtHR, *Salman v. Turkey,* Application no. 21986/93 (27 June 2000) (hereafter *Salman*).

65. AG/RES 443 (IX-0/79) (31 October 1979); AG/RES 510 (X-0/80) (27 November 1980); AG/RES 618 (XII-0/82) (20 November 1982); AG/RES 666 (XIII-0/83) (18 November 1983); AG/RES 742 (XIV-0/84) (17 November 1984); and AG/RES 890 (XVII-0/87) (14 November 1987).

66. IACHR, *Annual Report 1978,* 24–27; IACHR, *Annual Report, 1980–1981,* 113–114; IACHR, *Case of Disappeared Persons in Argentina,* Resolution no. 1/83, Argentina (8 April 1983); OAS/Ser.L/V/II.61; Doc. 22, rev. 1, 46–47 (27 September 18 1983); IACHR, *Case of Disappeared Persons in Chile,* Resolution no. 11/83, Chile (1 July 1983); OAS/Ser.L/V/II.61; Doc. 22, rev. 1, 47–49 (27 September 1983); IACHR, *Gallardo et al.,* Resolution no. 13/83, Costa Rica (30 June 1983) (hereafter *Gallardo*); OAS/Ser.L/V/II.61; Doc. 22, rev. 1, 49–53 (27 September 1983); IACHR, *Ford et al.,* Resolution no. 17/83, Case 7575, El Salvador (30 June 1983); OAS/Ser.L/V/II.61; Doc. 22, rev. 1, 53–63 (27 September 1983); IACHR, *Bazile et al.,* Resolution no. 37/82, Case 2401, Haiti (9

March 1982); OAS/Ser.L/V/II.61; Doc. 22, rev. 1, 63–67 (27 September 1983); IACHR, Resolution no. 25/86, *Cases of Disappearance of Persons in Guatemala* (9 April 1986); OEA/Ser.L/II.68, Doc. 8, rev. 1, 37–40 (26 September 1986); OEA/Ser.L/V/II.71, Doc. 9, rev. 1, *Annual Report, 1986–1987,* 277–84 (22 September 1987); and in Country Reports: OEA/Serv. L/V/II.49, doc. 19, 1980 (Argentina), OEA/Ser.L/V/II.66, doc. 17, 1985 (Chile), and OEA/Ser.L/V/II.66, doc. 16, 1985 (Guatemala).

67. In the Inter-American system *crime against humanity* is used not in relation to a systematic or widespread human rights against civil population but to a human rights violation that is abominable, for example, against humanity.

68. See *Velasquez Rodriguez;* Id., *Godínez Cruz,* §162.

69. *Third Report Colombia,* §30.

70. *Missing persons* is used in the broadest sense: The Missing/Conf/02.2003/EN/82, *The Missing: Action to resolve the problem of people unaccounted for as a result of armed conflict or internal violence and to assist their families International Conference of Governmental and Non-Governmental Experts* Geneva, 19–21 February 2003, Working Group on the Observations and Recommendations Report by the Chairman Mr. Nicolas Michel, Director, Directorate of Public International Law, Federal Department of Foreign Affairs, Switzerland, at 1 (hereafter *The Missing*).

71. Report of Manfred Nowak, §71, 30.

Chapter 2

1. *Velasquez Rodriguez,* §134. A student "was violently detained without a warrant for his arrest by members of the National Office of Investigations (DNI) and G-2 of the Armed Forces of Honduras." He was "accused of alleged political crimes and subjected to harsh interrogation and cruel torture." There was no further news about him.

2. E/CN.4/2002/71,§75.

3. *Velasquez Rodríguez,* §150, and *Godínez Cruz,* §158.

4. *Velasquez Rodríguez,* §155. See *Godínez Cruz,* §163.

5. A/RES/47/133.

6. OAS/Ser.P AG/doc.3114/94 Rev. 1.

7. International Covenant on Civil and Political Rights, General Assembly Resolution 2200A (XXI) of 16 December 1966.

8. American Convention on Human Rights, Inter-American Specialized Conference on Human Rights, San José, Costa Rica, 22 November 1969.

9. *Godínez Cruz,* §169 et ss.

10. *Velasquez Rodriguez,* §162.

11. Id., §164.

12. Id., §166 et ss.

13. Jochen A. Frowein. "The European and the American Conventions on Human Rights; A Comparison," *Human Rights Law Journal,* vol. 1 no. 1–4, 44, at 45 (1980).

14. E/CN.4/2003/WG.22/CRP.2, §14.

15. E/CN.4/2001/68, §31.

16. OEA/Ser.L/V/II.98, Doc. 6, Report No. 40/97 *Camilo Alarcón* et al., Cases 10.941, 10.942, 10.944, and 10.945 (Peru), IACHR, 17 February 1998, §82.

17. E/CN.4/2001/69/Add.1, p. 6.

18. OEA/Ser.L/V/II.98, Doc. 6, Report No. 1/97, *Manuel García Franco,* Case 10.258 (Ecuador), *Annual Report 1997,* 17 February 1998, §76.

19. OEA/Ser.L/V/II.66, Doc.17, *Report on the Situation of Human Rights in Chile,* 9 September 1985, §125.

20. OEA/Ser.L/V/II.106, Doc. 3, Report No. 7/00, *Amparo Tordecilla Trujillo,* Case 10.337 (Colombia), IACHR, 24 February 2000. Id., OEA/Ser./L/V/II.111, doc. 20 rev., Report No. 60/01, *Ileana del Rosario Solares Castillo* et al., Case 9111 (Guatemala), IACHR, 4 April 2001, §31.

21. *Caballero Delgado & Santana Case* (Merits), Judgment of 8 December 1995, IACtHR, Ser. C, No. 22 (1995).

22. *Godínez Cruz,* p. 12; *Garrido and Baigorria Case,* 2 February 1996, IACtHR, Ser. C, No. 26 (1996).

23. OEA/Ser.L/V/II.76, Doc. 10, *Annual Report 1988–1989,* Report No. 10/89, Case 9802, Peru, 14 April 1989; OEA/Ser.L/V/II.79.rev. 1, Doc. 12, *Annual Report 1990–1991,* Report No. 2/91, Case 10.000, El Salvador, 13 February 1991, §9; Report No. 60/01 (Solares), §33; Id., *Annual Report 1988–1989,* Resolution No. 9/89 Case 9799; Id., *Annual Report 1990–1991,* Report No. 76/90, Case 10.202; IACHR, Luis F. Lalinde, Report No. 24/87, Case 9620, Colombia, 16 September 1988.

24. *Çakici v. Turkey* (Application No. 23657/94), ECtHR, 8 July 1999; *Akdeniz v. Turkey,* Application No. 23954/94, ECtHR, 31 May 2001

25. Communication No. 449/1991: Dominican Republic, 10/08/94, CCPR/C/51/D/449/1991; Communication No. 563/1993: Colombia, 13/11/95, CCPR/C/55/D/563/1993; Communication No. 540/1993: Peru, 16/04/96, CCPR/C/56/D/540/1993.

26. OEA/Ser.L/V/II.79.rev.1, *Annual Report 1990–1991,* Report No. 60/90, Case 9956, 13 February 1991; Case 10.464; OEA/ser. L/V/II.68, doc. 8, rev. 1, *Annual Report 1985–1986,* Case 9233, 105, (1986); Id., *Annual Report 1990–1991,* Report No. 1/91, Case 9999; Id., Report

No. 68/90, Case 9988, Report No. 3/91, Case 10.001, Report No. 75/90, Case 10.163, Report No. 79/90, Case 10.460, Report No. 88/90, Case 10.487, Report No. 89/90, Case 10.493, Report No. 85/90, Case 10.470, Report No. 55/90, Case 9935.

27. Communication No. 30/1978: Uruguay, 29/03/82, CCPR/C/15/D/30/1978; Communication No. 612/1995: Colombia, 19/08/97, CCPR/C/60/D/612/1995.

28. *Neira Alegría & al. Case,* January 19, 1995, IACtHR, Series C, No. 20 (1995).

29. OEA/Ser.L/V/II.79. rev. 1, *Annual Report 1990–1991,* 13 February 1999, Report No. 9/90, Case 9804; Report No. 10/90, Case 9805; Report No. 11/90, Case 9806; Report No. 12/90, Case 9807; Report No. 13/90, Case 9809; Report No. 14/90, Case 9814; Report No. 15/90, Case 9815; Report No. 16/90, Case 9816; Report No. 17/90, Case 9817; Report No. 18/90, Case 9824; Report No. 19/90, Case 9842; Report No. 20/90, Case 9859; Report No. 21/90, Case 9878; Report No. 22/90, Case 9881; Report No. 23/90, Case 9883; Report No. 24/90, Case 10.014; Report No. 26/90, Case 10.166; Report No. 27/90, Case 10.183; Report No. 28/90, Case 10.185; Report No. 29/90, Case 10.186; Report No. 30/90, Case 10.220; Report No. 33/90, Case 10.260; Report No. 32/90, Case 10.222; Report No. 34/90, Case 10.263; Report No. 35/90, Case 10.278; Report No. 37/90, Case 10.308; Report No. 38/90, Case 10.317; Report No. 39/90, Case 10.321; Report No. 40/90, Case 10.326; Report No. 41/90, Case 10.370; Report No. 42/90, Case 10.380; Report No. 9/91.

30. El Salvador, Case 10.323 — Mesias Elias Hernandez Anzora, Report No. 12/92, *Annual Report 1991,* IACHR, 4 February 1992; Id., El Salvador, Case 10.571— Erik Felipe Romero Canales, Report No. 15/92.

31. OEA/ser. L/V/II.85, doc. 9 rev., *Annual Report 1993,* Cases 11.106, 11.108, 11.109, 11.115, 11.119, 11.121, 232.

32. OEA/Ser./L/V/II.83, doc. 14 corr. 1, *Annual Report 1992–1993,* Report No. 10/93, Teófilo Rimac Capcha, Case 10.443, Peru, 12 March 1993; Id., Report No. 12/93, Simmerman Rafael Navarro, Case 10.531, Peru; Report No. 8/92, Cases 10.227 and 10.333, El Salvador, 4 February 1992, Julio Ernesto Fuentes Perez, William Fernandez Rivera, and Raquel Fernandez Rivera; Report No. 24/93, Olga Esther Bernal Dueñas, Case 10.537, Colombia, *Annual Report 1993;* Report No. 33/92, Alirio de Jesús Pedraza, Case 10.581, Colombia, *Annual Report 1992.*

33. *Castillo Páez Case,* 3 November 1997, IACtHR, Ser. C, No. 34 (1997).

34. *Calloccunto v. Peru* [OEA/Ser.L/V/II.85, *Annual Report 1993,* Report No. 37/93, Case 10.563 (1 February 1993)]. *Martín Javier Roca Casas v. Peru* (OEA/Ser.L/V/II.98 Doc. 6, Report No. 39/97, Case 11.233, Peru, *Annual Report 1997,* 98th Session, 17 February 1998); *Oscar Manuel Gramajo López v. Guatemala* (OEA/Ser./ L/V/II.111 doc. 20 rev., Report No. 58/01, Case 9207, 16 April 2001); *Catalán Nicoleo v. Chile* (OEA/Ser./L/V/II.111, doc. 20 rev., Report No. 61/01, Case 11.771, 16 April 2001).

35. *Caballero Delgado & Santana; Paniagua Morales,* 8 March 1998, Series C, No. 37.

36. IACtHR, *El Caracazo,* Series C, No. 58, 11 November 1999.

37. Case 1757, IACHR. 136 (1974) (Ten Years of Activities 1971–81).

38. American Declaration of the Rights and Duties of Man, Approved by the Ninth International Conference of American States, Bogotá, Colombia, 1948.

39. See note 37, Cases 1702, 1748, 1755, at 128.

40. OEA/Ser.L/V/II.102, Doc. 9 rev. 1, §32–33.

41. OEA/Ser.L/V/II.106, Doc. 3, *Isabela Velásquez et al.,* Report No. 40/00, Case 10.588, 10.608, 10.796, 10.856, 10.921, Guatemala, 13 April 2000.

42. *Bamaca Velasquez (Merits),* Judgment of 25 November 2000, IACtHR, Series C, No. 70 (2000).

43. *Annual Report 1996,* Francisco Pratdesaba, Report No. 53/96, Case 8074, Guatemala 6 December 1996; Luis Gustavo Marroquín, Report No. 54/96, Case 8075, Guatemala, 6 December 1996; Axel Lemus García, Report No. 55/96, Case 8076, Guatemala; Ana Orellana Stormont, Report No. 56/96, Case 9120, Guatemala; Report No. 11/98 (Samuel de la Cruz Gómez); Francisco Guarcas Cipriano, Report No. 22/98, Case 11.275, Guatemala, 2 March 1998; Report No. 56/98 (Manrique); Raúl Zevallos Loayza, Report No. 52/99, Cases: 10.544, 10.745, 11.098, Peru, 16 April 1999; David Palomino Morales, Report No. 53/99, Cases: 10.551, 10.803, 10.821, 10.906, 11.180, 11.322, Peru, 16 April 1999; Romer Morales Zegarra, Report No. 57/99, Cases: 10.827, 11.984, Peru, 16 April 1999; see Report No. 40/00; Alcides Julio César et al., Report No. 43/00, Case 10.670, Peru, 13 April 2000; Report No. 44/00, Americo Zavala Martínez, Case 10.820, Peru, 13 April 2000; Report No. 45/00, Manuel Mónago, Case 10.826, Peru, 13 April 2000; Report No. 46/00, Manuel Meneses, Case 10.904, Peru, 13 April 2000; Report No. 47/00, Manuel Pacotaype, Case 10.908, Peru, 13 April 2000; OEA/Ser./L/V/II.111, doc. 20 rev., Report No. 112/00; Yone Cruz Ocalio, Case 11.099, Peru, 4 December 2000.

44. Case No. CH/99/3196, *Palic v. Republika Srpska,* 11 January 2001.

45. Case No. CH/01/8365 et al., *the "Srebrenica Cases"* (49 applications), 7 March 2003, §173 et ss.

46. Optional Protocol to the International Covenant on Civil and Political Rights, GA Resolution 2200A (21) of 16 December 1966.

47. See the jurisprudence cited in notes 22 to 44.

48. See the jurisprudence cited in notes 22 to 25, 29, 32–44.

49. CONADEP, *Nunca Más–Informe de la Comisión Nacional sobre la Desaparición de Personas,* Eudeba, Buenos Aires, 5th ed., 1997.

50. See the jurisprudence cited in notes 22–44.

51. See the jurisprudence cited in notes 40–44.

52. See note 44, *Palic,* and 45, *Matanovic.*

53. See the jurisprudence cited in notes 29–42.

Chapter 3

1. HRI/GEN/1/Rev.1 at 6, *Compilation of General Comments and General Recommendations Adopted by Human Rights Treaty Bodies,* HRC, General Comment 6, Article 6 (16th session, 1982), 1994.

2. Manfred Nowak, *U.N. Covenant on Civil and Political Rights,* N. P. Engel, Kehl, 1993, 105 et ss.

3. Id., 106.

4. A/RES/47/133.

5. *Principles on the Effective Prevention and Investigation of Extra-legal, Arbitrary and Summary Executions,* Recommended by Economic and Social Council resolution 1989/65 of 24 May 1989.

6. Convention (I) for the Amelioration of the Condition of the Wounded and Sick in Armed Forces in the Field, Geneva, 12 August 1949; Convention (II) for the Amelioration of the Condition of Wounded, Sick and Shipwrecked Members of Armed Forces at Sea, Geneva, 12 August 1949; Convention (III) relative to the Treatment of Prisoners of War, Geneva, 12 August 1949; Convention (IV) relative to the Protection of Civilian Persons in Time of War, Geneva, 12 August 1949.

7. Protocol Additional to the Geneva Conventions of 12 August 1949, and relating to the Protection of Victims of Non-International Armed Conflicts (Protocol II), 8 June 1977.

8. Protocol Additional to the Geneva Conventions of 12 August 1949, and relating to the Protection of Victims of International Armed Conflicts (Protocol I), 8 June 1977.

9. *Godínez Cruz Case,* §165.

10. Id., §198.

11. See also *Trujillo Oroza* (Merits), 26 January 2000, IACtHR, Series C, No. 64; *Bena-vides Cevallos* (Merits), 19 June 1998, Series C, No. 38 (1998); *Garrido and Baigorria;* and *El Caracazo.*

12. *Neira Alegría et al., Durand and Ugarte,* Series C, No. 68, 16 August 2000, §71.

13. Id., §74.

14. Id.

15. Id., §76.

16. *Castillo Páez Case,* §68.

17. Id., §73

18. *Blake,* §84.

19. *Paniagua Morales et al.,* §119 et ss.

20. *Villagrán Morales et al.,* 19 November 1999, IACtHR, No. 63, §137 et ss.; Id. in HRLJ 21 (2000), 195.

21. IACtHR, *Villagrán Morales et al. Case, Reparations* (Article 63 of the American Convention of Human Rights), 26 May 2001, §92.

22. *Bamaca Velasquez* (Merits), §167 et ss.

23. *Kurt v. Turkey,* §106–107.

24. ECtHR, *McCann and others v. the United Kingdom,* 27/09/1995; ECtHR, *Kaya v. Turkey,* 19/02/1998.

25. *Kurt v. Turkey,* § 108.

26. Id., §109.

27. Id., p. 27 §68.

28. *Ertak v. Turkey* (Application No. 20764/92), ECtHR, 9 May 2000.

29. Id., §131.

30. Id., §134.

31. *Çakici v. Turkey,* p. 66.

32. Id., §85.

33. Id., §96.

34. Id., §87.

35. *Mahmut Kaya v. Turkey,* §84.

36. Id., p. 24.

37. Id., §87.

38. Id., §89.

39. Id., §91.

40. Id., §96.

41. Id., §108–109.

42. *Timurtaş v. Turkey,* §81.

43. Id., §82.

44. Id., §83.

45. Id., §84.

46. Id., §86.

47. Id., §90.

48. *Orhan v. Turkey,* Application No. 25656/94, 18 June 2002, §331 et ss., §348.

49. See Chapter I; *Timurtaş v. Turkey,* §63.

50. See Chapter I; *Taş v. Turkey,* §64.

51. Id., §67.

52. Id., §68.

53. Id., §69.

54. Id., §71.

55. *Salman v. Turkey,* §14.

56. Id., §19.

57. Id., §20.

58. Id., §21.

59. Id., §24.

60. Id., §26.
61. *Çiçek v. Turkey* (Application No. 25704/94), ECtHR, 27 February 2001.
62. Id., §136.
63. Id., §146.
64. Id., §146.
65. Id., §147.
66. Id., §150.
67. *Cyprus v. Turkey*, Application No. 25781/94, ECtHR, 10 May 2001.
68. Id.
69. *Bilgin v. Turkey*, Application No. 25659/94, ECtHR, 17 July 2001.
70. Id., §132.
71. Id., §137–138.
72. Id., §140, p. 82.
73. Id., §141.
74. See Communication No. 30/1978, §14, 11.2.
75. CCPR/C/37/D/181/1984, Communication No. 181/1984 (Jurisprudence) Colombia, (22/11/89.)
76. Id., §10 and 11.
77. Communication No. 449/1991.
78. Id., §5.5.
79. Id., §5.6.
80. Communication No. 563/1993.
81. Id., §8.3.
82. Communication No. 612/1995.
83. Id., §8.3.
84. Communication No. 540/1993.
85. Id., §8.3.
86. Rules of Procedure of the Inter-American Commission on Human Rights, 4–8 December 2000.
87. OEA/Ser.L/V/II.96, Doc. 10, rev. 1, *Report on the Situation of Human Rights in Ecuador,* 24 April 1997.
88. Id., *Report on the Situation of Human Rights in Dominican Republic,* §135.
89. OEA/Ser.L/V/II.66, Doc. 17, §134 et ss.
90. Id., §181.
91. OEA/ser. L/V/II.47, Doc. 13 rev. 1, *Patrick Rice & Fatima Edelmira Cabrera,* Case 2450, IACHR 33 (1978), *Annual Report 1978;* see id., *Esteban Cabrera et al.*, Case 2291 and Case 2662.
92. Report No. 24/93.
93. *Annual Report 1991,* Report No. 1/92, García Villamizar, Case 10.235, IACHR, 6 February 1992.
94. Report No. 7/00 (Tordecilla).
95. OEA/Ser.L/V/II.98, Doc. 6, Report No. 3/98, Medina Charry, Case 11.221, Annual Report 1997, 17 February 1998.
96. Id., §39.
97. Case 1790, Enrique Paris Roa, IACHR, 147 (1977) (Ten Years of Activities 1971–81).
98. Report No. 1/97 (García Franco).
99. OEA/Ser.L/V/II.74, Doc. 10, rev. 1, Report No. 28/88, Rivas Hernandez, Case 9844, IACHR, 13 September 1988, 140–145; Report No. 1/91; Report No. 2/91; Report No. 3/91.
100. Annual Report *1990–1991,* Report No. 49/90, Case 9918; Report No. 50/90, Case 9922; Report No. 51/90, Case 9925; Report No. 52/90, Case 9926; Report No. 53/90, Case 9932; Report No. 54/90, Case 9933; Report No. 56/90, Case 9936; Report No. 55/90; Report No. 57/90, Case 9946; Report No. 58/90, Case 9948; Report No. 59/90, Case 9955; see Report No. 60/90; Report No. 61/90, Case 9960; Report No. 62/90, Case 9961; Report No. 63/90, Case 9963; Report No. 64/90, Case 9964; Report No. 65/90, Case 9967; Report No. 66/90, Case 9968; Report No. 67/90, Case 9983; Report No. 68/90; Report No. 69/90, Case 9989; Report No. 70/90, Case 9991; Report No. 71/90, Case 9992; Report No. 30/96, Arnoldo Cruz, Case 10.897, *Annual Report* 1996, §44; Report No. 53/96; Report 54/96, §27; Report 55/96, §25; Report 56/96, §29; Report No. 11/98 (Samuel de la Cruz Gómez); Report No. 22/98, §34; Report No. 40/00, §70; Report No. 58/01, §29; Id., Report No. 60/01 (Solares).
101. Report No. 7/91, Case 9905, 17 February 1991.
102. OEA/Ser.L/V/II.100, Doc. 7, rev. 1, *Report on the Situation of Human Rights in Mexico,* 24 September 1998, §145 et ss., in particular §161.
103. OEA/ser. L/V/II.61, Doc. 22, rev. 1, *Annual Report 1982–1983,* Case 7245, 105 (1982).
104. Report No. 13/90, Case 9809; Report No. 32/90; Report No. 34/90; Report No. 37/90; Report No. 42/90; Report No. 75/90; Report No. 77/90, Case 10.203; Report No. 79/90; *Id.,* Report No. 81/90, Case 10.463, 22 February 1991; Report No. 83/90, Case 10.466; Report No. 84/90, Case 10.467; Report No. 85/90; Report No. 86/90, Case 10.475; Report No. 88/90; Report No. 89/90; Report No. 9/91. See also Report No. 40/97 (Alarcón), §78 and §81; Report No. 41/97 (Ruiz Davila), §19; Report No. 42/97 (Escobar Jurado), §17; Report No. 43/97 (Pérez Salazar), §12; Report No. 56/98 (Manrique), §107; Report No. 19/99 (Juscamaita Laura), §21; Report No. 51/99, Cases 10.471, 11.014, 11.067, 11.070, §113; Report No. 52/99, §89; Report No. 53/99, §115; Report No. 54/99, Cases 10.807, 10.808, 10.809, 10.810, 10.879, 11.307, §113; Report No. 55/99, Cases 10.815, 10.905, 10.981, 10.995, 11.042, 11.136, §107; Report No. 57/99, §73; Report No. 43/00, §47; Report No. 44/00, §40.; Report No. 45/00, §41; Report No. 46/00, §50; Report No. 47/00, §48; Report No. 80/90, Case 10.461, 22 February 1991; Report No. 112/00, §40.
105. *Kurt.*
106. *Ertak.*
107. *Timurtaş.*

108. *Taş.*
109. *Cyprus v. Turkey.*
110. *Rafael Mojica* and *Velasquez Rodriguez.*

Chapter 4

1. HRI/GEN/1/Rev.1 at 6, *Compilation of General Comments and General Recommendations Adopted by Human Rights Treaty Bodies,* HRC, General Comment 6, Article 6 (16th session, 1982), 1994.
2. Manfred Nowak, *U.N. Covenant on Civil and Political Rights,* N. P. Engel, Kehl, 1993, 105 et ss.
3. Id., 106.
4. A/RES/47/133.
5. *Principles on the Effective Prevention and Investigation of Extra-legal, Arbitrary and Summary Executions,* Recommended by Economic and Social Council resolution 1989/65 of 24 May 1989.
6. Convention (I) for the Amelioration of the Condition of the Wounded and Sick in Armed Forces in the Field, Geneva, 12 August 1949; Convention (II) for the Amelioration of the Condition of Wounded, Sick and Shipwrecked Members of Armed Forces at Sea, Geneva, 12 August 1949; Convention (III) relative to the Treatment of Prisoners of War, Geneva, 12 August 1949; Convention (IV) relative to the Protection of Civilian Persons in Time of War, Geneva, 12 August 1949.
7. Protocol Additional to the Geneva Conventions of 12 August 1949, and relating to the Protection of Victims of Non-International Armed Conflicts (Protocol II), 8 June 1977.
8. Protocol Additional to the Geneva Conventions of 12 August 1949, and relating to the Protection of Victims of International Armed Conflicts (Protocol I), 8 June 1977.
9. *Godínez Cruz Case,* §165.
10. Id., §198.
11. See also *Trujillo Oroza* (Merits), 26 January 2000, IACtHR, Series C, No. 64; *Benavides Cevallos* (Merits), 19 June 1998, Series C, No. 38 (1998); *Garrido and Baigorria;* and *El Caracazo.*
12. *Neira Alegría et al., Durand and Ugarte,* Series C, No. 68, 16 August 2000, §71.
13. Id., §74.
14. Id.
15. Id., §76.
16. *Castillo Páez Case,* §68.
17. Id., §73
18. *Blake,* §84.
19. *Paniagua Morales et al.,* §119 et ss.
20. *Villagrán Morales et al.,* 19 November 1999, IACtHR, No. 63, §137 et ss.; Id. in HRLJ 21 (2000), 195.

21. IACtHR, *Villagrán Morales et al. Case, Reparations* (Article 63 of the American Convention of Human Rights), 26 May 2001, §92.
22. *Bamaca Velasquez* (Merits), §167 et ss.
23. *Kurt v. Turkey,* §§106–107.
24. ECtHR, *McCann and others v. the United Kingdom,* 27/09/1995; ECtHR, *Kaya v. Turkey,* 19/02/1998.
25. *Kurt v. Turkey,* § 108.
26. Id., §109.
27. Id., p. 27 §68.
28. *Ertak v. Turkey* (Application No. 20764/92), ECtHR, 9 May 2000.
29. Id., §131.
30. Id., §134.
31. *Çakici v. Turkey,* p. 66.
32. Id., §85.
33. Id., §96.
34. Id., §87.
35. *Mahmut Kaya v. Turkey,* §84.
36. Id., p. 24.
37. Id., §87.
38. Id., §89.
39. Id., §91.
40. Id., §96.
41. Id., §108–109.
42. *Timurtaş v. Turkey,* §81.
43. Id., §82.
44. Id., §83.
45. Id., §85.
46. Id., §86.
47. Id., §90.
48. *Orhan v. Turkey,* Application No. 25656/94, 18 June 2002, §331 et ss., §348.
49. See Chapter I; *Timurtaş v. Turkey,* §63.
50. See Chapter I; *Taş v. Turkey,* §64.
51. Id., §65.
52. Id., §67.
53. Id., §68.
54. Id., §69.
55. Id., §71.
56. *Salman v. Turkey,* §14.
57. Id., §19.
58. Id., §20.
59. Id., §21.
60. Id., §24.
61. Id., §26.
62. *Çiçek v. Turkey* (Application No. 25704/94), ECtHR, 27 February 2001.
63. Id., §136.
64. Id., §146.
65. Id., §146.
66. Id., §147.
67. Id., §150.
68. *Cyprus v. Turkey,* Application No. 25781/94, ECtHR, 10 May 2001.
69. Id.
70. *Bilgin v. Turkey,* Application No. 25659/94, ECtHR, 17 July 2001.
71. Id., §132.

72. Id., §137–138.
73. Id., §140, p. 82.
74. Id., §141.
75. See Communication No. 30/1978, §14, 11.2.
76. CCPR/C/37/D/181/1984, Communication No. 181/1984 (Jurisprudence) Colombia, (22/11/89.)
77. Id., §10 and 11.
78. Communication No. 449/1991.
79. Id., §5.5.
80. Id., §5.6.
81. Communication No. 563/1993.
82. Id., §8.3.
83. Communication No. 612/1995.
84. Id., §8.3.
85. Communication No. 540/1993.
86. Id., §8.3.
87. Rules of Procedure of the Inter-American Commission on Human Rights, 4–8 December 2000.
88. OEA/Ser.L/V/II.96, Doc. 10, rev. 1, *Report on the Situation of Human Rights in Ecuador,* 24 April 1997.
89. Id., *Report on the Situation of Human Rights in Dominican Republic,* §135.
90. OEA/Ser.L/V/II.66, Doc. 17, §134 et ss.
91. Id., §181.
92. OEA/ser. L/V/II.47, Doc. 13 rev. 1, *Patrick Rice & Fatima Edelmira Cabrera,* Case 2450, IACHR 33 (1978), *Annual Report 1978;* see id., *Esteban Cabrera et al.,* Case 2291 and Case 2662.
93. Report No. 24/93.
94. *Annual Report 1991,* Report No. 1/92, García Villamizar, Case 10.235, IACHR, 6 February 1992.
95. Report No. 7/00 (Tordecilla).
96. OEA/Ser.L/V/II.98, Doc. 6, Report No.3/98, Medina Charry, Case 11.221, Annual Report 1997, 17 February 1998.
97. Id., §39.
98. Case 1790, Enrique Paris Roa, IACHR, 147 (1977) (Ten Years of Activities 1971–81).
99. Report No. 1/97 (García Franco).
100. OEA/Ser.L/V/II.74, Doc. 10, rev. 1, Report No. 28/88, Rivas Hernandez, Case 9844, IACHR, 13 September 1988, 140–145; Report No. 1/91; Report No. 2/91; Report No. 3/91.
101. Annual Report *1990–1991,* Report No. 49/90, Case 9918; Report No. 50/90, Case 9922; Report No. 51/90, Case 9925; Report No. 52/90, Case 9926; Report No. 53/90, Case 9932; Report No. 54/90, Case 9933; Report No. 56/90, Case 9936; Report No. 55/90; Report No. 57/90, Case 9946; Report No. 58/90, Case 9948; Report No. 59/90, Case 9955; see Report No. 60/90; Report No. 61/90, Case 9960; Report No. 62/90, Case 9961; Report No. 63/90, Case 9963; Report No. 64/90, Case

9964; Report No. 65/90, Case 9967; Report No. 66/90, Case 9968; Report No. 67/90, Case 9983; Report No. 68/90; Report No. 69/90, Case 9989; Report No. 70/90, Case 9991; Report No. 71/90, Case 9992; Report No. 30/96, Arnoldo Cruz, Case 10.897, *Annual Report* 1996, §44; Report No. 53/96; Report No. 54/96, §27; Report 55/96, §25; Report 56/96, §29; Report No. 11/98 (Samuel de la Cruz Gómez); Report No. 22/98, §34; Report No. 40/00, §70; Report No. 58/01, §29; Id., Report No. 60/01 (Solares).
102. Report No. 7/91, Case 9905, 17 February 1991.
103. OEA/Ser.L/V/II.100, Doc. 7, rev. 1, *Report on the Situation of Human Rights in Mexico,* 24 September 1998, §145 et ss., in particular §161.
104. OEA/ser. L/V/II.61, Doc. 22, rev. 1, *Annual Report 1982–1983,* Case 7245, 105 (1982).
105. Report No. 13/90, Case 9809; Report No. 32/90; Report No. 34/90; Report No. 37/90; Report No. 42/90; Report No. 75/90; Report No. 77/90, Case 10.203; Report No. 79/90; *Id.,* Report No. 81/90, Case 10.463, 22 February 1991; Report No. 83/90, Case 10.466; Report No. 84/90, Case 10.467; Report No. 85/90; Report No. 86/90, Case 10.475; Report No. 88/90; Report No. 89/90; Report No. 9/91. See also Report No. 40/97 (Alarcón), §78 and §81; Report No. 41/97 (Ruiz Davila), §19; Report No. 42/97 (Escobar Jurado), §17; Report No. 43/97 (Pérez Salazar), §12; Report No. 56/98 (Manrique), §107; Report No. 19/99 (Juscamaita Laura), §21; Report No. 51/99, Cases 10.471, 11.014, 11.067, 11.070, §113; Report No. 52/99, §89; Report No. 53/99, §115; Report No. 54/99, Cases 10.807, 10.808, 10.809, 10.810, 10.879, 11.307, §113; Report No. 55/99, Cases 10.815, 10.905, 10.981, 10.995, 11.042, 11.136, §107; Report No. 57/99, §73; Report No. 43/00, §47; Report No. 44/00, §40.; Report No. 45/00, §41; Report No. 46/00, §50; Report No. 47/00, §48; Report No. 80/90, Case 10.461, 22 February 1991; Report No. 112/00, §40.
106. *Kurt.*
107. *Ertak.*
108. *Timurtaş.*
109. *Taş.*
110. *Cyprus v. Turkey.*
111. *Rafael Mojica* and *Velasquez Rodriguez.*

Chapter 5

1. E/CN.4/Sub.2/1994/23, *The Administration of Justice and the Human Rights of Detainees: Question of Human Rights and States of Emergency, Seventh revised annual report and list of States which, since 1 January 1985, have proclaimed, extended or terminated a state of emergency,*

presented by Mr. Leandro Despouy, Special Rapporteur appointed pursuant to Economic and Social Council resolution 1985/37*/§14 (3 June 1994).

2. Manfred Nowak, at 129.

3. For international armed conflict: I GC, Article 12; II GC, Article 12, III GC, Article 13, IV GC, Article 32; AP I, Article 75.2.a.ii. Concerning internal armed conflict: common Article 3.1.a to the four GC and AP II, Article 4.2.a.

4. Code of Conduct for Law Enforcement Officials Adopted by General Assembly, resolution 34/169 of 17 December 1979.

5. *Velasquez Rodriguez* (Merits).

6. *Godínez Cruz*, §164, 186, 197.

7. *Caballero Delgado & Santana*, §65.

8. *Castillo Páez*, §62.

9. Id., §66.

10. *Neira Alegría*, §60.

11. Id., §86.

12. *Paniagua Morales et al.*, §133.

13. *Blake*, §110.

14. Id., §112.

15. Id., §114.

16. Id., §115.

17. Id., §116. *Trujillo Oroza* (Merits); *Benavides Cevallos; Garrido and Baigorria Case;* and *El Caracazo*.

18. *Villagrán Morales et al.*, §148 et ss.

19. Id., §239.

20. Id.

21. *Bamaca Velasquez* (Merits).

22. Id., §148.

23. Id., §150.

24. Id., §154.

25. Id., §158.

26. Id., §160.

27. *Kurt v. Turkey*, §68.

28. Communication No. 107/1981, §14.

29. *Kurt v. Turkey*, §114.

30. *Çakici v. Turkey*, §92.

31. Id., §98.

32. *Mahmut Kaya v. Turkey*, §117.

33. Id., §119.

34. Id., §115.

35. Id., §116.

36. *Timurtaş v. Turkey*, §94.

37. Id., §95.

38. Id., §96.

39. Id., §98.

40. *Orhan v. Turkey*, §360.

41. *Taş v. Turkey*, §74.

42. Id., §75.

43. Id., §80.

44. *Çiçek v. Turkey*, §152.

45. Id., §154.

46. Id., §155.

47. Id., §172.

48. Id., §173.

49. Id.

50. Case No. CH/99/2150, *Unkovic v. Federation of Bosnia Herzegovina* (9 November 2001).

51. Case No. CH/99/2150, *Decision on Request for Review, Dordo Unkovic vs. The Federation of Bosnia Herzegovina*, 10 January 2002.

52. *Srebrenica Cases*, §182 et ss.

53. ICTY, Case No. IT-98–33-T, *Prosecutor v. Krstic*, Judgment of 2 August 2001, §2.

54. *Srebrenica Cases*, §178 et ss.

55. Communication No. 30/1978.

56. Communication No. 107/1981.

57. Id.

58. Communication No. 449/1991.

59. Id., §5.7.

60. Communication No. 540/1993, §8.5.

61. Id., §8.4.

62. Communication No. 612/1995, §8.4.

63. Id., §8.5.

64. *Report on the Situation of Human Rights in Chile*, §121.

65. Report No. 28/88.

66. Report No. 2/91; Report No. 54/96, §28; Report No. 53/96, §27 et ss.; Report No. 55/96, §27; Report No. 3/98, §67.

67. Report No. 1/92.

68. Report No. 11/98 (Samuel de la Cruz Gómez), §46.

69. Id., §47.

70. Report No. 22/98, §30–31.

71. Report No. 30/96, §47; Report No. 40/97 (Alarcón); Report No. 56/98 (Manrique), §103; Id., Report No. 51/99, §110; Report No. 52/99, §86 et ss.; Report No. 53/99, §112 et ss.; Report No. 54/99, §110; Report No. 57/99, §70; Report No. 44/00, §36.

72. Report No. 9/92.

73. OEA/ser. L/V/II.85, doc. 9 rev.

74. Report No. 56/96, §31.

75. Report No. 1/97 (García Franco).

76. Id., §63.

77. Report No. 7/00 (Tordecilla).

78. Report No. 40/00, §68.

79. Report No. 43/00, §41.

80. Report No. 45/00, §40; Report No. 46/00, §46; Report No. 47/00, §44; Report No. 112/00, §36; Report No. 111/00, §51.

81. Report No. 60/01 (Solares).

82. Id., §35.

83. Manfred Nowak, at 187.

84. Basic Principles for the Treatment of Prisoners Adopted and proclaimed by General Assembly, resolution 45/111 of 14 December 1990.

85. CCPR/C/9/D/8/1977, Communication No. 8/1977 (03/04/80).

86. See Communication No. 107/1981.

87. CCPR/C/20/D/83/1981, Communication No. 83/1981 (04/11/83).

88. The court had only enumerated the right to life and the right to physical integrity.

Chapter 6

1. *Bamaca Velasquez (Merits),* §176 et ss.; *Trujillo Oroza* (Merits); id., *Benavides Cevallos, El Caracazo.*
2. *Bamaca Velasquez* (Merits), §179.
3. Report No. 30/96, §42 et ss.
4. Report No. 53/96, §24.
5. Report No. 54/96, §26.
6. Report No. 55/96.
7. Report No. 56/96.
8. Report No. 1/97 (García Franco), §76.
9. Report No. 3/98, §123.
10. Report No. 11/98 (Samuel de la Cruz Gómez), §57.
11. Report No. 22/98, §41; Report No. 56/98 (Manrique), §110; Report No. 51/99, §117; Report No. 52/99, §93 et ss.; id., Report No. 53/99, §119 et ss.; Report No. 54/99, §117; Report No. 55/99, §111; Report No. 57/99, §77; Report No. 43/00, §49; Report No. 40/00, §81; Report No. 44/00, §43; Report No. 47/00, §53; Report No. 46/00, §55; Report No. 111/00, §57; see Report No. 112/00, §44.
12. CCPR/C/53/D/400/1990, Communication No. 400/1990: Argentina. 27/04/95, 27 April 1995.
13. CCPR/C/66/D/717/1996, Communication No. 717/1996: Chile. 16/09/99, 16 September 1999.
14. CCPR/C/66/D/718/1996/Rev.1, Communication No. 718/1996: Chile. 24/09/99, 24 September 1999.
15. A/4625, para. 25; also Nowak, at 283–284.
16. CCPR/C/75/D/902/1999, Communication No. 902/1999: New Zealand. 30/07/2002.
17. Antonio Cassesse, *Los Derechos Humanos en el Mundo Contemporáneo,* trans. A. Pentimalli Melacrino and B. Ribera, Ariel, Barcelona, 1993, 189.
18. Paul Reuter, *Introducción al Derecho de los Tratados,* traducción de Eduardo Suárez, Fondo de Cultura Económica, Mexico, 1999, 117 et ss.

Chapter 7

1. CCPR/C/19/D/107/1981, Communication No. 107/1981 (21/07/83).
2. Priscilla Hayner, "Fifteen Truth Commissions — 1974 to 1994," *Human Rights Quarterly,* November 1994.
3. Juan E. Méndez, *Accountability for Past Abuses.* Working paper #233, Notre Dame University, September 1996; Juan E. Méndez, "El derecho a la verdad frente a graves violaciones de derechos humanos"; and Carlos Chipoco, *"El derecho a la verdad,"* *Paz,* No. 28, 83–106, Lima, March 1994, cited by Esteban Cuya, *Las Comi-*

siones de la Verdad en América Latina, Menschenrechtezentrum, Nürnberg.
4. Juan E. Méndez, "El derecho a la verdad frente a las graves violaciones a los derechos humanos," *Revista de la Defensoría del Pueblo Debate Defensorial,* No. 3, May 2001, 10–30, 20.
5. Id., 10–11.
6. E/CN.4/2001/69, Question of enforced or involuntary disappearances, 21 December 2000, p. 36.
7. Id., 38–39.
8. See E/CN.4/2000/64, Report of the Working Group on Enforced or Involuntary Disappearances, 21 December 1999, §74 concerning Morocco.
9. E/CN.4/1994/26, 22 December 1993, Argentina (§105), Saudi Arabia (§424); E/CN.4/1997/34, 13 December 1996, India (§181); E/CN.4/1998/43, 12 January 1998, in particular §101 concerning Argentina, §129 concerning Chile, §146 (Colombia), §170 (El Salvador), §190 (Guatemala), §202 (Honduras), §269 (Mexico), §288 (Nicaragua), §292 (Pakistan); E/CN.4/1999/62, 28 December 1998, §88 (Colombia), §112 (El Salvador), §144 (Honduras).
10. E/CN.4/Sub.2/1998/19, Report of the sessional working group on the administration of justice, Annex, 19 August 1998.
11. E/CN.4/2002/71, Report submitted by Mr. Manfred Nowak, independent expert charged with examining the existing international criminal and human rights framework for the protection of persons from enforced or involuntary disappearances, pursuant to paragraph 11 of Commission resolution 2001, §63 (p. 27).
12. Principles on the Effective Prevention and Investigation of Extra-legal, Arbitrary and Summary Executions Recommended by Economic and Social Council resolution 1989/65, 24 May 1989.
13. E/CN.4/1435, 26 January 1981, §30.
14. E/CN.4/1995/36, 21 December 1994, §442.
15. E/CN.4/1996/36, Special process on missing persons in the territory of the former Yugoslavia, Report submitted by Mr. Manfred Nowak, expert member of the Working Group on Enforced or Involuntary Disappearances, responsible for the special process, pursuant to paragraph 4 of Commission resolution 1995/35, *4 March 1996,* §84.
16. E/CN.4/1996/38, 15 January 1996, §33 *et ss.*
17. E/CN.4/1997/34, 13 December 1996.
18. E/CN.4/1997/55, Special process on missing persons in the territory of the former Yugoslavia, Report submitted by Mr. Manfred Nowak, expert member of the Working Group on Enforced or Involuntary Disappearances, responsible for the special process, pursuant to Commission resolution 1996/71, 15 January 1997, §2.

19. Id., §4, and Conclusions and Recommendations.

20. E/CN.4/1997/34, *13 December 1996,* §121.

21. §101, 105, citing *Aguiar de Lapacó.*

22. Id., §124.

23. §43; also §88, concerning Peru.

24. This is the argumentation of Judge Garzón.

25. E/CN.4/2002/L.57, *15 April 2002,* Draft resolution: Question of Enforced or Involuntary Disappearances, 4a and 5a; Resolution 2001/46 and 2000/37, 20 April 2000 (adopted without a vote), §4.d.

26. Case No. CH/99/3196, *Palic v. Republika Srpska,* 11 January 2001.

27. Case No. CH/99/2150, *Unkovic v. Federation of Bosnia Herzegovina,* 9 November 2001, §101.

28. Case No. CH/99/2150, *Unkovic v. the Federation of Bosnia and Herzegovina, Decision on Review of 6 May 2002,* §126.

29. Case No. CH/01/8365 et al., The "Srebrenica Cases" (49 applications), 7 March 2003, §173 et ss.

30. OEA/ser.L/V/II.43, doc. 21, *Annual Report of the Inter-American Commission on Human Rights,* Case 2029, 42 (1977).

31. *Castillo Páez,* Judgment of 3 November 1997, IACtHR, Ser. C, No. 34 (1997), §85–86.

32. *Cyprus v. Turkey,* Application No. 25781/94, ECtHR, 10 May 2001.

33. *Velasquez Rodriguez (Merits),* 29 July 1988, IACtHR, Ser. C, No. 4, §177.

34. *Godínez Cruz (Merits),* 20 January 1989, IACtHR, Ser. C, No. 5, §188.

35. *Caballero Delgado & Santana Case (Merits),* 8 December 1995, IACtHR, Ser. C, No. 22 (1995).

36. OEA/Ser.L/V/II.68 doc. 8 rev. 1, *Annual Report 1985–86,* 26 September 1986, 193.

37. *OEA/Ser.L/V/II.66, Doc. 17, Report on the Situation of Human Rights in Chile,* 9 September 1985, §126.

38. OEA/Ser.L/V/II.98, Doc. 6, Report No. 1/97, *Manuel García Franco,* Case 10.258 (Ecuador), *Annual Report 1997,* 17 February 1998, §73.

39. *Velasquez Rodriguez (Merits),* 29 July 1988, IACtHR, Ser. C, No. 4, §166.

40. *Francisco Guarcas Cipriano,* Report No. 22/98, Case 11.275, Guatemala, 2 March 1998, §40.

41. *David Palomino Morales,* Report No. 53/99, Cases 10.551, 10.803, 10.821, 10.906, 11.180, 11.322, Peru, 16 April 1999, §136.

42. OEA/Ser.L/V/II.106, Doc. 3, *Isabela Velásquez et al.,* Report No. 40/00, Case 10.588, 10.608, 10.796, 10.856, 10.921, Guatemala, 13 April 2000, §80.

43. OEA/Ser.L/V/II.98, Doc. 6, Report No. 11/98, *Samuel de la Cruz Gómez,* Case 10.606 (Guatemala), *Annual Report 1997* (17 February 1998), §56.

44. *Castillo Páez,* 3 November 1997, IACtHR, Ser. C, No. 34 (1997), §85–86.

45. *Bamaca Velasquez (Merits),* 25 November 2000, IACtHR, Series C, No. 70, §197 et ss.

46. *Bamaca Velasquez (Merits),* §201.

47. *Barrios Altos (Merits),* 14 March 2001, IACtHR, Series C, No. 70, §48.

48. *Mignone Emilio F. s/ presentación en causa 761* E.S.M.A., published in El Derecho 20–4-95.

49. C.S.J.N., U. 14. XXXIII. *Urteaga, Facundo Raúl c/ Estado Nacional*—Estado Mayor Conjunto de las FF.AA., s/ amparo ley 16.986. 15/10/98 T. 321, P. 2767.

50. C.S.J.N., "*Ganora Mario E. Y otra,*" 16/09/99 (Diario LA LEY, 1/3/00, 10/14).

51. Case 070/00— FCCA, Salta, Case No. 820/00, June 2000.

52. Aguiar de Lapacó Carmen on writ of certiorari (case No. 450) Suárez Mason, S. 1085, LXXXI, 13–8-98.

53. The Bassiouni/van Boven Principles include the right to a remedy, "access the factual information concerning the violation" (E/CN.4/2000/62, Annex, Basic Principles and Guidelines on the Right to a Remedy and Reparation for Victims of Violations of International Human Rights and Humanitarian Law, §11.c, p. 8–9, 18 January 2000). See, in addition, the proposed Article 20, E/CN.4/Sub.2/1998/19, Report of the sessional working group on the administration of justice, Annex, 19 August 1998. The right to the truth of the society has also been asserted as derived form the right to information (Article 13.1 ACHR, 19.2 ICCPR), a nonderogable right (Article 27 ACHR; Article 4 ICCPR). Juan E. Méndez, "Accountability for Past Abuses," 19 *Human Rights Quarterly* 2, May 1997.

Chapter 8

1. Theo van Boven, *Report to the U.N. on the Prevention of the Disappearances of Children in Argentina,* U.N. doc. E/CN.4/Sub.2/1988/19.

2. OEA/Ser.L/V/II.74, doc. 10, Rev. 1.

3. *Reggiardo Tolosa,* Provisional Measures, Serie E, doc. XVII, IACtHR, Resolution of the President of the IACtHR, 19 November 1993.

4. E/CN.4/Sub.2/1998/19.

5. E/CN.4/2001/69.

6. See Communication 400/1990.

7. Communication No. 540/1993, §8.7.

8. *Villagrán Morales,* §178.

9. Report No. 67/90.

10. Report No. 56/90.

11. Report No. 58/90.

12. Report No. 61/90.

13. Report No. 49/90.

Chapter 9

1. E/CN.4/2003/63, The right to a remedy and reparation for victims of violations of international human rights and humanitarian law (27 December 2002), §6.

2. Manfred Nowak, "The Right of Victims of Gross Human Rights Violations to Reparation," in *Rendering Justice to the Vulnerable: Liber Amicorum in Honour of Theo van Boven,* ed. Fons Coomans, The Hague, Kluwer, 2000, 203–224, 203.

3. A/RES/56/83, Chapter I, p. 16, Article I.

4. Cees Flinterman & Jeroes Gutter, *The United Nations and Human Rights: Achievements and Challenges,* UNDP, New York, www.undp. org/hdro/occ.htm, paper No. 48, 2000, at 11.

5. E/CN.4/2003/63, §7.

6. *Chorzow Factory (Indemnity)*, 1928 P.C.I.J. (ser. A) No. 17, at 29. P.C.I.J., Series A, No. 9, *Case concerning the Factory at Chorzów Claim for indemnity.*

7. E/CN.4/Sub.2/1990/10, para. 33.

8. Cherif Bassiouni, *International Criminal Law and Human Rights,* Transnational Publishers, New York, vol. I, pp. 16 and 17.

9. Resolution 2002/44, the CHR requested the Secretary General to circulate to all member States, intergovernmental groups and NGOs in consultative status with the ECOSOC the text of the "Basic principles and guidelines on the right to a remedy and reparation for victims of violations of international human rights and humanitarian law," annexed to the last report of the Independent Expert, Cherif Bassiouni, and to send their comments to the UNHCHR.

10. The ICJ asserted: "An essential distinction should be drawn between the obligations of a State towards the international community as a whole, and those arising vis-à-vis another State in the field of diplomatic protection. By their very nature the former are the concern of all States. In view of the importance of the rights involved, all States can be held to have a legal interest in their protection; they are obligations erga omnes.... Such obligations derive, for example, in contemporary international law, from the outlawing of acts of aggression, and of genocide, as also from the principles and rules concerning the basic rights of the human person, including protection from slavery and racial discrimination. Some of the corresponding rights of protection have entered into the body of general international law ... others are conferred by international instruments of a universal or quasi universal character." *ICJ Reports* (1970), at 32.

11. Vojin Dimitrijevi, "Dimensions of state responsibility for gross violations of human rights and fundamental freedoms following the introduction of democratic rule," in Theo van Boven, Fred Grünfeld Cees Flinterman, and Ingrid Westendorp (eds.), *Seminar on the Right to Restitution, Compensation and Rehabilitation for Victims of Gross Violations of Human Rights and Fundamental Freedoms,* Maastricht, 11–15 March 1992. Utrecht: SIM No. 12, 1992, 219.

12. E/CN.4/Sub.2/1993/8 Study concerning the right to restitution, compensation and rehabilitation for victims of gross violations of human rights and fundamental freedoms Final report submitted by Mr. Theo van Boven, Special Rapporteur, 2 July 1993.

13. E/CN.4/2003/WG.22/CRP.2, §15.

14. Dimitrijevi, §26.

15. United Nations Declaration on the Elimination of All Forms of Racial Discrimination Proclaimed by General Assembly resolution 1904 (18) of 20 November 1963.

16. International Convention on the Elimination of All Forms of Racial Discrimination Adopted and opened for signature and ratification by General Assembly resolution 2106 (20) of 21 December 1965, entry into force 4 January 1969, in accordance with Article 19.

17. Convention (No. 169) concerning Indigenous and Tribal Peoples in Independent Countries, Adopted on 27 June 1989 by the General Conference of the International Labour Organisation at its 76th session, entry into force 5 September 1991.

18. E/CN.4/Sub.2/1994/22, The Administration of Justice and the Human Rights of Detainees Question of the Human Rights of Persons Subjected to Any Form of Detention or Imprisonment Report of the Sessional Working Group on the Administration of Justice and the Question of Compensation, Chairman-Rapporteur: Mrs. Claire Palley, 15 August 1994, §20.

19. Dimitrijevi.

20. Pascualacci.

21. Communication No. 30/1978.

22. Communication No. 45/1979, *Pedro Pablo Camargo v. Colombia* (31 March 1982), U.N. Doc. CCPR/C/OP/1 at 112 (1985).

23. Communication No. 84/1981, *Guillermo Ignacio Dermit Barbato and Hugo Haroldo Dermit Barbato v. Uruguay,* 27 February 1981, U.N. Doc. Supp. No. 40 (A/38/40) at 124 (1983).

24. Communication No. 107/1981.

25. Communication No. 110/1981, *Antonio Viana Acosta v. Uruguay* (31 March 1983), U.N. Doc. Supp. No. 40 (A/39/40) at 169 (1984).

26. Communication Nos. 146/1983 and 148–154/1983, *John Khemraadi Baboeram, Andre Kamperveen, Cornelis Harold Riedewald, Gerald Leckie, Harry Sugrim Oemrawsingh, Somradj Robby Sohansingh, Lesley Paul Rahman and Edmund Alexander Hoost v. Suriname* (4 April 1985), U.N. Doc. Supp. No. 40 (A/40/40) at 187 (1985).

27. *Aloeboetoe,* Reparations (Article 63.1 ACHR), 10 September 1993, Series C, No. 15.

28. E/CN.4/Sub.2/1994/7/Add.1, *Review of Further Developments in Fields with which the Sub-Commission has been Concerned,* Report of the Secretary-General Prepared Pursuant to Sub-Commission Resolution 1993/29, 22 July 1994.

29. Christian Tomuschat, "Individual Reparation Claims in Instances of Grave Human Rights Violations: The Position under General International Law," in A. Randelzhofer and C. Tomuschat (eds.), *State Responsibility and the Individual,* Kluwer Law International, London, 1–25, at 1011.

30. Daillier and Pellet, 828, where asserting that "[d]ans l'ordre international, le recours à une procédure jurisdictionelle ou arbitrale est subordonné au consentement de toutes les parties à un litige, il sera difficile d'établir une justice internationale obligatoire, autorisant chaque Etat à citer unilatéralement un autre Etat devant une jurisdiction internationale à propos de n'importe quel différend." If states, subjects of international law in full extent, are not able to submit a claim against another state if the last state has not expressed its consent (and this question does not imply the denial of the substantive law that would have been breached by the defendant state), one cannot understand why a higher standard is claimed concerning individuals, whose role in international law is clearly limited. On the partial subjectivity of the individual or "Grauzone," Hanspeter Neuhold, *Österreichisches Handbuch des Völkerrechts,* I, 2. Auflage, Manz, Wien, 1991, p. 3, §8.

31. E/CN.4/Sub.2/1994/22, §19 et ss.

32. E/CN.4/Sub.2/1993/8, section IX.

33. E/CN.4/Sub.2/1996/17, The Administration of Justice and the Human Rights of Detainees, Revised set of basic principles and guidelines on the right to reparation for victims of gross violations of human rights and humanitarian law, prepared by Mr. Theo van Boven, pursuant to Sub-Commission decision 1995/117, 24 May 1996.

34. E/CN.4/1997/104, Question of the Human Rights of All Persons Subjected to Any Form of Detention or Imprisonment, Noted by the Secretary-General, 16 January 1997.

35. E/CN.4/1999/65, *Civil and Political Rights, Including the Question of Independence of the Judiciary, Administration of Justice, Impunity — Report of the independent expert on the right to restitution, compensation and rehabilitation for victims of grave violations of human rights and fundamental freedoms,* Mr. M. Cherif Bassiouni, submitted pursuant to Commission on Human Rights resolution 1998/43, 8 February 1999, §3.

36. Commission on Human Rights Resolution 1998/53 on impunity, 17 April 1998.

37. E/CN.4/Sub.2/1997/20, Question of the impunity of perpetrators of human rights violations (civil and political). Report prepared by Mr. Joinet pursuant to Sub-Commission Decision 1996/119, 26 June 1997; E/CN.4/Sub.2/1997/20/Rev.1 of 2 October 1997). ("Joinet Guidelines" and "revised Joinet Guidelines.")

38. E/CN.4/Sub.2/1997/20/Rev. 1.

39. E/CN.4/1999/65, §59.

40. E/CN.4/Sub.2/1993/10, *Review of Further Developments in Fields with Which the Sub-Commission Has Been Concerned Definition of Gross and Large-Scale Violations of Human Rights as an International Crime.* Working Paper Submitted by Mr. Stanislav Chernichenko in Accordance with Sub-Commission Decision 1992/109, 8 June 1999.

41. Id., §14 et ss.

42. The question of international crimes of states was linked to the Ago Project on State Responsibility, Article 19.

43. E/CN.4/1999/65, §25.

44. Id., §52 and 53.

45. Dinah L. Shelton and Thordis Ingadottir, The International Criminal Court Reparations to Victims of Crimes (Article 75 of the Rome Statute) and the Trust Fund (Article 79), Recommendations for the Court Rules of Procedure and Evidence, Reparations to Victims at the International Criminal Court by Dinah L. Shelton, Center on International Cooperation, New York University for the 26 July–13 August 1999 Meeting of the Preparatory Commission for the International Criminal Court.

46. E/CN.4/1999/65, §72.

47. *International Seminar on access of victims to the International Criminal Court* (Paris, 27–29 April 1999), Report of workshops, 29 April 1999.

48. *Declaration of Basic Principles of Justice for Victims of Crime and Abuse of Power.* Adopted by General Assembly, Resolution 40/34, 29 November 1985.

49. E/CN.4/2001/69.

50. *Aloeboetoe;* David J. Padilla, "Reparations in *Aloeboetoe v. Suriname,*" 17 *Human Rights Quarterly* 541–555, at 545 et ss. (1995).

51. *Kurt v. Turkey,* §68.

52. *Çakici v. Turkey,* §92.

53. *Timurtaş v. Turkey,* §75.

54. Pp. 6–7.

55. *Velásquez Rodríguez. Compensatory Damages* (Article 63(1) American Convention on Human Rights), 21 July 1989, §53.

56. *Caballero Delgado and Santana,* Reparations (Article 63(1) American Convention on Human Rights), 29 January 1997.

57. *Blake Reparations* (Article 63(1) American Convention on Human Rights), 22 January 1999.

58. *Castillo Páez Reparations* (Article 63(1) American Convention on Human Rights), 27 November 1998, §54.

59. *Durand and Ugarte,* Reparations (Article 63(1) American Convention on Human Rights), 3 December 2001, §26.

60. *Barrios Altos,* Reparations (Article 63(1) American Convention on Human Rights), 30 November 2001, §26 et ss.

61. *Bámaca Velásquez,* Reparations (Article 63(1) American Convention on Human Rights), 22 February 2002, §30 et ss.

62. *Trujillo Oroza,* Reparations (Article 63(1) American Convention on Human Rights), 27 February 2002, §55.

63. *El Caracazo,* Reparations (Article 63.1 ACHR), 29 August 2002, §68.

64. Id., §69.

65. Id., §72.

66. *Palic.*

67. Henkin, *Human Rights,* 315.

68. Monica Pinto, *Temas de Derechos Humanos,* Ediciones del Puerto, Buenos Aires, 1997, 47 et ss.

69. *Velasquez Rodriguez.* See also the opinion of judge Barberis in *Cantos,* IACtHR, 28 November 2002, who asserts that the interpretation of the IACtHR on Article 1.1 implies that the rule establishes the self-obligatoriness of the ACHR, at §7.

70. E/CN.4/Sub.2/1996/17.

71. *Series A, No. 7. Enforceability of the Right to Reply or Correction (*Articles 14(1), 1(1), and 2, American Convention on Human Rights), Advisory Opinion OC-7/86 of 29 August 1986.

72. E/CN.4/2000/62.

73. §26.

74. The ICC would only deal with enforced disappearances as crimes against humanity.

75. E/CN.4/Sub.2/1998/19.

76. TheMissing/Conf/02.2003/EN/1.

77. Commission on Human Rights, openended Working Group to elaborate a draft legally binding normative instrument for the protection of all persons from enforced disappearance, First session, Geneva, 6–17 January 2003.

78. Nowak.

79. Rene Provost, *International Human Rights and Humanitarian Law,* Cambridge, 2002, at 44.

80. E/CN.4/Sub.2/1996/17.

81. E/CN.15/1996/16/Add.3, Commission on Crime Prevention and Criminal Justice, Fifth Session Vienna, 21–31 May 1996; United Nations Standards and Norms in the Field of Crime Prevention and Criminal Justice, Report of the Secretary-General, Addendum, Use and Application of the Declaration of Basic Principles of Justice for Victims of Crime and Abuse of Power, 10 April 1996.

82. Bassiouni, §51 et ss.

83. E/CN.4/Sub.2/1997/20.

84. *Luyeye Magana ex-Philibert v. Zaire,* Communication No. 90/1981, 30 March 1981, U.N. Doc. Supp. No. 40 (A/38/40) at 197 (1983), 21–7–83; *Carmen Améndola and Graciela Baritussio v. Uruguay,* Communication No. 25/1978 (26 July 1982), U.N. Doc. CCPR/C/OP/1 at 136 (1985). See also the cases of *Bleier* and *Nydia Bautista.*

85. Communication No. 275/1988: Argentina. 04/04/90. CCPR/C/38/D/275/1988.

86. Communication No 612/1995.

87. Communication No. 322/1988: Uruguay. 09/08/94. CCPR/C/51/D/322/1988.

88. General Comment 20, Replaces general comment 7 concerning prohibition of torture and cruel treatment or punishment (Article 7): 10/03/92.

89. *Aksoy v. Turkey,* ECtHR, Reports 1996-VI, 18 December 1996; *Kurt.*

90. *Kurt v. Turkey,* §114.

91. *Çakici v. Turkey,* §111.

92. Id., §121.

93. *Timurtaş v. Turkey,* §110.

94. *Taş v. Turkey,* §92–93; *Salman v. Turkey; Çiçek v. Turkey,* §179; *Akdeniz v. Turkey.*

95. Report No. 34/00, Case 11.291, Carandiru*, Brazil, 13 April 2000, §95.

96. *Castillo Páez,* §82–83; *Suárez Rosero,* 12 November 1997, Series C, No. 35; *Paniagua Morales et al.,* §164; *Blake,* §63 et ss.

97. *Paniagua Morales,* §173; *Blake,* §64.

98. The remedy in the Inter-American system is *amparo.*

99. *Castillo Páez,* §80 et ss.

100. *Trujillo Oroza* (Merits); *Benavides Cevallos,* and *Garrido and Baigorria.*

101. *Paniagua Morales,* §157 et ss.

102. Id., §164.

103. *Villagrán Morales v. Guatemala,* §199 et ss.

104. *Bamaca Velasquez (Merits),* §185 et ss.

105. *Cantoral Benavides,* Reparations (Article 63(1) American Convention on Human Rights), 3 December 2001.

106. *Barrios Altos,* §41 et ss.

107. Report No. 1/92; Report No. 24/93; Report No. 57/99, §89.

108. OEA/Ser.L/V/II.83, Doc. 14 corr. 1, *Reports 28/92* (Argentina) and 29/92 (Uruguay) in Annual Report 1992–93, 12 March 1993, at 49–51, 161–65.

109. Report No. 1/97 (García Franco), §70.

110. *Durand* and *Ugarte,* §128.

111. Id., §129–130.

112. *Blake v. Guatemala,* §91.

113. Id., §96–97.

114. Report No. 28/92, §32 et ss.

115. Id., §35 et ss.

116. See Report No. 53/96, §51; Report No. 54/96, §31.

117. Report No. 40/97 (Alarcón); Report No. 1/97 (García Franco), §70; Report No. 53/99, §121 et ss.; Report No. 56/98 (Manrique), §112–17; Report 56/96, §36; Report No. 55/99, §113; Report No. 51/99, §119; Report No. 54/99, §119; Report No. 43/00, §52; Report No. 47/00, §53; Report No. 52/99, §95.

118. *See* Report No. 40/00, §74; Report No. 11/98 (Samuel de la Cruz Gómez), §50 et ss.; Report No. 22/98, §34.

119. See Report No. 60/01.

120. Id., §39.

121. Id., §40.

122. Report No. 46/00, §58; Report No. 57/99, §79; Report No. 45/00, §50; Report No. 44/00, §47 et ss.; Report No. 112/00, §47.

123. *Gómez López v. Guatemala,* Case 11.303, Report No. 29/96, IACHR, OEA/Ser.L/V/II.95 Doc. 7 rev. at 425 (1997), §84 et ss.

124. *Velásquez Rodríguez, Fairén Garbi y Solís Corrales, Godínez Cruz,* Preliminary Objections, Judgment of 26 June 1987, paragraphs 91, 90, and 92, respectively.

125. Report No. 1/99, Case 10.480, Lucio Parada Cea et al., El Salvador, 27 January 1999, §128 et ss.

126. Luis Huerta Guerrero, "El Debido Proceso y la Corte Interamericana de Derechos Humanos: tendencias actuales y posibilidades de aplicación por las defensorías del pueblo," (La Revista del Defensor del Pueblo), 79, at 82.

127. Report No. 28/96, Case 11.297 Guatemala, 16 October 1996, §70 et ss.

128. E/CN.4/sub.2/1997/20, §54 et ss.

129. General Assembly resolution 2391 (23) of 26 November 1968.

130. E/CN.4/sub.2/1997/20, §55.

131. Id.

132. E/CN.4/2003/63.

133. Habeas Corpus in Emergency Situations (Articles 27(2) and 7(6) of the American Convention on Human Rights), Advisory Opinion OC-8/87 of 30 January 1987, IACtHR (ser. A) No. 8 (1987).

134. Judicial Guarantees in States of Emergency (Articles 27(2), 25 and 8 of the American Convention on Human Rights), Advisory Opinion OC-9/87 of 6 October 1987, IACtHR (ser. A) No. 9 (1987).

135. *Castillo Páez,* §80 et ss.; *Paniagua Morales,* §157 et ss., in particular, §164; Report No. 1/92; Report No. 24/93; Report No. 57/99, §89; Report No. 1/97 (García Franco), §70; Report No. 40/97 (Alarcón); Report No. 1/97 (García Franco), §70; Report No. 53/99, §121 et ss.; Report No. 56/98 (Manrique), §112–17; Report No. 56/96, §36; Report No. 55/99, §113; Report No. 51/99, §119; Report No. 54/99, §119;

Report No. 43/00, §52; Report No. 47/00, §53; Report No. 52/99, §95; Report No. 40/00, §74; Report No. 11/98 (Samuel de la Cruz Gómez), §50 et ss.; Report No. 22/98, §34; Report No. 60/01 (Solares). See also Article 9 DED, first paragraph; Article 25/Article 7.6, ACHR.

136. E/CN.4/Sub.2/1994/24; *Advisory Opinions 8* and *9* of the IACtHR.

137. Article 13, DED; Principle 20, Joinet Principles; Communication No. 275/1988; Communication No. 322/1988; Principles on Prevention, §9; *Kurt v. Turkey,* §114; *Çakici v. Turkey,* §111; *Timurtaş v. Turkey,* §110; *Ylhan v. Turkey;* Arg. Article 1.1, Article 2 and Article 25, ACHR; *Villagrán Morales v. Guatemala,* §199 et ss.; *Barrios Altos,* §41 et ss.; Report No. 1/92; Report No. 24/93; Report No. 57/99, §89; Report No. 1/97 (García Franco), §70; *Durand and Ugarte,* §129–30; *Blake v. Guatemala,* §91; Report No. 28/92, §32 et ss.; Report No. 29/92, §35 et ss.; Report No. 40/00, §74; Report No. 11/98 (Samuel de la Cruz Gómez), §50 et ss.; Report No. 22/98, §34; Report No. 60/01 (Solares); Report No. 46/00, §58; Report No. 57/99, §79; Report No. 45/00, §50; Report No. 44/00, §47 et ss.; Report No. 112/00, §47; Report No. 28/96, §70 et ss.

138. Report No. 29/92, §35 et ss.

139. Bassiouni Guidelines; Joinet Principles, Principle 21; Article 14 DED; Draft Article 6; Article 4 IACFD; Article 12 IACAT; Article 5 CAT; Report No. 28/92, §32 et ss.

140. Report No. 29/92, §35 et ss.

141. Principle 29, Joinet Principles.

142. Bassiouni Guidelines.

143. Bassiouni Guidelines; Joinet Principles, Principle 19; *Paniagua Morales,* §173; *Blake Case,* §64 and §91; *Durand and Ugarte,* §129–30; Report No. 1/99, in special, §128 et ss.; Article 24 Draft IC.

144. Article 17, DED, Article 26 Draft IC, Article 7, IACFD; Bassiouni Guidelines; Principles on Impunity, Joinet.

Chapter 10

1. E/CN.4/1997/104.

2. E/CN.4/Sub.2/1996/17.

3. Van Boven, Flinterman, Grünfeld, and Westendorp (eds.), *Seminar on the Right to Restitution, Compensation and Rehabilitation for Victims of Gross Violations of Human Rights and Fundamental Freedoms,* Maastricht, 11–15 March 1992: SIM No. 12, 1992, Conclusions, at 16. (Hereafter, van Boven, *Seminar*).

4. Id.

5. The Principles on Impunity prepared by Joinet include in Principle 36 the following text: "Any human rights violation gives rise to a right

to reparation on the part of the victim or his beneficiaries, implying duty on the part of the State to make reparation and the possibility of seeking redress from the perpetrator." E/CN.4/Sub.2/1997/20.

6. Nowak; van Boven, *Rapporteur, Appendice: E/CN.4/Sub.2/1993/8, Study Concerning the Right to Restitution, Compensation and Rehabilitation for Victims of Gross Violations of Human Rights and Fundamental Freedoms: Final Report Submitted by Mr. Theo van Boven, Special Rapporteur*, 59 *Law & Contemp. Prob.* 283, note 4.

7. R.S.J. MacDonald, "Supervision of the Execution of the Judgements of the European Court of Human Rights," *Droit et Justice Mélanges Nicolas Valticos, ed.* René Jean Dupuy, 1999, Pédone, Paris, 418–31, at 426 (1999).

8. E/CN.4/1998/38; E/CN.4/1998/68; E/CN.4/1998/54; E/CN.4/Sub.2/1998/13; E/CN.4/1998/10; E/CN.4/1998/15; E/CN.4/1998/39/Add.1; E/CN.4/1998/43; E/CN.4/Sub.2/1997/8; A/CONF.187/PM.1

9. E/CN.4/2001/69, at 18.

10. §67.

11. This position opposes the IACtHR in *Aloeboetoe:* only the direct consequences of the human rights violations deserve reparation.

12. E/CN.4/Sub.2/1997/20.

13. E/CN.4/1999/65, §43.

14. Id., §45.

15. Id., §60.

16. E/CN.4/2000/62.

17. IACtHR, *Las Palmeras,* Reparations (Article 63.1 ACHR); Judgment of 26 November 2002, §39.

18. IACtHR, *Cantos,* §67.

19. Case No. CH/97/82, *Decision on the Admissibility and Merits, Velimir Ostojic and 31 Other JNA cases against Bosnia and Herzegovina and the Federation of Bosnia and Herzegovina* (15 January 1999); Case No. CH/97/46, Decision on the Claim for Compensation, Delivered in Writing on 24 August 1999, *Ivica Kevesevic v. The Federation of Bosnia and Herzegovina,* 15 May 1999.

20. E/CN.4/2000/62.

21. Felipe Paolillo, "Derechos Humanos y Reparación (con especial referencia al sistema interamericano)," *Héctor Gros Espiell amicorum liber: persona humana y derecho internacional,* vol. 2, p. 988, Bruylant, Brussels, 1997.

22. F. A. Mann, "The Consequences of an International Wrong in International and National Law," 48 B.Y.I.L., 1–65, at 3 (1976–77).

23. Report No. 54/96; Report No. 42/97 (Escobar Jurado); Report No. 53/96; Report No. 56/96; Report No. 55/96.

24. Article 34 and Article 38.1.

25. A/CN.4/488, State responsibility — Comments submitted by States, 25 March 1998.

26. Report No. 56/98 (Manrique); Report No.

53/99; Report No. 52/99; Report No. 55/99; Report No. 51/99; Report No. 54/99; Report No. 57/99, §73; Report No. 43/00.

27. Report No. 22/98, §92.

28. Report No. 28/92, §51–52.

29. Report No. 40/00, §88.

30. Report No. 43/00; Report No. 44/00; Report No. 45/00; Report No. 46/00; Report No. 47/00; Report No. 112/00; Report No. 7/00 (Tordecilla); Report No. 61/01.

31. Report No. 58/01.

32. Juan Méndez, "Derecho a la verdad frente a las graves violaciones de derechos humanos," in *La Aplicación de los Tratados sobre Derechos Humanos por los Tribunales Locales, CELS,* Buenos Aires, 1997.

33. *Bamaca Velasquez,* §56; *Cantoral Benavides,* §56.

34. Nowak, 18.

35. E/CN.4/RES/2000/37, Question of enforced or involuntary disappearances, 20 April 2000; E/CN.4/RES/2001/46, Question of enforced or involuntary disappearances, 23 April 2001; E/CN.4/2002/41.

36. *Lusitania Cases (United States v. Germany),* Mixed Claims Commission, Reports of International Arbitral Awards, vol. 7, pp. 256 and 257 (1924).

37. *Loayza Tamayo Case,* Reparations (Article 63(1) American Convention on Human Rights), Judgment of 27 November 1998, Inter-Am. Ct. H.R. (Ser. C) No. 42 (1998).

38. §76.

39. p. 988.

40. Id.

41. Juan Méndez, "Position of Americas Watch, a division of Human Rights Watch, on the right of victims of gross violations of human rights to reparations and on measures to prevent such violations," in van Boven, *Seminar,* 43.

42. A/CN.4/SR.2612 to SR.2662, *Fifty-second session provisional Summary Records International Law Commission,* 17 August 2000.

43. *Matanovic,* §63.

44. Cecilia Medina Quiroga, "The Experience of Chile," in van Boven, *Seminar,* 101.

45. §79.

46. The ILC included the criteria to determine compensation in Article 39: the contribution to the injury by willful or negligent action or omission of the injured state or any person or entity in relation to whom reparation is sought.

47. E/CN.4/1998/43.

48. Id.

49. E/CN.15/1996/16/Add.3.

50. Nowak, p. 19.

51. E/CN.4/1999/65, 22.

52. IACtHR, *Loayza Tamayo — Interpretation of the Judgement of Reparations* (Article 67 of the ACHR), 3 June 1999.

53. P. 43.

54. Id.

55. Yael Danieli, "Preliminary reflections from a psychological perspective," in van Boven, *Seminar*.

56. Report No. 28/92, §51–52.

57. Paolillo, p. 991.

58. Report No. 15/92; Report No. 54/96; Report No. 41/97 (Ruiz Davila).

59. Report No. 19/99 (Juscamaita Laura).

60. Report No. 3/98, §136 et ss.; Report No. 42/97 (Escobar Jurado); Report No. 56/98 (Manrique); Report No. 53/99; Report No. 52/99; Report No. 55/99; Report No. 51/99; Report No. 54/99; Report No. 57/99, §73; Report No. 43/00.

61. See Report No. 24/93; Report No. 1/92; Report No. 10/93.

62. Report No. 22/98.

63. Report No. 56/98 (Manrique); Report No. 53/99; Report No. 52/99; Report No. 55/99; Report No. 51/99; Report No. 54/99; Report No. 57/99, §73; Report No. 43/00; Report No. 39/97; Report No. 3/98, §136 et ss.

64. *Alabama Claims Arbitration*, in Moore, *International Arbitration* (1871), 1, 496.

65. *Pedro Pablo Camargo*, p. 991.

66. Communication 84/1981.

67. Communication 107/1981.

68. CH/96/30, *Damjanovic* decision of 11 March 1998, Decisions and Reports, January–June 1998, chapter 1, paragraph 23.

69. Decision on the Claim for Compensation in Cases Nos. CH/96/3 and CH/96/9 *Branko Medan and Radosav Markovic against Bosnia and Herzegovina and the Federation of Bosnia and Herzegovina*, 15 May 1999, §12. See id., Decision on the Claim for Compensation, Delivered on 29 July 1998 by Notification in Writing in the *Case of Stjepan Bastijanovic, against the State of Bosnia and Herzegovina and the Federation of Bosnia and Herzegovina*, Case No. CH/96/8.

70. Decision on the Claim for Compensation, Delivered on 29 July 1998 by Notification in Writing in the *Case of Milivoje Bulatovic, against the State of Bosnia and Herzegovina and the Federation of Bosnia and Herzegovina*, Case No. CH/96/22; Decision on the Claim for Compensation, Delivered in Writing on 22 July 1998 in the *Case of Rifat Bejdic against the Republika Srpska*, Case No. CH/96/27.

71. *Palic*, at 18–19.

72. Id.

73. *Supra Srebrenica Cases*, §211 et ss.

74. *Bámaca Velásquez*, §56; *Cantoral Benavides*, §53.

75. *Velasquez Rodriguez*, Reparations.

76. *Godínez Cruz*, Compensatory Damages (Article 63(1) American Convention on Human Rights), 21 July 1989, §49.

77. *Neira Alegría et al.*, Reparations (Article 63(1) American Convention on Human Rights), 19 September 1996, §53.

78. *Caballero Delgado*, §48.

79. *Garrido and Baigorria*, Reparations (Article 63(1) American Convention on Human Rights), 27 August 1998, §62.

80. *Castillo Páez*, Reparations, §78.

81. *Loayza Tamayo*, Reparations, §125 et ss.

82. *Blake*, Reparations, §113 et ss.

83. *Bamaca Velasquez v. Guatemala*, Reparations (22 February 2002), §60. *Cantoral Benavides*, §57; *Cesti Hurtado*, Reparations, 31 May 2001, §51. *Paniagua Morales*, Reparations, 25 May 2001, §105; *Villagrán Morales* et al., §88.

84. *Bamaca Velasquez*, §62.

85. *Trujillo Oroza*, §77.

86. Id., §85.

87. *Paniagua Morales*, §104 et ss.

88. Id., §108.

89. *Cesti Hurtado*, §111.

90. *Villagrán Morales*, Reparations, §93.

91. *Las Palmeras*, Reparations, §54–55.

92. Id., §58.

93. *Çakici v. Turkey*, §128.

94. *Ertak v. Turkey*, §146.

95. *Mahmut Kaya*, §16.

96. Decision on the Claim for Compensation, Case No. CH/96/28, *"M.J.,"* against the *Republika Srpska*, 14 October 1998.

97. *Palic*, §90.

98. *Unkovic*, §68.

99. Id., §106.

100. *Damjanovic*, §23.

101. *Srebrenica Cases*, §211 et ss.

102. *Cantoral Benavides*, §80.

103. *Loayza Tamayo*, Reparations, §144.

104. *Bámaca Velásquez*, §69 et ss.

105. *Castillo Paez*, §91.

106. *Trujillo Oroza*, §76.

107. *Las Palmeras*, Reparations, §47.

108. *Velasquez Rodriguez*, Reparations, §34.

109. *Godinez Cruz*, Reparations, §39 et ss.

110. *Bámaca Velásquez*, §54.

111. *Trujillo Oroza*, §65 et ss.

112. *El Caracazo*, Reparations, §85 et ss.

113. *Çakici v. Turkey*, §123 et ss.

114. See §9.

115. Joinet Guidelines, p. 990.

116. *El Amparo Case*, Reparations, 14 September 1996, Inter-Am. Ct. H.R.

117. *Neira Alegría*, Reparations, §43.

118. *Caballero Delgado and Santana*, §26.

119. *Villagrán Morales*, §78 et ss.

120. *Cantoral Benavides*, §48.

121. *Blake*, §43 et ss.

122. *Loayza Tamayo*, §125 et ss.

123. *Castillo Páez*, §71.

124. *Suarez Rosero*, §55.

125. *Paniagua Morales*, §85 et ss.

126. *Bámaca Velásquez*, §44 et ss.
127. Id., §51.
128. *Kaya v. Turkey*, §13.
129. *Ertak v. Turkey*, §146.
130. *Kaya v. Turkey*, §23.
131. *Çakici v. Turkey*, §132.
132. *Cesti Hurtado*, §43 et ss.
133. Id., §46.
134. *Neira Alegría v. Perú*, §70.
135. *Loayza Tamayo*, §172 et ss.
136. *Bámaca Velásquez*, §30 et ss. §88.
137. *Suárez Rosero*, Reparations (Article 63(1) American Convention on Human Rights), 20 January 1999, §88.
138. *Cesti Hurtado*, §68.
139. *Villagrán Morales*, §212.
140. *Trujillo Oroza*, §123.
141. *Castillo Páez*, §109.
142. *Blake*, §69 et ss.
143. *Cantoral Benavides*, §82.
144. *Çakici v. Turkey*, §128.
145. *Ertak v. Turkey*, §152.
146. *Kaya v. Turkey*, §211.
147. *Damjanovic*, §23.
148. Philippe Frumer, "La Réparation des Atteintes aux Droits de l'Homme Internationalement Protégés — Quelques Données Comparatives," *Rev.Trim. Dr.H* (1996), pp. 329–352, at 335.
149. E/CN.4/1997/104.
150. Agnes Camacho, *Reparations of victims of conflict and human rights violations*, HURIDOCS International Conference on Human Rights Information, Gammarth (Tunisia), 22–25 March 1998 (www.huridocs.org).
151. E/CN.4/2001/69.
152. *Durand and Ugarte*, §35.
153. Jean-Marie Simon, "The Alien Tort Claims Act: Justice or Show Trials?" *Boston University International Law Journal*, vol. 11:1, 2–79, at 16 et ss. (1993).
154. G. Hackworth, *Digest of International Law*, vol. 2, 703, 708 (1941) and M. Whiteman, *Damages in International Law*, 722 (1937).
155. 577 F. Supp. at 865, citing *Letelier v. Republic of Chile*, 502 F. Supp. 259, 266 (D.D.C. 1980).
156. Lillich, at 234.
157. *Hilao v. Estate of Marcos*, 103 F.3d 767 (9th Cir.1996).
158. *Forti v. Suarez-Mason*, 1541.
159. *Martinez-Baca v. Suarez-Mason*, No. 87–2057, slip op. at 4–5 (N.D. Cal. 22 April 1988).
160. *Quiros de Rapaport v. Suarez-Mason*, No. 87–2266 (N.D. Cal. 11 April 1989).
161. Upendra Baxi, "A perspective from India," in van Boven, *Seminar*, at 77.
162. *Godínez Cruz*, §33.
163. *Garrido and Baigorria*, §43.

164. Juan Méndez, at 43.
165. Nowak, at 20.
166. Report No. 78/90; Report No. 75/90; Report No. 77/90; Report No. 79/90; Report No. 88/90; Report No. 89/90; Report No. 81/90; Report No. 85/90; Report No. 76/90; Report No. 41/97 (Ruiz Dávila); Report No. 15/92.
167. Margriet Blauw, "'Denial and silence' or 'acknowledgement and disclosure,'" *IRRC Review*, December 2002, vol. 84 no. 848, 767–783.
168. A/RES/51/134.
169. ICJ, Case Concerning United States Diplomatic and Consular Staff in Tehran, Order of December 15, 1979, Provisional Measures; ICJ, Case Concerning Military and Paramilitary Activities in and against Nicaragua, June 27, 1986, p. 149, resolutive point 12.
170. Catherine Deman, "La céssation de l'acte illicite," *Revue Belge de Droit International*, 1990/2, 478–495, at 477.
171. Ian Brownlie, §192 et ss. *See also* Joost Pauwelyn, 415.
172. *Velasquez Rodriguez*, §155 and 158; and *Godínez Cruz Case*, §163 and 166.
173. Cf. *El Caracazo*, Reparations, §76; *Hilaire, Constantine y Benjamin et al*. Corte I.D.H., 21 June 2002, §202; *Trujillo Oroza*, §60; and *Cantos*, §67.
174. *Loizidou v. Turkey* (Article 50), 28 July 1998.
175. E/CN.4/2002/79, §362.
176. Report on the Situation of Human Rights in Brazil (1997), Report on the Situation of Human Rights in Colombia (1998).
177. OEA/Ser.L/V/II.34, doc. 21 corr.1.
178. Amnesty International, Ecuador, Torture and "disappearance" of Elías Elint López and Luis Alberto Shinin Laso (1), AMR 28/008/2001, 09/04/2001; 14-Point Program for the Prevention of disappearances online at http://web.amnesty.org/web/aboutai.nsf/5451236ceac8ca36802567750034ca9a/472772b3583aa3028025677f004c3f00,OpenDocument, December 1992; *Turkey: No security without human rights*, London, October 1996. AI Index: EUR/44/84/96.
179. Id., §17 et ss.
180. Report No. 22/98.
181. *Las Palmeras*, Reparations, §67.
182. Eric Stover and Rachel Shigekane, "The missing in the aftermath of war: When do the needs of victims' families and international war crimes tribunals clash?" *IRRC Review*, December 2002, vol. 84 no. 848, 845 et ss., at 860.
183. Alex Kirasi Olumbe, and Ahmed Kalebi Yakub, "Management, exhumation and identification of human remains: A viewpoint of the developing world," IRRC, December 2002, vol. 84 no. 848, 983 et ss., 896–897.

184. Reports of the WG cited in Chapter I.
185. Report No. 54/96; Report No. 41/97 (Ruiz Davila); Report No. 53/96; Report No. 56/96; Report No. 55/96; Report No. 58/01.
186. *Bámaca Velásquez*, §82.
187. *Villagrán Morales*, §204.
188. *El Caracazo*, §123 et ss.
189. *Las Palmeras*, Reparations, §71.
190. Id., §77.
191. Report No. 29/90.
192. Report No. 28/88.
193. Luigi Migliorino, "Sur la déclaration d'illicité comme forme de satisfaction: à propos de la sentence arbitral du 30 avril 1990 dans l'affaore du *Rainbow Warrior*," *R.G.D.I.P.* 96, 61–73, at 72 et ss. (1992).
194. Report No. 40/90.
195. Report No. 15/92.
196. *Las Palmeras*, Reparations, §75.
197. *Loayza Tamayo*, Reparations, §157.
198. *Suárez Rosero*, §68.
199. *Cantoral Benavides*, §65.
200. Jann K. Kleffner, "Conflict Related Crimes Under International Law: Legal Obligations To Prosecute?" Forthcoming in: Horst Fischer (ed.), *International and national criminal jurisdictions as a means of conflict resolution.*
201. Diane Orentlicher, "Settling Accounts: The Duty to Prosecute Human Rights Violations of a Prior Regime," 100 *Yale L.J.* 2537 (1991), at 2568, quoted by Henry J. Steiner and Philip Alston, *International Human Rights in Context: Law, Politics, Morals—Texts and Materials*, Clarendon Press, Oxford, 1996, at 1091.
202. Lillich and Paxman, 287.
203. Id., 290 et ss.
204. J. B. Moore, *History and Digest of the International Arbitrations to which the United States has been a Party (1898)*, 2050, cited by Lillich.
205. *Mallén Case* (*México v. United States*), 4 R.I.A.A. 173, 175 (1925).
206. At 1438.
207. See Kleffner.
208. *Bámaca Velásquez*, §70 et ss.
209. *Blake*, §65; *Suárez Rosero*, §80; *Loayza Tamayo*, Reparations, §161; *Castillo Páez*, §107.
210. *Cesti Hurtado*, §60.
211. *El Caracazo*, §115 et ss.
212. *Las Palmeras*, Reparations, §65 et ss.
213. Communication No. 30/1978.
214. HRC, *Joaquin David Herrera Rubio v. Colombia*, Communication No. 161/1983 (1983).
215. Report No. 28/88.
216. Report No. 41/90.
217. *Cesti Hurtado*, §62.
218. Report No. 28/88; Report No. 16/90; Report No. 39/90; Report No. 29/90; Report No. 10/93.
219. Report No. 49/90; Report No. 50/90; Report No. 51/90; Report No. 68/90.

220. Report No. 78/90; Report No. 75/90; Report No. 77/90; Report No. 79/90; Report No. 88/90; Report No. 89/90; Report No. 81/90; Report No. 85/90; Report No. 76/90.
221. Report No. 54/96; Report No. 53/96; Report No. 56/96; Report No. 55/96; Report No. 7/00 (Tordecilla); Report No. 58/01.
222. Report No. 3/98, §136 et ss.; Report No. 11/98 (Samuel de la Cruz Gómez); Report No. 56/98 (Manrique); Report No. 53/99.
223. Report No. 15/92.
224. Report No. 68/90; Report No. 3/91; Report No. 12/93.
225. Report No. 22/98; Report No. 40/00, §88.
226. Report No. 43/00; Report No. 44/00; Report No. 45/00; Report No. 46/00; Report No. 47/00; Report No. 112/00.
227. Report No. 12/92.
228. Nowak, at 20.
229. E/CN.4/2002/L.57; E/CN.4/2002/41.
230. E/CN.4/RES/1999/34, 23 April 1999, *Impunity,* Resolution of the CHR 1999/34.
231. The ECtHR has not ordered a state to proceed to investigate a case.
232. Agneta Pallinder, *Impunity and Challenges of the Post-Conflict Healing Process, HURIDOCS International Conference on Human Rights Information,* Gammarth (Tunisia), 22–25 March 1998 (www.huridocs.org).
233. *Cyprus v. Turkey,* at 209.
234. *Interim Report of the Commission of Inquiry into Involuntary Removal or Disappearance of Persons in the Western, Southern and Sabaragamuwa Provinces* (Department of Government Printing, Sri Lanka, September 1997).
235. *Srebrenica Cases*, §133 et ss.
236. §33, A/CONF.157/23; A/52/469, *Human Rights Questions, Including Alternative Approaches for Improving the Effective Enjoyment of Human Rights and Fundamental Freedoms,* United Nations Decade for Human Rights Education, 1995–2004, and public information activities in the field of human rights Report of the Secretary-General, 15 October 1997, in particular §68, §105–106, §110; Statement by the chairperson on behalf of the Commission on Human Rights (55th session) Geneva, 22 March–30 April 1999, Agenda item 3, Colombia.
237. 1998 Commission on Human Rights Report; January–December 1998.
238. Asia-Pacific Human Rights Information Center, "The Human Rights Education Situation in Sri Lanka" in "Human Rights Education in Asian Schools. Volume Four" (Osaka, 2001), online at *http://erc.hrea.org/Library/curriculum_methodology/hurights01.html.*
239. *Villagrán Morales*, §202.
240. E/CN.4/1992/18/Add.1, para. 204(k) and E/CN.4/1993/25/Add.1, para. 133.

241. E/CN.4/1992/18/Add.1, para. 204(a).

242. Report of the Working Group on Enforced or Involuntary Disappearances, Addendum — Sri Lanka, §38 (21 December 1999).

243. Id., in the report, NGOs stated that this provision was often ignored.

244. Id., §47.

245. *Cantoral Benavides,* §81.

246. *Caballero Delgado,* §53.

247. *Garrido & Baigorria,* §66.

248. Report No. 56/98 (Manrique); Report No. 53/99; Report No. 52/99; Report No. 55/99; Report No. 51/99; Report No. 54/99; Report No. 57/99, §73; Report No. 43/00.

249. Report No. 19/99 (Juscamaita Laura).

250. Report No. 53/99.

251. Report No. 61/01.

252. E/CN.4/1992/18/Add.1, para. 204(e) and E/CN.4/1993/25/Add.1, para.146 (a).

253. *Cantoral Benavides,* §72.

254. *Villagrán Morales,* §203.

255. IACtHR, *Bamaca Velasquez.*

256. Nowak.

257. Sir Humprey Waldock, "The Effectiveness of the System Set Up by the European Convention on Human Rights," 1 *Human Rights Law Journal,* No. 14, 1–12, at 5 (1980).

258. Directorate of Human Rights, *Proceedings of the Sixth International Colloquy about the European Convention on Human Rights,* Sevilla, 13–16 November 1985, Nijhoff, Dordrecht, at 583.

259. Heribert Golsong, "Quelques Reflexions à Propos du Pouvoir de la Cour Européenne des Droits de l'Homme d'accorder une Satisfaction Equitable," *René Cassin Amicorum Discipulorumque Liber,* 88, at 91, vol. 1, Paris, 1969.

260. ECtHR, *Le Compte, van Leuven et De Meyere,* Série A, vol. 54, 18 October 1982, §15; Montserrat Enrich Mas, "Right to Compensation under Article 50," *European System for the Protection of Human Rights,* edited by R. St. J. MacDonald, F. Matcher, H. Petrol, 776–90.

261. Hector Fix-Zamudio, "Judicial Protection of Human Rights in Latin America and the Inter-American Court of Human Rights," *Judicial Protection of Human Rights at the National and International Level — International Congress on Procedural Law for the Ninth Centenary of the University of Bologna (22–24 September 1988),* vol. I, General Reports, 387, at 443; Gruffer, Milan, 1991.

262. Id., at 441.

263. Resolution of the IACtHR, 27 November 2002, Case Castillo Páez, Follow-up of the Judgement. Resolution of the IACtHR 22 November 2002, Barrios Altos, Follow-up of the Judgement. Resolution of the IACtHR, 27 November 2003, Case Durand and Ugarte, Follow-up of the Judgement. Resolution of the IAC-

tHR, 27 November 2002, Case Garrido and Baigorria, 27 November 2002, Follow-up of the Judgement. Resolution of the IACtHR, 27 November 2002, Case of Loayza Tamayo, Follow-up of the Judgement. Resolution of the IACtHR, 28 November 2002, Neira Algeria case, Follow-up of the Judgement. Resolution of the IACtHR, 27 November 2002, Case Caballero Delgado and Santana, Follow-up of the Judgement. Resolution of the IACtHR, 27 November 2002, Blake Case, Follow-up of the Judgement.

264. *Blake,* §33; *Suárez Rosero Case,* §40; *Case Castillo Páez,* §50; *Loayza Tamayo,* §84; *Case Garrido y Baigorria,* §40; *Caballero Delgado and Santana,* §15; *Neira Alegría,* §36; *Aloeboetoe,* §43; *Cantoral Benavides,* §40; *Cesti Hurtado* Reparations, §35; *Villagrán Morales,* §62; *Bámaca Velásquez,* §38; and IACtHR, *Trujillo Oroza Case,* §60.

265. Communication No. 45/1979, p. 987.

266. Fix-Zamudio, at 451.

267. Decision on the Admissibility and Merits, Delivered on 18 February 1998 in Case No. CH/97/45, *Sammy Hermes against the Federation of Bosnia and Herzegovina,* §117.

268. *Damjanovic,* §23.

269. *Matanovic,* §63.

270. ECtHR, *Ireland v. United Kingdom,* 18 January 1978, §244 et ss.

271. *De Wilde, Rooms and Very ("Vagrancy") v. Belgium (Article 50),* 10/03/1972: paragraph 20: "No doubt, the treaties from which the text of Article 50 (Article 50) was borrowed had more particularly in view cases where the nature of the injury would make it possible to wipe out entirely the consequences of a violation but where the internal law of the State involved precludes this being done. Nevertheless, the provisions of Article 50 (Article 50), which recognise the Court's competence to grant to the injured party a just satisfaction, also cover the case where the impossibility of restitutio in integrum follows from the very nature of the injury; indeed, common sense suggests that this must be so a fortiori. The Court sees no reason why, in the latter case just as in the former, it should not have the right to award to the injured persons the just satisfaction that they had not obtained from the Government of the respondent State"; paragraph 21: "Where the consequences of a violation are only capable of being wiped out partially, the affording of 'just satisfaction' in application of Article 50 (Article 50) requires that: (i) the Court has found 'a decision or measure taken' by an authority of a Contracting State to be 'in conflict with the obligations arising from the ... Convention'; (ii) there is an 'injured party'; (iii) the Court considers it 'necessary' to afford just satisfaction."

272. *Cases of Srebrenica,* §220 et ss.
273. CCPR/C/3/Rev.6 and Corr.1, Rule 95.
274. Case No. 30/1978.
275. Communication No. 107/1981.
276. Communication No. 181/1984.

Chapter 11

1. E/CN.4/Sub.2/1997/20/Rev.1.
2. CIRC, "Personnes disparues: Mécanismes destinés à résoudre les problèmes relatifs aux personnes portées disparues," Atelier, Genève, 19–21 September 2002 (available online at www.icrc.org).
3. *Antonella Notari,* "War and Accountability — Missing," *Forum,* April 2002.
4. *Las Palmeras,* Reparations, §68 et ss.
5. See, e.g., the claim of the petitioner in *Unkovic,* decided by the HRCBH.

6. Vasuki Nesiah, "Overcoming Tensions between Family and Judicial Procedures," *IRRC Review,* December 2002, vol. 84 no. 848, 823, at 826.
7. Amnesty International, *Annual Report 2000,* Argentina, 2000.
8. Report No. 21/00,* Case 12.059 Carmen Aguiar de Lapacó, Argentina, 29 February 2000.
9. S. 1085. XXXI, Suárez Mason, Carlos Guillermo s/ homicidio, privación ilegal de la libertad, etc., 13 August 1998.
10. *Ganora.*
11. See id., opinion of Judge Vasquez.
12. *Urteaga,* concurrent opinion, Minister Petracchi.
13. Id., opinion of Boggiano.
14. CIRC.

Bibliography

Documents

United Nations

CONFERENCE DOCUMENTS

A/CONF.183/2/Add.1, United Nations Diplomatic Conference of Plenipotentiaries on the Establishment of an International Criminal Court, Report of the Preparatory Committee, Addendum, 1998.

A/CONF.157/23, Vienna Declaration and Programme of Action, 1993.

A/CONF.187/PM.1, Tenth United Nations Congress on the Prevention of Crime and the Treatment of Offenders, 1999.

GENERAL ASSEMBLY

A/810 (III), Universal Declaration of Human Rights, Res. 217A, of 10 December 1948.

A/5515, Declaration on the Elimination of All Forms of Racial Discrimination, Resolution 1904 (18) of 20 November 1963.

International Convention on the Elimination of All Forms of Racial Discrimination, Resolution 2106 (20) of 21 December 1965.

A/6316, International Covenant on Civil and Political Rights, Resolution 2200A, 1966.

A/6316, Optional Protocol to the International Covenant on Civil and Political Rights, Resolution 2200A (21) of 16 December 1966.

A/7218, Convention on the Non-Applicability of Statutory Limitations to War Crimes and Crimes Against Humanity, Res. 2391 (23), 1968.

A/34/46, Code of Conduct for Law Enforcement Officials, Resolution 34/169 of 17 December 1979.

A/34/583/Add.1, Protection of Human Rights in Chile, 21 November 1979.

A/40/34, Declaration of Basic Principles of Justice for Victims of Crime and Abuse of Power, 29 November 1985.

A/43/49, Body of Principles for the Protection of All Persons under Any Form of Detention or Imprisonment, Resolution 43/173 of 9 December 1988.

A/RES/47/133, Declaration on the Protection of all Persons from Enforced Disappearance, 18 December 1992.

A/52/469, Human Rights Questions, Including Alternative Approaches for Improving the Effective Enjoyment of Human Rights and Fundamental Freedoms United Nations Decade for Human Rights Education, 1995–2004, and public information activities in the field of human rights, Report of the Secretary-General, 15 October 1997.

A/RES/55/103, Question of enforced or involuntary disappearances (2 March 2001).

A/RES/56/83, Responsibility of States for internationally wrongful acts, 28 January 2002, Annex.

A/RES/57/215, Question of enforced or involuntary disappearances (28 February 2003).

ECOSOC

E/1989/89, Principles on the Effective Prevention and Investigation of Extra-legal, Arbitrary and Summary Executions, Resolution 1989/65 of 24 May 1989.

E/5988, Standard Minimum Rules for the Treatment of Prisoners Adopted by the First United Nations Congress on the Prevention of Crime and the Treatment of Offenders, Geneva, 1955, and approved by the ECOSOC by its resolution 663 C (24) of 31 July 1957 and 2076 (62) of 13 May 1977.

E/RES/1997/33, Elements of Responsible Crime Prevention: Standards and Norms, 1997.

E/2004/260, Enforced or involuntary disappearances.

INTERNATIONAL LAW COMMISSION

A/CN.4/488, State responsibility — Comments submitted by States, 25 March 1998.

A/CN.4/SR.2612 to SR.2662, Fifty-second session provisional Summary Records International Law Commission, 17 August 2000.

A/CN.4/L.602/Rev.1, State Responsibility, 26 July 2001

COMMISSION ON HUMAN RIGHTS

E/CN.4/1992/18/Add.1, Report of the Working Group on Enforced or Involuntary Disappearances, December 1991.

E/CN.4/1993/25/Add.1, Report of the Working Group on Enforced or Involuntary Disappearances, December 1992.

E/CN.4/1994/26, Report of the Working Group on Enforced or Involuntary Disappearances, 22 December 1993.

E/CN.4/1995/36, Report of the Working Group on Enforced or Involuntary Disappearances, 21 December 1994.

E/CN.4/1996/38, Report of the Working Group on Enforced or Involuntary Disappearances, 15 January 1996.

E/CN.4/1996/36, Special process on missing persons in the territory of the former Yugoslavia, Report submitted by Mr. Manfred Nowak, expert member of the Working Group on Enforced or Involuntary Disappearances, responsible for the special process, pursuant to paragraph 4 of Commission resolution 1995/35, 4 March 1996.

E/CN.4/1997/34, Report of the Working Group on Enforced or Involuntary Disappearances, 13 December 1996.

E/CN.4/1997/55, Special process on missing persons in the territory of the former Yugoslavia, Report submitted to Mr. Manfred Nowak, expert member of the Working Group on Enforced or Involuntary Disappearances, responsible for the special process, pursuant to Commission resolution 1996/71, 15 January 1997.

E/CN.4/1997/104, Report of the Working Group on Enforced or Involuntary Disappearances, 16 January 1997.

E/CN.4/1998/10, Adverse effects of the illicit movement and dumping of toxic and dangerous products and wastes on the enjoyment of human rights Progress report submitted by Mrs. Fatma-Zohra Ksentini, Special Rapporteur, pursuant to Commission resolution 1997/9, 20 January 1998.

E/CN.4/1998/15, Report on the Situation of Human Rights in the Territory of the Former Yugoslavia, 31 October 1997.

E/CN.4/1998/38, Report of the Special Rapporteur on Torture, 24 December 1997.

E/CN.4/1998/39/Add.1, Report of the Special Rapporteur of the Commission on Human Rights on the Independence of Judges and Lawyers, 1997.

E/CN.4/1998/43, Report of the Working Group on Enforced or Involuntary Disappearances, 12 January 1998.

E/CN.4/1998/54, Report of the Special Rapporteur on violence against women, its causes and consequences, Ms. Radhika Coomaraswamy, submitted in accordance with Commission resolution 1997/44, 26 January 1998.

E/CN.4/1998/68, Extrajudicial, summary or arbitrary executions, Report of the Special Rapporteur, Mr. Bacre Waly Ndiaye, submitted pursuant to Commission on Human Rights resolution 1997/61, 23 December 1997.

E/CN.4/RES/1998/53, Impunity, 17 April 1998.

E/CN.4/1999/62, Report of the Working Group on Enforced or Involuntary Disappearances, 28 December 1998.

E/CN.4/1999/65, Report of the independent expert on the right to restitution, compensation and rehabilitation for victims of grave violations of human rights and fundamental freedoms, Mr. M. Cherif Bassiouni, submitted pursuant to Commission on Human Rights resolution 1998/43, 8 February 1999.

E/CN.4/RES/1999/34, Impunity, 23 April 1999.

E/CN.4/2000/62, Annex, Basic Principles and Guidelines on the Right to a Remedy and Reparation for Victims of Violations of International Human Rights and Humanitarian Law, 18 January 2000.

E/CN.4/2000/64, Report of the Working Group on Enforced or Involuntary Disappearances, 21 December 1999.

E/CN.4/2000/64/Add.1, Report of the Working Group on Enforced or Involuntary Disappearances, Addendum–Sri Lanka, 2000.

E/CN.4/RES/2000/37, Question of enforced or involuntary disappearances, 20 April 2000.

E/CN.4/2001/68, Report of the Working Group on Enforced or Involuntary Disappearances, 18 December 2000.

E/CN.4/2001/69, Question of enforced or involuntary disappearances, 21 December 2000.

E/CN.4/2001/69/Add.1, Question of enforced or involuntary disappearances, Switzerland, 14 March 2001.

E/CN.4/RES/2001/46, Question of enforced or involuntary disappearances, 23 April 2001.

E/CN.4/2002/L.57, Draft resolution: Question of Enforced or Involuntary Disappearance, 15 April 2002.

E/CN.4/RES/2002/41, Question of enforced or involuntary disappearances, 23 April 2002.

E/CN.4/2002/79, Report of the Working Group on Enforced or Involuntary Disappearances, 18 January 2002.

E/CN.4/2002/71, Report submitted by Mr. Manfred Nowak, independent expert charged with examining the existing international criminal and human rights framework for the protection of persons from enforced or involuntary disappearances, pursuant to paragraph 11 of Commission resolution 2001, 8 January 2002.

E/CN.4/2003/WG.22/CRP.2, Groupe de travail intersessions à composition non limitée, chargé d'élaborer un projet d'instrument normatif juridiquement contraignant pour la protection de toutes les personnes contre les disparitions forcées, Première session, Project de Rapport, Organisation des travaux, 13 January 2003.

E/CN.4/2003/63, The right to a remedy and reparation for victims of violations of international human rights and humanitarian law (27 December 2002).

E/CN.4/2003/70, Question of enforced or involuntary disappearances. Report of the Working Group on Enforced or Involuntary Disappearances, Submitted in accordance with Commission resolution 2002/41, 21 January 2003.

E/CN.4/2003/71, Report of the intersessional open-ended working group to elaborate a draft legally binding normative instrument for the protection of all persons from enforced disappearance, 12 February 2003.

E/CN.4/2003/WG.22/CRP.3, Intersessional open-ended Working Group to elaborate a draft legally binding normative instrument for the protection of all persons from enforced disappearance, 13 January 2003.

E/CN.4/2004/40, Enforced or involuntary disappearances, 19 April 2004.

E/CN.4/2004/59, Report of the intersessional open-ended working group to elaborate a draft legally binding normative instrument for the protection of all persons from enforced disappearance, 23 February 2004.

E/CN.4/WG.22/WP.2, Working Paper, Intersessional open-ended Working Group to elaborate a draft legally binding normative instrument for the protection of all persons from enforced disappearance, October 2004.

SUB-COMMISSION ON THE PROMOTION AND PROTECTION OF HUMAN RIGHTS

E/CN.4/Sub.2/1988/19, Report to the U.N. on the Prevention of the Disappearances of Children in Argentina.

E/CN.4/Sub.2/1990/10, Preliminary Report Concerning the Right to Restitution, compensation and rehabilitation for victims of gross violations of human rights and fundamental freedoms, 1989.

E/CN.4/Sub.2/1993/8, Study concerning the right to restitution, compensation and rehabilitation for victims of gross violations of human rights and fundamental freedoms, Final report submitted by Mr. Theo van Boven, Special Rapporteur, 2 July 1993.

E/CN.4/Sub.2/1993/10, Definition of Gross and Large-Scale Violations of Human Rights as an International Crime. Working Paper Submitted by Mr. Stanislav Chernichenko in Accordance with Sub-Commission Decision 1992/109, 8 June 1992.

E/CN.4/Sub.2/1994/7/Add.1, Review of Further Developments in Fields with Which the Sub-Commission Has Been Concerned, Report of the Secretary-General Prepared Pursuant to Sub-Commission Resolution 1993/29, 22 July 1994.

E/CN.4/Sub.2/1994/22, The Administration of Justice and the Human Rights of Detainees, Question of the Human Rights of Persons Subjected to Any Form of Detention or Imprisonment, Report of the sessional working group on the administration of justice and the question of compensation, Chairman-Rapporteur: Mrs. Claire Palley, 15 August 1994.

E/CN.4/Sub.2/1994/23, The Administration of Justice and the Human Rights of Detainees: Question of Human Rights and States of Emergency, Seventh revised annual report and list of States which, since 1 January 1985, have proclaimed, extended or terminated a state of emergency, presented by Mr. Leandro Despouy, Special Rapporteur appointed pursuant to Economic and Social Council resolution 1985/37, 3 June 1994.

E/CN.4/Sub.2/1994/24, The Administration of Justice and the Human Rights of Detainees, The right to a fair trial: Current recognition and measures necessary for its strengthening. Final report prepared by Mr. Stanislav Chernichenko and Mr. William Treat, 3 June 1994.

E/CN.4/Sub.2/1996/17, The Administration of Justice and the Human Rights of Detainees, Revised set of basic principles and guidelines on the right to reparation for victims of gross violations of human rights and humanitarian law, prepared by Mr. Theo van Boven pursuant to Sub-Commission decision 1995/117, 24 May 1996.

E/CN.4/Sub.2/1997/8, Final report on the question of the impunity of perpetrators of human rights violations (economic, social and cultural rights), prepared by the Special Rapporteur, 27 June 1997.

E/CN.4/Sub.2/1997/20, Question of the impunity of perpetrators of human rights violations (civil and political). Report prepared by Mr. Joinet pursuant to Sub-Commission Decision 1996/119, of 26 June 1997.

E/CN.4/Sub.2/1997/20/Rev.1, Revised Final Report on the Question of the Impunity of Perpetrators of Human Rights Violations (Civil and Political), 2 October 1997.

E/CN.4/Sub.2/1998/13, Systematic rape, sexual slavery and slavery-like practices during armed conflict. Final report submitted by Ms. Gay J. McDougall, Special Rapporteur, 22 June 1998.

E/CN.4/Sub.2/1998/19, Report of the sessional working group on the administration of justice, Annex, 19 August 1998.

COMMISSION ON CRIME PREVENTION AND CRIMINAL JUSTICE

E/CN.15/1996/16/Add.3, Commission on Crime Prevention and Criminal Justice, Fifth Session, Vienna, 21–31 May 1996, United Nations Standards and Norms in the Field of Crime Prevention and Criminal Justice, Report of the Secretary-General, Addendum, Use and Application of the Declaration of Basic Principles of Justice for Victims of Crime and Abuse of Power, 10 April 1996.

HUMAN RIGHTS COMMITTEE

HRI/GEN/1/Rev.1, Compilation of General Comments and General Recommendations Adopted by Human Rights Treaty Bodies (1994).

CCPR/C/3/Rev.6 and Corr.1, Rules of Procedure of the Human Rights Committee.

PREPARATORY COMMISSION FOR THE INTERNATIONAL CRIMINAL COURT
PCNICC/2000/1/Add.2, Elements of Crimes, 2 November 2000. International Seminar on access of victims to the International Criminal Court (Paris, 27–29 April 1999) Report of workshops 29 of April 1999.

Regional Systems

COUNCIL OF EUROPE
Convention for the Protection of Human Rights and Fundamental Freedoms, ETS no. 005, Rome, 4 November 1950.

ORGANIZATION OF AMERICAN STATES
OEA/Ser.L/V/II.23, doc. 21, rev. 6, American Declaration of the Rights and Duties of Man, Ninth International Conference of American States, Bogotà, Colombia, 1948.
OAS/Ser.P AG/doc.3114/94 rev.1, The Inter-American Convention on Forced Disappearance of Persons, 7th Plenary Session, 9 June 1994.
Rules of Procedure of the Inter-American Commission on Human Rights (Commission, 109th special session, 4–8 December 2000, and amended at the 116th ordinary period of sessions, 7–25 October 2002).

Books and Articles

Books

American Law Institute, Restatement (Third) of the Foreign Relations Law of the United States (Section 702), 1987.
Bassiouni, Cherif, International Criminal Law and Human Rights, Transnational Publishers, New York, vol. I, 1999.
Blanc Altemir, Antonio, La violación de los derechos humanos fundamentales como crimen internacional, Bosch, Barcelona, 1990.
Brownlie, Ian, Principles of Public International Law, Oxford, Fifth edition, 1998.
Brownlie, Ian, State Responsibility, Part I, Oxford, 1983.
Cassesse, Antonio, Los Derechos Humanos en el Mundo Contemporáneo, trans. A. Pentimalli Melacrino and B. Ribera de Madariaga, Ariel, Barcelona, 1993.
Dailler, Patrick, and Allain Pellet, Droit International Public, 6th edition, L.G.D.J., Paris, 1999.
Directorate of Human Rights, Proceedings of the Sixth International Colloquy about the European Convention on Human Rights, Seville, 13–16 November 1985, Nijhoff, Dordrech.
Guest, Iain, Behind the disappearances: Argentina's dirty war against human rights and the United Nations, Philadelphia, 1990.
Henkin, Louis, Gerald Neuman, Diane F. Orentlicher, and David Leebron, Human Rights, Foundation Press, New York, 1999.
Krausnick, H., and M. Broszat, Anatomy of the SS State, Paladin, London, 1970.
Moore, J. B., History and Digest of the International Arbitrations to which the United States has been a Party, Washington, DC, 1898.
Neuhold, Hanspeter et al, Österreichisches Handbuch des Völkerrechts, I, 2. Auflage, Manz, Wien, 1991.
Nowak, Manfred, U.N. Covenant on Civil and Political Rights, N.P. Engel, Kehl, 1993.
Pinto, Monica Temas de Derechos Humanos, Ediciones del Puerto, Buenos Aires, 1997.
Provost, Rene, International Human Rights and Humanitarian Law, Cambridge, 2002.
Randelzhofer, A., and C. Tomuschat (eds.), State Responsibility and the Individual, Kluwer Law International, London, 1999.
Reuter, Paul, Introducción al Derecho de los Tratados, rev. ed. by Peter Haggenmacher, trans. Eduardo Suárez, Fondo de Cultura Económica, Mexico, 1999.

Rodley, Nigel S., The treatment of prisoners under international law, Clarendon Press, Oxford, 2nd ed., 1999.

Steiner, Henry J., and Philip Alston, International Human Rights in Context: Law, Politics, Morals — Texts and Materials, Clarendon Press, Oxford, 1996

Van Boven, Theo, Cees Flinterman, Fred Grünfeld and Ingrid Westendorp (eds.), Seminar on the Right to Restitution, Compensation and Rehabilitation for Victims of Gross Violations of Human Rights and Fundamental Freedoms, Maastricht, 11–15 March 1992, Utrecht: SIM no 12, 1992.

Articles in Collective Pieces

Abellán Honrubia, V., "Aspectos Jurídico Internationales de la Desaparición Forzada de Personas como práctica política del Estado," Estudios Jurídicos en Honor del Profesor Octavio Pérez-Vitoria, Volume I, Madrid, 1983.

Baigun, David, "La desaparición forzada de personas: su ubicación en el ambito penal," in Asamblea Permanente por los Derechos Humanos (eds.), La Desaparición, Crimen contra la Humanidad, ed. Asamblea Permanente por los Derechos Humanos, Buenos Aires, 1987.

Enrich Mas, Montserrat, "Right to Compensation under Article 50," European System for the Protection of Human Rights, ed. R. St. J. MacDonald, F. Matscher, H. Petzold, 776–790.

Fernández de Soto, Guillermo, "La desaparicion forzada de personas: un crimen de lesa humanidad," Derechos humanos en las Americas, Homenaje a la memoria de Carlos A. Dunshee de Abranches, 1985.

Fix-Zamudio, Héctor, "Judicial Protection of Human Rights in Latin America and the Inter-American Court of Human Rights," Judicial Protection of Human Rights at the National and International Level — International Congress on Procedural Law for the Ninth Centenary of the University of Bologna (22–24 September 1988), vol. I, General Reports, 387.

Frouville, Olivier de, "Les disparitions forcées," Droit Pénal International, CEDIN — Paris X, ed. A. Pedone, Paris, 2000.

Golsong, Heribert "Quelques Réflexions à Propos du Pouvoir de la Cour Européenne des Droits de l'Homme d'accorder une Satisfaction Equitable," René Cassin Amicorum Discipulorumque Liber, volume I, Problèmes de Protection Internationale des Droits de l'Homme, Pedone, Paris, 1969, 88.

Kleffner, Jann K. "Conflict related crimes — legal obligations to prosecute?" Forthcoming in International and national criminal jurisdictions as a means of conflict resolution, ed. Horst Fischer.

Macdonald, R. St. J., "Supervision of the Execution of the Judgments of the European Court of Human Rights," Droit et Justice Mélanges Nicolas Valticos, ed. René Jean Dupuy, 1999, Pédone, Paris, 418–431.

Méndez, Juan, "Derecho a la verdad frente a las graves violaciones de derechos humanos," in La Aplicación de los Tratados sobre Derechos Humanos por los Tribunales Locales, CELS, Buenos Aires, 1997.

Molina Theissen, Ana Lucrecia, "La desaparición forzada de personas en America Latina," Estudios Básicos de Derechos Humanos 7, IIDH, San José, 1996.

Nowak, Manfred, "The Right of Victims of Gross Human Rights Violations to Reparation," in Rendering Justice to the Vulnerable: Liber Amicorum in Honor of Theo van Boven, ed. Fons Coomans, The Hague, Kluwer, 2000, 203–24.

Paolillo, Felipe, "Derechos Humanos y Reparación (con especial referencia al sistema interamericano)," Héctor Gros Espiell amicorum liber: persona humana y derecho internacional, volume 2, Bruylant, Brussels, 1997, 988.

Tomuschat, Christian, "Individual Reparation Claims in Instances of Grave Human Rights Violations: The Position under General International Law," in State Responsibility and the

Individual, eds. A. Randelzhofer and C. Tomuschat, Kluwer Law International, London, 1999, 1–25.

Articles in Reviews

Andreu-Guzman, Federico, "Le Groupe de travail sur les disparitions forcées des Nations Unies," *IRRC Review,* December 2002, vol. 84 no. 848, 803–818.

Andreu-Guzman, Federico, "The draft international convention on the protection of all persons from forced disappearance. Impunity, crimes against humanity and forced disappearance," *ICJ Review,* no. 62–63, September 2001.

Bailey-Wiebecke, Ilka, "The United Nations Working Group on Disappearances: After 15 years, focus on Asia," *Human Rights Forum* (Philippines), vol. 5/1, 1995.

Blaw, Margriet, "'Denial and silence' or 'acknowledgement and disclosure,'" *IRRC Review,* December 2002, vol. 84 no. 848, 767–783.

Brody, Reed, "Commentary on the draft United Nations declaration on the protection of all persons from enforced or involuntary disappearances," *Netherlands Quarterly of Human Rights,* 8, 1990.

Brody, Reed, and Felipe Gonzalez, "Nunca más: an analysis of international instruments on 'disappearances,'" *Netherlands Quarterly of Human Rights,* vol. 19, no. 2, May 1997.

Deman, Catherine, "La céssation de l'acte illicite," *Revue Belge de Droit International* 1990/2, 478–495

Frowein, Jochen A., "The European and the American Conventions on Human Rights — A Comparison," *Human Rights Law Journal,* vol. 1 no. 1–4, 44, at 45 (1980).

Frumer, Philippe "La Réparation des Atteintes aux Droits de l'Homme Internationalement Protégés — Quelques Données Comparatives," *Rev. Trim. Dr.H,* (1996), 329–352.

Hayner, Priscilla, "Fifteen Truth Commissions — 1974 to 1994," *Human Rights Quarterly,* November 1994.

Huerta Guerrero, Luis, "El Debido Proceso y la Corte Interamericana de Derechos Humanos: tendencias actuales y posibilidades de aplicación por las defensorías del pueblo," *La Revista del Defensor del Pueblo,* 2000, 79.

Kaur, Jaskaran, "A Judicial Blackout: Judicial Impunity for Disappearances in Punjab, India," *Harvard Human Rights Journal,* Spring 2002, 269.

Kramer, David, and David Weissbrodt, "The 1980 United Nations Commission on Human Rights and the disappeared," *Human Rights Quarterly,* vol. 18, 1981.

Lillich, Richard B., and John M. Paxman, "State Responsibility for Injuries to Aliens Occasioned by Terrorist Activities," 25 *Amer. Univ. L. Rev* 2 (1979), 219.

Lillich, Richard B., "The United States Constitution and International Human Rights Law," 3 *Harv. Hum. Rts. J.* 53.

Mann, F. A., "The Consequences of an International Wrong in International and National Law," 48 *B.Y.I.L.,* 1–65, at 3 (1976–77).

Méndez, Juan E. "El derecho a la verdad frente a las graves violaciones a los derechos humanos," *Revista de la Defensoría del Pueblo Debate Defensorial* no. 3, May 2001, 10–30.

Méndez, Juan E., "Accountability for Past Abuses," 19 *Human Rights Quarterly* 2, May 1997.

Mendez, Juan E., and José Miguel Vivanco, "Disappearances and the Inter-American Court: reflections on a litigation experience," *Hameline Law Review,* vol. 13 no. 3, Summer 1990.

Migliorino, Luigi, "Sur la déclaration d'illicité comme forme de satisfaction: à propos de la sentence arbitral du 30 avril 1990 dans l'affaire du Rainbow Warrior," R.G.D.I.P. 96, 61–73.

Nesiah, Vasuki, "Overcoming tensions between family and judicial procedures," *IRRC Review,* December 2002, vol. 84 no. 848, 823, at 826.

Notari, Antonella, "War and Accountability — Missing," *Forum,* April 2002.

Nowak, Manfred, "Monitoring disappearances — the difficult path from clarifying past cases to effectively preventing future ones," *European Human Rights Law Review* 4, 1996.

Olumbe, Alex Kirasi, and Ahmed Kalebi Yakub, "Management, exhumation and identification of human remains: A viewpoint of the developing world," *IRRC Review,* December 2002, vol. 84 no. 848.

Oren, Laura, "Righting Child Custody Wrongs: The Children of the 'Disappeared' in Argentina," *Harvard Human Rights Journal,* Spring 2001, 123.

Orentlicher, Diane, "Settling Accounts: The Duty to Prosecute Human Rights Violations of a Prior Regime," 100 *Yale L.J.* 2537 (1991).

Padilla, David J., "Reparations in *Aloeboetoe v. Suriname,*" 17 *Human Rights Quarterly* (1995) 541–555.

Pascualacci, Jo M., "The Inter-American Human Rights System: Establishing Precedents and Procedure in Human Rights Law," 26 *U. Miami Inter-Am. L. Rev.* 297 (Winter 1994–1995).

Pauwelyn, Joost, "The Concept of a Continuing Violation of an International Obligation: Selected Problems," 66 *B.Y.I.L.* (1995) 415.

Punyasena, Wasana, "The Façade of Accountability: Disappearances in Sri Lanka," *Boston College Third World Law Journal,* Winter 2003, 115.

Rodley, Nigel S., "United Nations actions procedures against "disappearances, summary or arbitrary executions, and torture," *Human Rights Quarterly,* vol. 8, no. 4, November 1986.

Simon, Jean-Marie, "The Alien Tort Claims Act: Justice or Show Trials?" *Boston University International Law Journal,* 11:1, 2–79.

Stover, Eric, and Rachel Shigekane, "The missing in the aftermath of war: When do the needs of victims' families and international war crimes tribunals clash?" *IRRC Review,* December 2002, vol. 84 no. 848, 845.

Taqi, Irum, "Adjudicating Disappearance Cases in Turkey: An Argument for Adopting the Inter-American Court of Human Rights' Approach," *Fordham International Law Journal,* March 2001, 940.

Tayler, Wilder, "Background to the elaboration of the draft international convention for the protection of all persons from forced disappearance. Impunity, crimes against humanity and forced disappearance," *ICJ Review,* no. 62–63, September 2001.

Van Boven, Theo, "Rapporteur, Appendice: E/CN.4/Sub.2/1993/8, Study Concerning the Right to Restitution, Compensation and Rehabilitation for Victims of Gross Violations of Human Rights and Fundamental Freedoms: Final Report Submitted by Mr. Theo van Boven, Special Rapporteur," *Law & Contemp. Prob.,* 59 283.

Van Dongen, Toine, "Vanishing point — the problem of disappearances," *Human Rights Bulletin* 1990/1, United Nations, Centre for Human Rights, New York, 1991.

Waldock, Sir Humphrey, "The Effectiveness of the System Set Up by the European Convention on Human Rights," 1 *Human Rights Law Journal,* no. 14, 1–12.

Wyler, Eric, "Quelques Réflexions sur la Réalisation dans le Temps du Fait Internationalement Illicite," *R.G.D.I.P.,* 95, 881–914 (1991).

Papers

Black, Laura, "Forced disappearances in Sri Lanka constitute a crime against humanity." www.disappearances.org, 2000.

Camacho, Agnes, "Reparations of victims of conflict and human rights violations," HURIDOCS International Conference on Human Rights Information, Gammarth (Tunisia), 22–25 March 1998 (www.huridocs.org).

CIRC, "Personnes disparues: Mécanismes destinés à résoudre les problèmes relatifs aux personnes portées disparues," Atelier, Geneva, 19–21 September 2002 (www.icrc.org).

Cuya, Esteban, "Las Comisiones de la Verdad en América Latina," Menschenrechtezentrum, Nürnberg.

Flinterman, Cees, and Jeroes Gutter, "The United Nations and Human Rights: Achievements and Challenges," UNDP, New York, www.undp.org/hdro/occ.htm, paper no. 48, 2000, 26 pp.

Méndez, Juan E., "Accountability for Past Abuses," Working Paper #233, Helen Kellogg Institute, Notre Dame University, September 1996.

Pallinder, Agneta, "Impunity and Challenges of the Post-Conflict Healing Process," HURIDOCS International Conference on Human Rights Information, Gammarth (Tunisia), 22–25 March 1998 (www.huridocs.org).

Rodley, Nigel S., "The United Nations Declaration on the Protection of all Persons from Enforced or Involuntary Disappearances," Working paper 1 (doc. CEJE 022) presented to the International Conference on Political Killings and Disappearances organized by the Netherlands Section of Amnesty International, Amsterdam, 4–6 September 1992.

Shelton, Dihah L., and Thordis Ingadottir, "The International Criminal Court Reparations to Victims of Crimes (Article 75 of the Rome Statute) and the Trust Fund (Article 79) Recommendations for the Court Rules of Procedure and Evidence, Reparations to Victims at the International Criminal Court," Center on International Cooperation, New York University, for 26 July–13 August 1999 Meeting of the Preparatory Commission for the International Criminal Court.

Jurisprudence

ICJ

ICJ Reports (1970) Barcelona Traction Case.

ICJ Reports (1979), Case Concerning United States Diplomatic and Consular Staff in Tehran, Order of December 15th, 1979, Provisional Measures.

ICJ Reports (1986), Case Concerning Military and Paramilitary Activities in and against Nicaragua, 27 June 1986.

PCIJ

Chorzów Factory (Indemnity), 1928 P.C.I.J. (series A) no. 17.

Arbitral Tribunals

Alabama Claims Arbitration, in Moore, *International Arbitration* (1871), 1, 496.

Hackworth G., "I am alone," *Digest of International Law,* vol. II, 703, 708 (1941). M. Whiteman, Damages in International Law, 722 (1937).

Lusitania Cases (United States v. Germany), Mixed Claims Commission, R.I.A.A., vol. 7, pp. 256 and 257 (1924).

Mallén Case (México v. United States), R.I.A.A., vol. 4, 173.

HRC

CCPR/C/9/D/8/1977, Communication no. 8/1977, 03/04/80.

CCPR/C/OP/1 at 136, Communication no. 25/1978, 26 July 1982.

CCPR/C/15/D/30/1978, Communication no. 30/1978: Uruguay, 29/03/82.

Supp. No. 40 (A/36/40), Communication no. R.12/52, 6 June 1979.

CCPR/C/OP/1 at 112, Communication no. 45/1979, Colombia, 31 March 1982.

CCPR/C/OP/1 at 92, Communication no. 56/1979, Uruguay, 1984.

CCPR/C/20/D/83/1981, Communication no. 83/1981 (Jurisprudence) (04/11/83).

Supp. No. 40 (A/38/40) at 124, Communication no. 84/1981, Uruguay, 27 February 1981.

Supp. No. 40 (A/38/40) at 197, Communication no. 90/1981, Zaire, 30 March 1981.

CCPR/C/OP/2 at 138, Communication no. 107/1981, Uruguay, 21 July 1983.

Supp. No. 40 (A/39/40) at 169, Communication no. 110/1981, Uruguay, 31 March 1983.

Supp. No. 40 (A/40/40) at 187, Communication nos. 146/1983 and 148–154/1983, Suriname, 4 April 1985.

CCPR/C/OP/2 at 192, Communication no. 161/1983: Colombia (1983).

CCPR/C/37/D/181/1984, Communication no. 181/1984, Colombia, 22/11/89.

CCPR/C/38/D/275/1988, Communication no. 275/1988: Argentina, 04/04/90.

CCPR/C/51/D/322/1988, Communication no. 322/1988: Uruguay, 09/08/94.

CCPR/C/53/D/400/1990, Communication no. 400/1990: Argentina, 27/04/95.

CCPR/C/51/D/449/1991, Communication no. 449/1991: Dominican Republic, 10/08/94.

CCPR/C/56/D/540/1993, Communication no. 540/1993: Peru, 16/04/96

CCPR/C/55/D/563/1993, Communication no. 563/1993: Colombia, 13/11/95.

CCPR/C/60/D/612/1995, Communication no. 612/1995: Colombia, 19/08/97.

CCPR/C/66/D/717/1996, Communication no. 717/1996: Chile, 16/09/99.

CCPR/C/66/D/718/1996/Rev.1, Communication no. 718/1996: Chile, 24/09/99.

CCPR/C/75/D/902/1999, Communication no, 902/1999: New Zealand, 30/07/2002.

ECtHR

Akdeniz v. Turkey, Application no. 23954/94, 31 May 2001.

Aksoy v. Turkey, Application no. 21987/93, Reports 1996-VI, 18 December 1996.

Bilgin v. Turkey, Application no. 25659/94, ECtHR, 17 July 2001.

Çakici v. Turkey, Application no. 23657/94, Reports 1999-IV, 8 July 1999.

Çiçek v. Turkey, Application no. 25704/94, 27 February 2001.

Cyprus v. Turkey, Application no. 25781/94, ECtHR, 10 May 2001.

De Becker v. Belgium, Series A, vol. 4, 27 March 1962.

De Wilde, Ooms and Versyp ("Vagrancy") *v. Belgium* (Article 50), Applications 2832/66; 2835/66; 2899/66, Series A, vol. 14, 10 March 1972.

Ertak v. Turkey, Application no. 20764/92, Reports 2000-V, 9 May 2000.

Ylhan v. Turkey, Application no. 22277/93, Reports 2000-VII, 27 June 2000.

Kaya v Turkey, Application 22729/93, Reports 1998-I, 19 February 1998.

Kurt v. Turkey, 15/1997/799/1002, Reports 1998-III, 25 May 1998.

Le Compte, van Leuven et De Meyere, Series A, vol. 54, 18 October 1982.

Loizidou v. Turkey (Article 50), Application 15318/89, Reports 1998-IV, 28 July 1998.

Mahmut Kaya v. Turkey, Application no. 22535/93, Reports 2000-III, 28 March 2000.

McCann and others v. The United Kingdom, Series A, vol. 324, 27 September 1995.

Orhan v. Turkey, Application no. 25656/94, 18 June 2002.

Salman v. Turkey, Application no. 21986/93, Reports 2000-VII, 27 June 2000.

Tas v. Turkey, Application no. 24396/94, 14 November 2000.

Timurtas v. Turkey, Application no. 23531/94, Reports 2000-VI, 13 June 2000.

IACtHR

CONTENTIOUS JURISPRUDENCE

Aloeboetoe, Reparations (Article 63.1 ACHR) 10 September 1993, Series C, no. 15.

Bamaca Velasquez (Merits), 25 November 2000, IACtHR, Series C, no. 70 (2000).

Bámaca Velásquez Case. Reparations (Article 63[1] American Convention on Human Rights), 22 February 2002, Series C, no. 91.

Barrios Altos (Merits), 14 March 2001, IACtHR, Series C, no. 70 (2001).

Barrios Altos Case, Reparations (Article 63[1] American Convention on Human Rights). 30 November 2001, Series C, no. 87.

Barrios Altos, Resolution of the IACtHR, 22 November 2002, Follow up of the Judgment.

Benavides Cevallos (Merits), 19 June 1998, Series C, no. 38 (1998).

Blake (Merits), 24 January 1998, IACtHR, Series C, no. 36 (1998).

Blake Case, Reparations (Article 63[1] American Convention on Human Rights), 22 January 1999, Series C, no. 48.

Blake, Resolution of the IACtHR, 27 November 2002, Follow-up of the Judgment.

Caballero Delgado & Santana Case (Merits), 8 December 1995, Series C, no. 22 (1995).

Caballero Delgado & Santana, Reparations (Article 63[1] American Convention on Human Rights). 29 January 1997, Series C, no. 31.

Caballero Delgado & Santana, Resolution

of the IACtHR, 27 November 2002, Follow up of the Judgment.

Cantoral Benavides Case, 18 August 2000, no. 69, Series C (2000).

Cantoral Benavides Case. Reparations (Article 63[1] American Convention on Human Rights), 3 December 2001, Series C, no. 88.

Cantos, Merits and Reparations, 28 November 2002, Series C, no. 97 (2002).

Castillo Páez Case, 3 November 1997, Series C, no. 34 (1997).

Castillo Páez Case, Reparations (Article 63[1] American Convention on Human Rights). 27 November 1998, Series C, no. 43.

Castillo Páez, Resolution of the IACtHR, 27 November 2002, Follow-up of the Judgment.

Cesti Hurtado Case. Reparations, 31 May 2001, Series C, no. 56.

Durand and Ugarte, Resolution of the IACtHR, 27 November 2002, Follow-up of the Judgment.

Durand and Ugarte. Reparations (Article 63[1] American Convention on Human Rights), 3 December 2001, Series C, no. 89.

Durand and Ugarte, 16 August 2000, Series C, no. 68.

El Amparo, Reparations, 14 September 1996, Series C, no. 28.

El Caracazo, Judgment, Series C, no. 58, 11 November 1999.

El Caracazo. Reparations (Article 63.1 ACHR), 29 August 2002, Series C, no. 95.

Fairén Garbi y Solís Corrales, Preliminary Objections, 26 June 1987, Series C, no. 2.

Garrido & Baigorria, Reparations (Article 63[1] American Convention on Human Rights), 27 August 1998, Series C, no. 39.

Garrido & Baigorria, Resolution of the IACtHR, 27 November 2002, Follow-up of the Judgment.

Godínez Cruz, (Merits) 20 January 1989, Series C, no. 5 (1989).

Godínez Cruz. Compensatory Damages (Article 63[1] American Convention on Human Rights), July 21,1989, no. 8.

Godínez Cruz, Preliminary Objections, 26 June 1987, Series C, no. 3.

Hilaire, Constantine y Benjamin et al., 21 June 2002, Series C, no. 94.

Las Palmeras, Reparations (Article 63.1 ACHR), 26 November 2002, Series C, no. 95.

Loayza Tamayo, Reparations (Article 63[1] American Convention on Human Rights), Judgment of 27 November 1998, Series C, no. 42 (1998).

Loayza Tamayo, Resolution of the IACtHR, 27 November 2002, Follow-up of the Judgment.

Loayza Tamayo, Interpretation of the Judgment of Reparations (Article 67 of the ACHR), 3 June 1999.

Neira Alegria, Resolution of the IACtHR, 28 November 2002, Follow-up of the Judgment.

Neira Alegría et al., Reparations (Article 63[1] American Convention on Human Rights). Judgment of 19 September 1996, Series C, no. 29.

Paniagua Morales, Reparations, 25 May 2001, Series C, no. 76.

Paniagua Morales, 8 March 1998, Series C, no. 37.

Reggiardo Tolosa, Provisional Measures, Series E, doc. 17, Resolution of the President of the IACtHR, 19 November 1993.

Suárez Rosero, Reparations (Article 63[1] American Convention on Human Rights), Series C., no. 44. Judgment of 20 January 1999.

Trujillo Oroza (Merits), 26 January 2000, Series C, no. 64

Trujillo Oroza Case. Reparations (Article 63[1] American Convention on Human Rights). 27 February 2002, Series C, no. 92.

Velasquez Rodríguez (Merits), 29 July 1988, Series C, no. 4 (1988).

Velásquez Rodríguez. Compensatory Damages (Article 63[1] American Convention on Human Rights). 21 July 1989, Series C, no. 7.

Velásquez Rodríguez, Preliminary Objections, 26 June 1987, Series C., no. 1

Villagrán Morales et al., Reparations. 26 May 2001, Series C, no. 77.

Villagrán Morales et al., 19 November 1999, Series C, no. 63

ADVISORY OPINIONS

Enforceability of the Right to Reply or

Correction (Articles 14[1], 1[1] and 2 American Convention on Human Rights), Advisory Opinion OC-7/86 of 29 August 1986, Series A no. 7.

Habeas Corpus in Emergency Situations (Articles 27[2] and 7[6] of the American Convention on Human Rights), Advisory Opinion OC-8/87 of 30 January 1987, Inter-Am.Ct.H.R., Series A, no. 8 (1987).

Judicial Guarantees in States of Emergency (Articles 27[2], 25 and 8 of the American Convention on Human Rights), Advisory Opinion OC-9/87 of October 6, 1987, Inter-Am.Ct.H.R., Series A, no. 9 (1987).

IACHR

COUNTRY REPORTS

OEA/Ser.L/V/II.34 doc. 21 corr.1, Report on the Status of Human Rights in Chile, Chapter 9, 25 October 1974.

OEA/Ser.L/V/II.49, doc. 19, Informe sobre la Situación de los Derechos Humanos en Argentina, 1980.

OEA/Ser.L/V/II.66, doc. 16, Tercer Informe sobre la Situación de los Derechos Humanos en la República de Guatemala, 1985.

OEA/Ser.L/V/II.66, doc. 17, Report on the Situation of Human Rights in Chile, 1985.

OEA/Ser.L/V/II.96, Doc. 10, rev. 1, Report on the Situation of Human Rights in Ecuador, 24 April 1997.

Report on the Situation of Human Rights in Brazil (1997), available online at www.cidh.org/countryrep/brazil-eng/index%20-%20brazil.htm.

OEA/Ser.L/V/II.100, doc. 7, rev. 1, Report on the Situation of Human Rights in Mexico, 24 September 1998.

OEA/Ser.L/V/II.102, Doc. 9, rev. 1, Third Report on the Situation of Human Rights in Colombia, 26 February 1999.

OEA/Ser.L/V/II.104 Doc. 49, rev. 1, Report on the Situation of Human Rights in Dominican Republic, 7 October 1999.

ANNUAL REPORTS

OEA/Ser.L/V/II.47 doc. 13, rev.1, Informe Annual 1978, 29 June 1979.

OEA/Ser.L/V/II.54 doc. 9, rev. 1, Annual Report 1980–1981, 16 October 1981.

OEA/Ser.L/V/II.68 doc. 8, rev. 1, Annual Report 1985–86, 26 September 1986.

OEA/Ser.L/V/II.71, Annual Report, 1986–1987, doc. 9, rev.1, 22 September 1987.

OEA/Ser.L/V/II.74, doc. 10, rev.1, IACHR, Annual Report 1987–1988, Areas in Which Steps Need to be Taken towards full Observance of the Human Rights set forth in the American Declaration of the Rights and Duties of Man and the American Declaration on Human Rights, 16 September 1988.

OEA/ser. L/V/II.85, doc. 9 rev., Annual Report 1993, 11 February 1994.

INDIVIDUAL PETITIONS

IACHR, Ten Years of Activities 1971–1981 (1982) [Cases 1757, 1702, 1748, 1755 (1974); Case 1790 (1977)].

OEA/ser.L/V/II.43, doc. 21, Annual Report 1977, (1977) [Case 2029].

OEA/ser.L/V/II.47, doc. 13, rev. 1, Annual Report 1978 (1978) [Cases 2271, 2291, 2262, and 2450].

OEA/ser.L/V/II.50, doc. 13, rev. 1, Annual Report 1979–1980 [Case 2209].

OAS/Ser.L/V/II.61, doc. 22, rev.1, Annual Report 1982–83 (1983) [Cases 2401, 7245; Resolutions 1, 11, 13, 17 (1983)].

OEA/ser.L/V/II.68, doc. 8, rev. 1, Annual Report 1985–86 [Case 9233; Resolution 25/86].

OEA/Ser.L/V/II.74 doc. 10, rev. 1, Annual Report 1988–89 [Report no. 24/87].

OEA/Ser.L/V/II.76 doc. 10, Annual Report 1989–1990 [Reports no. 28/88, 30/88, 9/89 and 10/89].

OEA/Ser.L/V/II.79.rev.1 doc. 12, Annual Report 1990–1991 [Reports no. 9/90 to 24/90, 26/90 to 30/90, 32/90 to 35/90, 37/90 to 42/90, 49/90 to 72/90, 75/90 to 81/90, 83/90 to 86/90, 88/90 to 89/90, 1/91 to 3/91, 7/91, 9/91, 27/91].

OEA/Ser.L/V/II.83, doc. 14, corr. 1, Annual Report 1992–1993 [Cases 1/92, 9/92,12/92, 15/92,28/92, 29/92, 33/92, 10/93, 12/93, 24/93].

OEA/Ser.L/V/II.85, Annual Report 1993 [Report no. 37/93].

OEA/Ser.L/V/II.95 Doc. 7, rev., Annual

Report 1996 [Report no. 28/96 to 30/96, 53/96 to 56/96].

OEA/Ser.L/V/II.98, doc. 6, Annual Report 1997 [Report no. 1/97, 39/97 to 43/97, 3/98, 11/98, 22/98].

OEA/Ser.L/V/II.102, doc. 6, rev., Annual Report 1998 [Report no. 56/98, 1/99, 19/99, 51/99 to 55/99, and 57/99].

OEA/Ser.L/V/II.106, doc. 3, Annual Report 1999 [Report no. 7/00, 21/00, no. 34/00, 40/00, and 43/00 to 47/00].

OEA/Ser./L/V/II.111, doc. 20, rev.16, Annual Report 2000 [Report no. 111/00,112/00, 58/01, 60/01, 61/01].

OEA/Ser./L/V/II.114, doc. 5, Annual Report 2001 [Report no. 101/01].

HRCBH

Case no. CH/96/1, Josip, Bozana and Tomislav Matanovic against the Republika Srpska.

Cases nos. CH/96/3 and CH/96/9, Branko Medan and Radosav Markovic against Bosnia and Herzegovina and the Federation of Bosnia and Herzegovina, Decision on the Claim for Compensation, 15 May 1999.

Case no. CH/96/8, Decision on the Claim for Compensation in the Case Stjepan Bastijanovic, against the State of Bosnia and Herzegovina and the Federation of Bosnia and Herzegovina, 29 July 1998.

Case no. CH/96/22, Decision on the Claim for Compensation in the Case of Milivoje Bulatovic, against the State of Bosnia and Herzegovina and the Federation of Bosnia and Herzegovina, 29 July 1998.

Case no. CH/96/27, Decision on the Claim for Compensation in the Case of Rifat Bejdic against the Republika Srpska, 22 July 1998.

Case no. CH/96/28, "M.J.," against the Republika Srpska, Decision on the Claim for Compensation, 14 October 1998.

CH/96/30, Damjanovic, 11 March 1998.

Case no. CH/97/45, Samy Hermas against the Federation of Bosnia and Herzegovina Decision on the Admissibility and Merits, 18 February 1998.

Case no. CH/97/46, Decision on the Claim for Compensation, Delivered in Writing on 24 August 1999, Ivica

Kevesevic against the Federation of Bosnia and Herzegovina, 15 May 1999.

Case no. CH/97/82, Decision on the Admissibility and Merits, Velimir Ostojic and 31 Other JNA cases against Bosnia and Herzegovina and the Federation of Bosnia and Herzegovina, 15 January 1999.

Case no. CH/99/2150, *Unkovic v. Federation of Bosnia Herzegovina,* 9 November 2001.

Case no. CH/99/2150, Decision on Request for Review *Dordo Unkovic vs. The Federation of Bosnia Herzegovina,* 10 January 2002.

Case no. CH/99/3196, *Palic v. Republika Srpska,* 11 January 2001.

Case no. CH/01/8365 et al., The "Srebrenica Cases" (49 applications), 7 March 2003

Domestic Tribunals

ARGENTINA

Aguiar de Lapacó Carmen on writ of certiorari (case no. 450) Suárez Mason, S. 1085, 81, 13–8-98.

Case 070/00, FCCA, Salta, Case no. 820/00, June 2000.

Ganora Mario E. Y otra," 16/09/99, LA LEY, 1/3/00, 10/14.

Mignone Emilio F. s/ presentación en causa 761 E.S.M.A. El Derecho 20–4-95.

Suárez Mason, Carlos Guillermo s/ homicidio, privación ilegal de la libertad, etc., S. 1085. 31, 13 August 1998.

Urteaga, Facundo R. C. Estado Nacional 15/10/98, LA LEY, 1998, F, 237.

UNITED STATES

Filartiga v. Pena Irala, 577 F. Supp. at 865.

Forti v. Suarez Mason, 672 F. Supp. 1531 (1987).

Hilao v. Estate of Marcos, 103 F.3d 767 (9th Cir.1996).

Letelier v. Republic of Chile, 502 F. Supp. 259, 266 (D.D.C. 1980).

Martinez-Baca v. Suarez-Mason, no. 87–2057, slip op. at 4–5 (N.D. Cal. 22 April 1988).

Quiros de Rapaport v. Suarez-Mason, no. 87–2266 (N.D. Cal. 11 April, 1989).

Siderman de Blake v. Republic of Argentina, 965 F.2d 699 (9th Cir. 1992).

Reports of Commissions of Inquiry

Interim Report of the Commission of Inquiry into Involuntary Removal or Disappearance of Persons in the Western, Southern and Sabaragamuwa Provinces, Department of Government Printing, Sri Lanka, September 1997.

CONADEP, Nunca Más — Informe de la Comisión Nacional sobre la Desaparición de Personas, Eudeba, Buenos Aires, 5th edition, 1997.

Expert Conferences

El nunca más y la comunidad internacional — la desaparicion forzada como crimen de lesa humanidad, Coloquio de Buenos Aires, 10 al 13 de octubre de 1988. Buenos Aires, Paz Producciones, October de 1989.

Le refus de l'oubli — la politique de disparition forcée de personnes. Colloque de Paris, Jan.-Féb. 1981. Coll. Mondes en devenir, Ed. Berger-Levrault, Paris, 1982.

TheMissing/Conf/02.2003/EN/82, The Missing: Action to resolve the problem of people unaccounted for as a result of armed conflict or internal violence and to assist their families, International Conference of Governmental and Non-Governmental Experts, Geneva, 19–21 February 2003, Working Group on the Observations and Recommendations Report by the Chairman Mr. Nicolas Michel, Director, Directorate of Public International Law, Federal Department of Foreign Affairs, Switzerland.

NGO Documents

Amnesty International, Annual Report 2000, Argentina, 2000.

Amnesty International, Bosnia-Herzegovina Honouring the ghosts — challenging impunity for "disappearances," March 2003.

Amnesty International, Desapariciones, Fundamentos, Madrid, 1983.

Amnesty International, Disappearances: a workbook, 1981.

Amnesty International, Disappearances and political killings: human rights crisis of the 1990s, Amsterdam, 1994.

Amnesty International, Ecuador Torture and "disappearance" of Elías Elint López and Luis Alberto Shinin Laso(1), AMR 28/008/2001 09/04/2001.

Amnesty International, 14-Point Program for the Prevention of Disappearances, http://web.amnesty.org/web/aboutai.nsf/5451236ceac8ca3680256775003 4ca9a/472772b3583aa3028025677f 004c3f00!OpenDocument, adopted in December 1992.

Amnesty International, Turkey: No security without human rights, London, October 1996. AI Index: EUR/44/ 84/96.

Asia-Pacific Human Rights Information Center, The Human Rights Education Situation in Sri Lanka" in "Human Rights Education in Asian Schools. Volume Four" (Osaka, 2001), http://erc.hrea.org/Library/curriculum_methodology/hurights01.html.

Disparus, pourquoi? Rapport de la Commission indépendente sur les questions humanitaires internationales, ed. Berger-Lerault, Paris, 1986.

Index

239

www.ingramcontent.com/pod-product-compliance
Lightning Source LLC
Chambersburg PA
CBHW031127270326
41929CB00011B/1535